State of the eUnion

Government 2.0 and Onwards

Edited by
John Gøtze
Christian Bering Pedersen

Foreword by
Don Tapscott

21gov.net

AuthorHouse™
1663 Liberty Drive
Bloomington, IN 47403
www.authorhouse.com
Phone: 1-800-839-8640

© 2009 John Gøtze & Christian Bering Pedersen. All rights reserved.

No part of this book may be reproduced, stored in a retrieval system, or transmitted by any means without the written permission of the author.

First published by AuthorHouse 11/24/2009

ISBN: 978-1-4490-4730-6 (e)
ISBN: 978-1-4490-4729-0 (sc)

Printed in the United States of America
Bloomington, Indiana

This book is printed on acid-free paper.

TABLE OF CONTENTS

Section II: Opening Government

Section III: Democratizing Government

SECTION IV: CO-CREATION, INNOVATION & VALUES

CLOSING SECTION

Acknowledgements

First of all we would like to thank the contributing authors for joining this project. We are particularly grateful to Don Tapscott for writing the foreword.

We would also like to thank Gary Doucet, Executive Director within the Government of Canada, for inspiring comments and suggestions.

Thanks also to Freelancer.com users Demetris and Alex for helping with proofreading and index creation.

The cover image is created with the great Wordle.net service. This particular *wordle* is based on all text in the book.

We thank Forbes.com and *The New Republic* for permissions to use material from Tim O'Reilly resp. Lawrence Lessig.

John Gøtze and Christian Bering Pedersen, editors
Copenhagen, November 2009

All content is published under a Creative Commons
Attribution-Noncommercial-Share Alike 3.0 Denmark License

Content is available online at 21gov.net.

FOREWORD

GOVERNMENT 2.0: RETHINKING GOVERNMENT AND DEMOCRACY FOR THE DIGITAL AGE

Don Tapscott

Chairman, nGenera

This is a time of great peril and great promise for government. Around the world, governments are reeling under the strains of the financial meltdown and global economic crisis. Plummeting tax revenues, bank bailouts and infrastructure investments made to keep national economies from the brink of collapse have drained government coffers, causing in turn a crisis in the funding of basic operations. And in many parts of the world democracy itself is stalled, with low voter turnouts and cynical public attitudes towards government.

The irresistible force for cutbacks is meeting the immovable object of public expectations about what government should be and do: they should be better, providing better services, healthcare, safety and stability for our troubled economies. So while cost control measures may be necessary, they are clearly insufficient. We can no longer tinker with government – we need to reinvent it.

The idea of "reinventing government" dates back more than 15 years. As Osborne and Gaebler wrote in their landmark 1992 book, *Reinventing Government*, we need governments which are catalytic – steering and sparking action rather than doing things themselves; community-owned – empowering rather than serving; and mission-driven, results-oriented and customer-focused. Governments, they say, should inject competition into service delivery; focus on earning rather than spending; shift from hierarchy to teamwork and participation; and focus on prevention rather than cure.

In this spirit the US federal government initiated the National Performance Review led by Vice President Al Gore in 1993. A team developed a report and a set of accompanying documents which addressed key issues of reinvention. Since then, by most accounts, progress has been slow in implementing the approaches developed.

In recent years, governments in Europe and other parts of the world have embraced "citizen-centric" approaches to service delivery and emphasized inter-agency collaboration. Some governments have even extended new roles to citizens, community-based organizations and private businesses in a bid to reduce costs, harness new competencies and leverage untapped sources of innovation.

Despite significant progress, transforming the deeper structures of government is proving to be an intractable challenge. Deep and resilient traditions combine to frustrate progress, including conflicting timeframes and motives, a lack of incentives to innovate in the system, and deeply engrained cultural and institutional legacies. But just as new waves of innovation are washing over the private sector, the imperative to harness new models of collaboration and innovation is arriving on the doorstep of governments everywhere.

Today, in addition to the global economic crisis, four forces are bringing the urgency of public sector transformation to the fore:

A Technology Revolution – Web 2.0. The static, publish-and-browse Internet is being eclipsed by a new participatory Web that provides a powerful platform for the reinvention of governmental structures, public services and democratic processes. The Internet is no longer just a platform for web sites – the presentation of content. It is becoming a global platform for collaboration.

A Demographic Revolution – the Net Generation. The first generation to grow up immersed in digital technologies is coming of age and emerging as a major force in today's world – a generation that thinks differently about the role of government in society and will demand increasingly speedy, responsive, and customizable public services. The children of the post-WWII generation (sometimes called the baby boom) are the first generation to come of age in the digital age. Aged 13-30, this Net Generation learns, works, plays, communicates, shops and creates communities differently than their parents. As consumers of government services, young people have very different expectations about what governments should do and how they should operate. Moreover, their immersion in the interactive world of the Internet and digital technology has trained them to be activists – not passive readers, viewers or voters.

A Social Revolution – Social Networking. Online collaboration is exploding and citizens increasingly self-organize to peer produce everything from encyclopedias to operating systems, to advocacy campaigns, to stop global warming. With 300 million people on Facebook, collaboration and social networking are a phenomenon that no politician or public official can afford to ignore. Sadly, rather than embracing social media and tools as the new operating system of government, many governments have been doing the opposite - banning the use of these tools. Governments in many parts of the world for example have banned Facebook.

An Economic Revolution - Wikinomics. Mass collaboration is changing how enterprises innovate, orchestrate capability and engage with the rest of the world. Networked business models pioneered in the private sector hold promise for the public sector, but the unique public sector environment means the challenges of implementation are different. While the needs of citizens cannot be met by market forces alone, the principles of Wikinomics - openness, peering, sharing and acting globally - provide a powerful manifesto for public sector transformation. If governments are to ensure their relevance and authority, they must move quickly to meet rising expectations for openness, accountability, effectiveness and efficiency in the public sector.

For several years, my colleague Anthony D. Williams and I have had the pleasure of leading a multi-million Euro research program called Government 2.0. The program is funded by governments in North America, Europe and Asia and has been identifying best practices and lighthouse cases regarding the Internet-enabled transformation of government and democracy.

The program provides evidence that a new kind of government organization is emerging in response to these challenges—one that opens its doors to the world; co-innovates with everyone, especially citizens; shares resources that were previously closely guarded; harnesses the power of mass collaboration and behaves not as an isolated department or jurisdiction, but as something new: a truly integrated organization. The breakthrough enabled by new technologies is found in collaborative, cross-organizational governance webs that leave behind outmoded silos and structures.

Government 2.0 is an idea whose time has come.

Rethinking E-Government

There are vast new opportunities to improve the performance and effectiveness of government by harnessing the power of information technology, particularly the Internet. However, our research has shown that many governments at the National, Regional and Local levels are merely scratching at the surface.

In the private sector, the first era of the Net was "brochure-ware", followed by companies trying to sell products and services online. Similarly, the first government Web sites simply provided static information, followed by efforts to provide electronic delivery of existing government services – paving the cow path.

Today still, e-gov initiatives are mired in old thinking such as the creation of "government portals", "joined-up government" and "one stop government".

As such they are missing the much bigger opportunity to change the way governments orchestrate capability to create and deliver services – ultimately changing the division of labor in society for economic and social development and social justice.

Until now, governments were modeled after the command and control industrial organizations that dominated the landscape. If it was good enough for GM, it was good enough for bureaucrats. But in the digital economy, mammoth vertically integrated industrial corporations have started to unbundle. Today's most successful corporations aren't just speeded up versions of the old industrial behemoths. Instead we are seeing the rise of the business web, a much more supple and effective form of wealth creation.

An equally dramatic innovation is starting to happen throughout the public sector, paralleling the new forms of commercial value creation. Just as customers in the private sector move from passive consumers to active, value-adding participants in successful digital age business models, there is a similar transformation in governance.

Partnerships between government and external organizations that were previously impossible are beginning to materialize. Using the Internet to share power, forge new relationships, partner on service delivery – these are initiatives that deliver a bigger bang for the taxpayer and create the opportunity for injecting private sector innovation.

I call these new multi-stakeholder networks, governance webs. The big wins are not achieved simply by taking the status quo online, but instead by transforming the industrial age model into digital age governance.

The digital age allows the age-old question of "who does what" to be answered more creatively than ever before. "Public" value no longer needs to be provided by government alone. It can be provided by any combination of various public agencies, the private sector, a community group or citizens themselves, using the Internet as a mechanism for collaboration, process management and conducting transactions. The result is greater value and lower cost for the customers of government.

In Washington, the Obama administration codifies this thinking in its "Government as Platform" initiatives. Excitement is in the air about the potential for new, innovative information services to be created when data is made available through open government and transparency initiatives. Starting with their widespread use in political campaigns, Web 2.0 services are starting to tap government datasets and provide new communications and content services at the local level.

These new models change the way governments orchestrate capability to create and deliver services – ultimately changing the division of labor in society.

Rethinking Democracy

Far-reaching changes are underway, beyond the business of government, to the nature of governance itself.

The Geneva-based World Economic Forum has launched a bold new set of initiatives to provide leadership in redesigning the world's institutions. One of dozens of *Global Agenda Councils*, each comprised of leading thinkers on a topic, is a *Council on The Future of Government*. This Council noted that democracy is strong in the world because of a deep-seated human desire for freedom. But there are many storm warnings of danger due to four factors:

- **Collapse**. Basic democratic institutions are at risk and in danger of failing part due to the economic crisis in poor countries. The best predictor of democratic survival is per capita income.
- **Capture** (by interest groups). For example, the SEC was captured by the investment banking community leading the economic crisis of 2009. In developing countries, democracies have been captured by military, organized crime or tribes.
- **Competition**. There are fairly stable authoritarian regimes that make the case that democracy is inferior.
- **Constraints**. The current economic crisis shows that national governments and domestic regulation are inadequate to deal with the challenges of the global economy. There is also a danger of protectionism and isolationism.

Throughout the developed world there is an additional complicating factor. With the exception of the United States, young people are not engaged in the democratic process. Youth voting is dangerously low, and in many countries declining, as many young people are alienated from their governments and don't see how they can make a difference. Further, unlike their parents who grew up being the passive recipients of television, they have come of age interacting and collaborating using digital technologies.

In the traditional form of democracy enjoyed by previous generations, citizens listened to speeches, debates and television ads. They gave money and voted. But when it came to having input into policy and real decisions, they were relegated to the sidelines.

The Internet enables a new model of democracy – one appropriate for The Net Generation. Having grown up digital, they expect to collaborate with everyone – including politicians. They want to be involved directly: to interact with them, contribute ideas and scrutinize their actions, not just during elections, but as they govern. And they will insist on integrity from politicians; they will know very quickly if a politician says one thing and does another.

Barack Obama understood this and enabled citizens, largely youth, to organize a social movement that brought him to power. Now he's embracing these same principles to change the way government operates and engages its citizens.

Ultimately this promises to change the nature of democracy and the relationship between citizens and the state – for the better. The first wave of democracy established elected and accountable institutions of governance, but with a weak public mandate and an inert citizenry. The second wave is being characterized by strong representation and a new culture of public deliberation built on active citizenship.

Call it Democracy 2.0.

All of this requires leadership. Which is why the book "State of the eUnion" is so important and timely. John Gøtze and Christian Bering Pedersen have assembled a stellar cast of thinkers and practitioners who are pioneering the new possibilities for new paradigms in government and governance. Beginning with thoughtful definitional papers about Government 2.0, the book explores the topic of

"Open Government" which as much as any topic is central to the new thinking. It then delves into the issues of democratization and citizen engagement with stimulating and satisfying contributions based on real world experience.

Every government leader, every elected official and every government employee should read this book and get involved in one of the most exciting challenges of our times – transforming government for effectiveness, relevance and success, enabled by a new medium of communications and required for the emerging citizens of the 21st century. The stakes are very high.

Don Tapscott
Toronto, November 2009

Don Tapscott (@dtapscott) is Chairman of nGenera Insight and Executive Director of their research program "Government 2.0: Wikinomics Government and Democracy." Don is the author of many books, including Wikinomics *and* Grown Up Digital. *His next book (March 2010), with Anthony D. Williams, is a sequel to Wikinomics.*

#1

INTRODUCTION

John Gøtze
Lecturer, Copenhagen Business School

Christian Bering Pedersen
Consultant, Devoteam Consulting

In his famous Gettysburg Address on November 19, 1863, Abraham Lincoln stated that "government of the people, by the people, for the people, shall not perish from the earth".

In the same November days, but 146 years later, the 5th European Ministerial e-Government Conference[1] will be held in the city of Malmö in southern Sweden. EU Member State ministers responsible for e-Government will meet on the eve of the Conference, November 18, 2009, to agree on a Ministerial Declaration that will set out the path for the field of e-Government up until 2015. The Swedish EU Presidency and the European Commission will then present the signed Ministerial Declaration jointly on the first day of the conference under the heading *Teaming up for the eUnion*.

Perhaps it would be fitting for the European ministers to review the Gettysburg Address statement, and for them to consider whether this is still the quintessential statement about government – *of, by and for the people* – or whether the time has come for some rethinking? There are many other prepositions one could use, in addition to these three fine ones, but we suggest one in particular, and that is *with:* government *with* the people.

This idea does not come out of the blue. We are actually more describing the *zeitgeist* of 2009. The book's title, *State of the eUnion,* is of course a play on words and contexts. First and foremost, there is a reference to 'The State of the Union', the annual address presented by the President of the United States to Congress. This address not only reports on the condition of the nation, but also allows the President to outline his legislative agenda and national priorities to the Congress. In a similar way, this book is both about the current state of government and about ways to deal with the future state of government. The *eUnion* part of the title is a reference to the minister conference, *Teaming Up for the eUnion*. The book's reference to the eUnion, however, is not limited to any particular geographical 'union'. With contributions from Europe, North America and Australia, the book's perspective is international.

The subtitle, *Government 2.0 and Onwards*, indicates that the focus is more towards the future than the past. Government 2.0[2] is without doubt a concept that has made a breakthrough in government offices, vendor circles, media and, albeit slowly, in academia. In late September 2009, Gartner analyst Andrea DiMaio argued[3] that Government 2.0 is rapidly reaching what Gartner calls the "peak of inflated expectations", with maximum hype around it. This is the highest point in their classic hype cycle, which means the dreaded "trough of disillusionment" is coming up, and that there is still a long way to the "plateau of productivity", where measurable value is delivered.

Government 2.0 is oftentimes understood as social media and web 2.0 in government, or "how government is making use of web 2.0

technologies to interact with citizens and provide government services,"[4] but in our view it is more than that. As Don Tapscott et al[5] write:

> *The transition to 'Government 2.0' and governance webs begins with opening up formerly closed processes, embracing transparency and renovating tired rules that inhibit innovation. But that is merely the beginning. ... a new breed of public sector organization is emerging in response to these challenges: One that opens its doors to the world; co-innovates with everyone, especially citizens; shares resources that were previously closely guarded; harnesses the power of mass collaboration; and behaves not as an isolated department or jurisdiction, but as something new – a truly integrated organization.*

Government 2.0 therefore fundamentally challenges the way government works, and perhaps in particular, how government is managed. Being complex enterprises, governments – whether federal, national, regional or local governments – are generally characterized exactly as Gary Hamel describes[6] modern enterprises: they have 21st Century, Internet-enabled business processes, mid-20th-century management processes, all built atop 19th-century management principles. Hamel calls for Management 2.0, and argues that it is all about *management innovation* – new ways of mobilizing talent, allocating resources, and formulating strategies. Although his focus is on private companies, his message is clearly also relevant in a government context.

Many would argue that the US saw management innovation in practice when, as one of his first actions in office, President Obama on January 21, 2009, issued a *Memorandum on Transparency and Open Government*[7], in which he instructed that government should be more transparent, participatory and collaborative. The Obama Administration has since launched the *Open Government Initiative*[8] led by the White House Office of Science & Technology Policy, and hired law professor Beth Simone Noveck as *Deputy Chief Technology*

Officer for Open Government. Just as Obama set a new standard for using the internet in the election process (e-campaigning), his administration's recent initiatives such as the *IT Dashboard*[9] and *data.gov* are setting new standards for internet-supported open government.

The open government agenda at large, internationally, has of course been around for quite a number of years, probably as long as democracy has been around[10]. Sweden's *Freedom of the Press Act* of 1766 counts for the early legislation in the field, and all around the world, many 'Sunshine laws' (Freedom of Information legislation[11]) have followed since then.

For years, open government has been a key hallmark of democratic practice, and is by many considered the perhaps most important pillar in a well-functioning democracy. Open and transparent government is certainly an important area of concern for developing democracies, with corruption and coercion, but indeed also, always, of concern for so-called developed democracies. As such, open government has also seen its share of skepticism and controversy. In *Yes, Minister*, the wonderful satirical British sitcom from 1980, Sir Arnold Robinson, Cabinet Secretary, explains about open government: "My dear boy, it is a contradiction in terms: you can be open or you can have government."

Transparency is indeed a somewhat ambivalent concept[12]. It has, so to speak, an obvious light side, but also a sometimes very visible dark side. Transparency is related not only to enlightenment and freedom, but also to surveillance and control. The best example of the latter is perhaps the socio-optical *architecture of illumination* that Jeremy Bentham used in 1785, when he designed *Panopticon*[13], a prison that allows an observer to observe all prisoners without them being able to tell whether they are being observed. He invented, so to speak, CCTV (surveillance cameras) long before the video camera was invented.

In philosophic terms, *the public sphere* is the place where light comes from, namely the light thrown on things when they take place in public. In a 1958 lecture called *Man in Dark Times,* political philosopher Hannah Arendt[14] talked about her times as a darkening or obscuring of the light from the public sphere, and the withdrawal of the general public from the public world based on the "well-founded anger that makes you hoarse", anger towards a 'system' that does not listen; a system with freedom *from* politics, rather than freedom *to* take part and make *praxis* (action). The same argument, but now from a social and cultural perspective, was in 1961 put forward by English culture critic Raymond Williams[15]:

> *"If man is essentially a learning, creating and communicating being, the only social organisation adequate to his nature is a participatory democracy, in which all of us, as unique individuals, learn, communicate and control."*

Carole Pateman, 2009-2010 President-Elect of the American Political Science Association[16], in her early career (1970) formulated a theory of participatory democracy[17] based on the argument that participation fosters human development, enhances a sense of political efficacy, reduces a sense of estrangement from power centers, nurtures a concern for collective problems and, not least, that it contributes to the formation of an active and knowledgeable citizenry capable of taking an active interest in governmental and managerial affairs. These are all good arguments for climbing Arnstein's ladder of participation[18] – from non-participation over tokenism (e.g., consultation) to citizen power. Over the past 40 years, both theory and practice of democracy have continued to climb up – but sometimes also down – that ladder.

Tim O'Reilly coined the concept *architecture of participation*[19] to describe the nature of systems that are designed for user contribution, noting that the Internet and the World Wide Web have this participatory architecture in spades, for example in big open source projects. As he explains in this book, time has come for government to embrace the architecture of participation.

We know there is a lot of value[20] for all kinds of companies in adopting co-creation, the practice of developing systems, products, or services through collaboration with customers. But we are indeed also seeing a trend in government's adoption of co-creation and participatory collaboration, for example at the US Patent Office who embraced user-generated content with their Peer-to-Patent Program[21].

There are many ways to interpret the famous quote from Thomas Jefferson, "information is the currency of democracy", but it certainly implies that government data is valuable. And something of value can be made into a commodity. The European Directive on the re-use of public sector information ('the PSI Directive'[22]) meant that certain government data should be regarded as a commodity that government can sell to the private sector. Not all government data, of course, the EU promised those with privacy and other concerns. But government, the public sector as such, has lots of data, and surely some of it can be exhibited and sold to those who want it, the underlying logic said. Examples are geographical information, environmental data, certain statistics and a whole lot of data residing in the many government IT systems, databases and archives. A recent Gartner survey for the Danish National Telecom and IT Agency[23] predicted an economic potential of almost €100m for Denmark alone in letting public and private actors have access to government data, which arguably could spur a wave of innovation as private companies compete to build services on top of the valuable data.

Other research[24] shows that public sector information and government data has a huge socioeconomic value, but also that the European PSI-approach (cost-recovery) may not be the most optimal way to maximize the value. Perhaps giving it all away for free[25] is a better alternative? It depends on how, and for whom you measure the value. The challenge is in the reaping and sowing of value, that sometimes, some (government) must make investments in order for others (business, citizens) to benefit, get value, from. Indeed, government needs an *architecture of fruition*[26].

Introducing the Contributions

The contributions to the book come from thought-leaders on three continents. Among the contributors you'll find battle-hardened practitioners with many years of experience, writing about what works and what does not work. Many of the contributors have been working with e-Government for many years, and are not fazed by the current attention to "government 2.0". Their contributions are based on what they have experienced and done, not on buzzwords and hype.

In structuring the book's contributions, we took inspiration in the Obama memo - that government should be transparent, participatory and collaborative - and ended up sorting the contributions in three related sections: "Opening Government," "Democratizing Government" and "Co-Creation, Innovation & Values," each with five chapters. Before we get to these, and to get into the context, we have a substantial "Government 2.0" section with ten chapters as well as the foreword by Don Tapscott.

The Government 2.0 section begins with a contribution from Mr. Web 2.0, *Tim O'Reilly*, who argues that Government 2.0 is a promise of innovation. Washington-based researcher and writer *Mark Drapeau* follows up and argues that Government 2.0 is about moving from what he calls the "goverati adhocracy," to "Government With the People."

Then follows three different examples of Government 2.0 in action. The first example is the hugely successful social networking site GovLoop, a "Facebook for feds," which is described by its founder, *Steve Ressler*. The second example is about crowdsourcing in a specific area, as *Dan Doney* from the US Office of the Director of National Intelligence introduces BRIDGE, the Intelligence Community's testbed for new community and analysis tools. The third example is about the State of Utah, which is recognized as one of the absolute leading US States when it comes to e-Government. State CTO, *David Fletcher*, describes how Utah deals with Government 2.0.

Having now seen a few examples of Government 2.0 in action, it is time to take a close look at the concept. "Is the concept of Government 2.0 really all that new?" asks *Steve Radick* from Booz Allen Hamilton. Inspired by the Cluetrain Manifesto, he presents Twenty Theses for Government 2.0.

The Government 2.0 agenda is not just on the table in the US, and the following chapters will take the reader around the world. First stop is Australia. *Stephen Collins* from AcidLabs introduces the Australian Government 2.0 agenda, and discusses how it relates to the traditional e-Government agenda. He also analyzes the cultural issues around Government 2.0. Next we come to Europe. *David Osimo* from Tech4i2 gives an overview of the progressive structuring of web 2.0 in government, and calls for Public Services 2.0. Returning to North America, now to Canada, *Alexandra Samuel* from Social Signal asks, "why do public agencies take so long to embrace social media?" and distills emergent opportunities and best practices for governments, seeking to tap the power of social media. Closing this section, from San Francisco, digital anthropologist *Ariel Waldman* suggests three reasons government isn't ready for 2.0 yet.

Ready or not, government is changing. The following section, Opening Government, deals with the changes induced by the transparency and openness agenda. The section opens with government strategist *W. David Stephenson*, who argues that time has come to make government data freely available and usable. He presents five principles to guide the process of democratizing data, and discusses the strategic shift that will be needed, since data triggers transformation.

The same logic can be found in the work of the UK Government's *Power of Information Taskforce;* they recently recommended sweeping reforms to how the civil service publishes, manages and engages with information. Taskforce Chair *Richard Allen* describes the Power of Information agenda and its impact on the way in which the UK

Government works with public sector information and internet-enabled innovation.

Another dimension in opening government is in the way government projects are handled, especially when they have IT components. *Tommy Dejbjerg Pedersen* from Danish GeekHouse argues for a fully transparent approach to government projects, right down to the code level.

Picking up on transparency, *Lawrence Lessig* from Harvard Law School argues that the age of transparency is upon us, for good and for worse. He looks into the perils of openness in government, and argues that we are not thinking critically enough about where and when transparency works, and where and when it may lead to confusion, or to worse.

David Weinberger from Harvard Berkman Center for Internet & Society puts forward the claim that transparency is the new objectivity, and discusses the challenges governments face, as hyperlinked transparency becomes the norm.

At this point, it should be clear to the reader that there is much more to be said about wider democratic issues, and this is exactly what the next section, Democratizing Government, deals with.

Michael Friis, Founder of *Folkets Ting*, a website covering the Danish parliament ("Folketinget"), discusses Democracy 2.0 and how we can go about building websites that support and strengthen democracy.

Joanne Caddy from the OECD identifies a need for governments to shift from their traditional "government-as-usual" to a broader governance perspective which builds on the twin pillars of openness and inclusion to deliver better policy outcomes and high quality public services not only for, but with, citizens.

Rolf Lührs, Bengt Feil and *Harald Rathmann* from German TuTech Innovation discuss the field of spatial planning. They argue that electronic tools can provide many advantages over the traditional analogue way of organising formal participation.

Matt Leighninger from the Deliberative Democracy Consortium finds that today's citizens are better at governing, and worse at being governed, than ever before. We need, he argues, to recast the relationship between citizens and government.

Lee Bryant from HeadShift in the UK argues that it is time to take a serious look at how we can leverage human talent, energy and creativity to begin rebooting the system to create sustainable, affordable, long-term mechanisms for public engagement.

In the last section, Co-Creation, Innovation & Values, the contributions cover a range of issues related to the collaborative and managerial aspects of government.

The section opens with *Olov Östberg* from Mid Sweden University, who looks at the challenge the Swedish Government faces as they aim to reclaim world leadership in the e-Government ranking circus by 2010. He argues that the main challenge for government is to become better at becoming better, together.

From the UK, *Tony Bovaird, Elke Löffler* and *James Downe* explore user co-production and community co-production, two very different theoretical strands in current thinking on co-production of public services and public policy.

Philipp S. Müller from Salzburg-based Center for Public Management and Governance argues that open value creation has become a mainstream strategic management approach, and that in order to fully utilize open value creation, radical transparency is necessary. He presents a framework for this approach.

Corporate strategist *Chris Potts* points out that government must be much more transparent about investments in government-led change. He analyzes the value dimension of government IT project portfolios and the importance of transparency.

Researchers *Kim Normann Andersen, Hanne Sørum* and *Rony Medaglia* look closer at how the e-government portfolio is recognized through various awards. They put forward five propositions on how to increase the value of e-government awards.

In the transparent, participatory and collaborative spirit, the book's content (over 75,000 words) has been published under a Creative Commons license ("Attribution-Noncommercial-Share Alike 3.0 Denmark"). This means that you can use it, share it, and remix it, but must always give attribution to the authors, and you may not use it for commercial purposes. All content is available at our website, *21Gov.net*, where you can also find more material and participate in debates.

Just a note on the book's references: There are many references to weblinks (URLs), and will note these links are all to *j.mp* (for example, http://j.mp/21gov). This is fully intentional: We use the popular j.mp URL-shortening service, which many twitters and others are using to avoid having to write the all-too-often much too long links we find everywhere on the web.

John Gøtze, PhD, (@gotze) is a lecturer at Copenhagen Business School and the IT University of Copenhagen, and an independent consultant as well as a partner in enterprise architecture consulting firm EA Fellows. He spent ten years working in government in Denmark and Sweden on e-government programs. His is a co-editor of Coherency Management – Architecting the Enterprise for Alignment, Agility and Assurance.

Christian Bering Pedersen (@bering) is an enterprise architect, working with requirement specification, system documentation, technical standards, IT-governance and collaboration tools. He works for Devoteam Consulting, guiding public and private sector customers in their work to get more out of their IT investments.

[1] See http://egov2009.se

[2] Digging into the history of the concept Government 2.0, it is a bit unclear who actually coined the concept, but Deloitte's William Eggers published a book called "Government 2.0" in late 2004. http://j.mp/MpUUM

[3] http://j.mp/efu1I

[4] http://j.mp/4wwC8z

[5] GOVERNMENT 2.0: Transforming Government and Governance for the Twenty-First Century, by Don Tapscott, Anthony D. Williams and Dan Herman. 2008 nGenera Corporation

[6] Hamel, Gary (2007) *The Future of Management*. Harvard Business School Press.

[7] *Memorandum on Transparency and Open Government*, see http://j.mp/PsWI1

[8] http://j.mp/CyuQS

[9] http://it.usaspending.gov/

[10] http://j.mp/HxSCN

[11] http://j.mp/PpoEL

[12] http://j.mp/3zRQ6u

[13] Foucault, Michel (1980) *The Eye of Power*. Power/Knowledge: Selected Interviews and Other Writings 1972-1977. Ed. Colin Gordon. Harvester.

[14] Hannah Arendt's critique of modern culture is related to Richard Sennett's, Oscar Negt's, Thomas Ziehe's and (other) branches of critical theory, such as the works of Walter Benjamin and T. W. Adorno.

[15] Williams, Raymond (1961) *The Long Revolution*. Columbia University Press.

[16] http://j.mp/1BLO6t

[17] Pateman, Carole (1970) *Participation and Democratic Theory*. Cambridge University Press.

[18] Arnstein, Sherry R. "A Ladder of Citizen Participation," JAIP, Vol. 35, No. 4, July 1969, pp. 216-224.

[19] http://j.mp/nQ5TY

[20] Prahalad & Ramaswamy (2004) *The Future of Competition: Co-Creating Unique Value with Customers*. Harvard Business Press.

[21] Beth Simone Noveck (2009) *Wiki Government. How Technology Can Make Government Better, Democracy Stronger, and Citizens More Powerful*. Brookings Institution Press.

[22] The PSI directive was approved by the Council of Ministers on 27 October 2003, and Member States had to implement the Directive into national law by 1 July 2005. http://j.mp/3NxK2p

[23] http://j.mp/eCdd3

[24] http://j.mp/4kwWpL

[25] http://j.mp/16Yjx

[26] On fruition, see Chris Potts' contribution here, and also his fruITion Strategy® http://j.mp/EQA2T

#2

GOV 2.0: A PROMISE OF INNOVATION[1]

Tim O'Reilly

Founder and CEO, O'Reilly Inc

Over the past 15 years, the World Wide Web has created remarkable new business models reshaping our economy. As the Web has undermined old media and software companies, it has demonstrated the enormous power of a new model, often referred to as Web 2.0.

Now, a new generation has come of age with the Web and is committed to using its lessons of creativity and collaboration to address challenges facing our country and the world. The Facebook Causes application has more than 60 million registered users who are leveraging the power of social networks to raise money for charity. Meetup.com helps interest groups formed on the Web get together in person – and a remarkable number of groups do so for civic purposes. A quick search turns up nearly 20,000 meetups devoted to cleaning up local parks, streets and neighborhoods. Twitter and

YouTube have played major roles in helping organize political protests in Iran's recent election. Everyblock and Stumblesafely take government crime statistics and turn them into public safety applications for the Web or iPhone. The list goes on.

Meanwhile, with the proliferation of issues and not enough resources to address them all, many government leaders recognize the opportunities inherent in harnessing a highly motivated and diverse population, not just to help them get elected, but to help them do a better job. By analogy, many are calling this movement Government 2.0.

President Obama exhorted us to rise to the challenge: "We must use all available technologies and methods to open up the federal government, creating a new level of transparency to change the way business is conducted in Washington, and giving Americans the chance to participate in government deliberations and decision-making in ways that were not possible only a few years ago."

There is a new compact on the horizon: Government maintains information on a variety of issues, and that information should rightly be considered a national asset. Citizens are connected like never before and have the skill sets and passion to solve problems affecting them locally as well as nationally. Government information and services can be provided to citizens where and when they need it. Citizens are empowered to spark the innovation that will result in an improved approach to governance.

This is a radical departure from the old model of government, which Donald Kettl so aptly named "vending machine government." We pay our taxes; we get back services. And when we don't get what we expect, our "participation" is limited to protest--essentially, shaking the vending machine.

In the vending-machine model, the full menu of available services is determined beforehand. A small number of vendors have the ability to get their products into the machine, and as a result, the choices are limited and the prices are high.

Yet there is an alternate model which is much closer to the kind of government envisioned by our nation's founders, a model in which, as Thomas Jefferson wrote in a letter to Joseph Cabel, "every man ... feels that he is a participator in the government of affairs, not merely at an election one day in the year, but every day." In this model, government is a convener and an enabler—ultimately, it is a vehicle for coordinating the collective action of citizens.

So far, you may hear echoes of the dialog between liberals and conservatives that has so dominated political discourse in recent decades. But big government versus small government is in many ways beside the point. To frame the debate in terms familiar to technologists, the question is whether government is successful as a platform.

If you look at the history of the computer industry, the most successful companies are those that build frameworks that enable a whole ecosystem of participation from other companies large and small. The personal computer was such a platform. So was the World Wide Web. But this platform dynamic can be seen most vividly in the recent success of the Apple iPhone. Where other phones have a limited menu of applications developed by the phone provider, and a few carefully chosen partners, Apple built a framework that allowed virtually anyone to build applications for the phone, leading to an explosion of creativity with more than 50,000 applications appearing for the phone in less than a year, and more than 3,000 new ones now appearing every week.

This is the right way to frame the question of "Government 2.0." How does government itself become an open platform that allows people inside and outside government to innovate? How do you design a system in which all of the outcomes aren't specified beforehand, but instead evolve through interactions between the technology provider and its user community?

The Obama administration's technology team has taken the first steps toward rethinking government as a platform provider. One of the first acts by Vivek Kundra, the national CTO, was to create data.gov, a catalog of all the federal government's Web services[2]. The Sunlight Foundation's Apps for America Contest (modeled on the successful Apps for Democracy program that Kundra ran while CIO of Washington, D.C.) is seeking to kick off the virtuous circle of citizen innovation using these data services.

Rather than licensing government data to a few select "value added" providers, who then license the data downstream, the federal government (and many state and local governments) are beginning to provide an open platform that enables anyone with a good idea to build innovative services that connect government to citizens, give citizens visibility into the actions of government and even allow citizens to participate directly in policy-making.

That's Government 2.0: technology helping build the kind of government the nation's founders intended: of, for and by the people.

Tim O'Reilly (@timoreilly) is the founder and CEO of O'Reilly Media, a premier computer book publisher. O'Reilly Media also hosts conferences on technology topics. Tim is chairing the upcoming Gov 2.0 Summit with Richard O'Neill, founder and president of The Highlands Group. Tim's blog, the O'Reilly Radar, "watches the alpha geeks" and serves as a platform for advocacy about issues of importance to the technical community.

---

[1] This article originally appeared on *Forbes.com* on August 10, 2009. Reprinted with permission.

[2] Web services, as opposed to static government Web sites, provide raw government data, allowing third parties to build alternate services and interfaces to government programs.

#3

GOVERNMENT 2.0: FROM THE GOVERATI ADHOCRACY TO GOVERNMENT WITH THE PEOPLE

Mark D. Drapeau

Associate Research Fellow, National Defense University

During the 2008 elections in the United States, then-candidate Barack Obama's campaign made excellent use of new media, not only to raise an unprecedented amount of money, but also to market him as the candidate that would bring change to the country. Inspired by this, citizens prominently used new media like YouTube, Flickr and Twitter to share their experiences during Obama's inauguration week celebration in Washington, D.C. And after President Obama took office, his first order of business was to reveal a modern White House website and to issue a memo[1] directing the Federal government to be more transparent, participatory and collaborative.

But the wheels of government do not turn merely because the President gives an order – even when that order comes from a leader as popular as Obama. Disagreements between people in the

Executive and Legislative branches over policy, strategy and tactics can delay progress for months, if not years; not to mention outside pressure from think tanks, special-interest groups and super-empowered individuals. Engaging in spirited debate is the core of democracy, but sometimes it feels like participating in a nationwide traffic jam.

An interesting by-product of leaders encouraging government to be more transparent, participatory and collaborative is that people are increasingly, if inadvertently, taking matters into their own hands. Encouraged by high-profile uses of social software, government employees previously hidden in "pockets of excellence" have used personal blogs, microsharing and other new communications technologies to promote their ideas with wider audiences than ever before, in the process circumventing to some extent their normal chains of command. And outsiders who have become enthusiasts regarding changing the way the government operates, have increasingly been sharing their ideas, hosting events and creating websites and applications that use government data to help people.

These evangelists for a transparent, participatory and collaborative Government 2.0 are a group of people I previously dubbed[2] the Goverati. They are a unique and empowered band of insiders and outsiders using an understanding of government, a passion for technology and a gift for communication in order to change governance and help people. What sets the Goverati apart from other special-interest groups that want to lobby or change government is two things. First, the technologies they are encouraging the government to use are the very things that enable them to communicate their messages better to their audience, increase their reach and gain recognition for their work. Practicing what they preach, they endorse technologies they use themselves (and criticize ones they dislike). Their personal passions feed back onto their mission in a positive way, and their messages come across as more authentic because of it.

Second, the Goverati are a loosely organized groundswell lacking formal organization or a designated leader. There are catalysts within the movement, to be sure; but while some persons have emerged as temporary thought leaders, many of them disagree with each other over various issues, and no one clearly leads the tribe by themselves. Nevertheless, modern communication technology has enabled the decentralized[3] Goverati to network with each other and empowered them to become very effective at educating people about the topic of Government 2.0 and its potential. As author Robert Waterman, Jr. would say, the Goverati is an "adhocracy" – a highly-adaptive organization[4] cutting across normal bureaucratic lines to capture opportunities, solve problems and get results. Adhocracies can be seen as everything bureaucracies are not, and they are perhaps what is needed most at a time when the world is grappling with many serious issues.

An interesting sub-phenomenon, perhaps crucial to the growing influence of the Goverati adhocracy, is that while some members have decades of experience in government, technology, or both, others have relatively little. Nevertheless, some fresh thinkers in this area, typically in their 30's, have become extraordinarily talented at using social technology to spread their views or innovate using pilot projects. Cynics sometimes judge this pattern as abuse of intellectual personal branding, or even annoyingly viral self-promotion; regardless, a new class of influencers[5] has risen from the bureaucratic ooze to network and partner with experienced and prominent leaders.

In perhaps the best-known example of a relatively young member of the Goverati having a major impact, an informal Government 2.0 social network named GovLoop was developed by a U.S. government employee in his spare time on the popular platform Ning. In the span of a just one year[6] it gained over 12,000 members at all levels of government, in and outside of the U.S., and its rate of growth seems to be accelerating as excitement about Government 2.0 spreads. Its membership includes advisors at the highest levels of the Obama Administration. Incredibly, GovLoop was made possible simply because one passionate, empowered young person filled a void that employees felt they needed, but that the government left empty. Now members of the government are some of its biggest fans.

There is, however, pushback on the ideals of Government 2.0, for many different reasons ranging from lack of understanding about emerging technologies, to ordinary resistance to change within a very large bureaucracy. It is often said that battles in government are usually won by the most persistent party; decentralized organizations like the Goverati have the ability to work on many things at once, adapt quickly to changing situations, replenish members and even leaders who move along to other passions, and reinforce their influence by using social media to spread their ideas. Increasingly, large (over 500 attendee) events like Government 2.0 Camp, Public Democracy Forum and Gov 2.0 Summit - formally organized independent of the government, but with their participation - are viewed as opportunities for networking and hearing the best ideas. Whereas the government previously held events to tell citizens about what it was doing, the government now more often finds itself in the position of taking advice from a subset of those very citizens who have more reach with their thoughts than ever before. And there is nothing wrong with this meta-pattern - who declared that government had to have all the answers? Citizens are smart too.

Government taking the lead from citizens about the benefits of using social software is also happening on a more individual scale, as government leaders in the U.S. and elsewhere continue to embrace new media tools, both personally and professionally. The examples set by senior leaders at the top of the hierarchy are trickling down throughout government, empowering others to start new projects or revive old ones shelved as unimportant in a more stovepiped era. One excellent new example of this is BRIDGE, an unclassified U.S. intelligence community virtual environment debuted[7] in 2009 to allow analysts to network with subject matter experts outside government. Not so long ago, collaboration between intelligence analysts and outsiders on national security challenges in an online environment would have been unthinkable to many; now, open collaboration is becoming the default place to start new projects.

Web-based social networking innovations like GovLoop and BRIDGE may result in the public-facing parts of government appearing more personable. At a time when citizens are thinking about government more than ever, this can almost certainly only be a good thing. As evidenced by the Goverati, however, this is a partnership of sorts – the government has the ability to be more personable towards citizens, and citizens have the ability to more easily tell the government what they think. The technology to make this possible is available. Decisions about who will take advantage of it, and when and how to utilize it, vary considerably. This two-way street is fraught with obstacles.

In the not-so-distant future, when a citizen is asked to name an individual government employee, the ideal end state should be that a person working in a micro-niche of interest to them (finance, farming, health, and so on) immediately comes to mind. Unfortunately, interesting and talented people working inside the government are often not known to the public despite the great importance of their work to everyday life. This state of affairs is mostly a vestige from the days when communications were controlled by professionally trained public relations staff dealing with mainstream media. This was understandable – equipment was expensive, channels were few, and citizens trusted authenticated, official sources for their information. But this media structure that worked well for half a century is now outdated. Reversing the obscurity of public servants[8] should be a principal goal of an open, transparent government.

In the Web 2.0 world[9] where the Internet is used as a platform, every individual is empowered to be not only a consumer of information, but a producer of it. Published words, pictures and video are searchable, discoverable, sharable, usable and alterable. The bloggers formerly known as kids in their parents' basements have morphed into a powerful society class of listeners, questioners, writers, editors, publishers and distributors; some bloggers have even become household names. Interestingly, this is beginning to happen not only outside the government, but within it. Take "Blogger Bob" from the U.S. Transportation Security Administration's blog – true, he isn't as famous as Tom Clancy, but he's been empowered by his organization to write with a personal viewpoint that showcases the personality of a human being rather than the coarseness of official jargon.

The developed global citizen is not an empty vessel waiting to be filled with press releases and government website updates. Even a sophisticated government website like the White House's can only expect to attract a subset of citizens a subset of the time, because there are simply too many avenues of information flowing towards these people formerly known as a captive audience. No matter how compelling the government information, they are not waiting to hear about it. Nor are they necessarily waiting to hear from the New York Times, BBC, or any other mainstream organization. From the government's viewpoint, rather than assuming citizens are eagerly awaiting government information, it is more productive to imagine them as interwoven networks of individuals having conversations over dinner with their families, in their workplace cafeteria and on social media websites.

Such online and offline social networks are increasingly an important and powerful force in the lives of adults.[10] But while governments have to some degree embraced new media in the form of publishing official blogs and reading comments, or utilizing Twitter and Facebook to accumulate "fans" and answer questions, they appear in many cases less adept at deploying individuals to become trusted members of microniche citizen networks based around the topics on which they work. Asking people to tune in to a live news chat on Facebook is not much different from asking them to tune into a televised news conference. Come-to-us is not being replaced by go-to-them, and yet trusted people within communities of interest have become filters for the multimedia vying for citizens' attention.

Bureaucracies cannot have conversations with citizens; only individual people who work within the bureaucracy can. Ideally, such people having conversations can become "lethally generous" trusted community members.[11] How does one know if someone has achieved that status? I posit that such lethally generous community leaders are known to the community by name. In other words, when a citizen who is passionate about environmental issues, or health care reform, or veterans' benefits, is asked to name a government staffer working on those topics, they should be able to answer, because that staffer is also a trusted member of their community of interest.

Anecdotally, few government employees consider "marketing" part of their job, and similarly most citizens don't think of "lobbying" as part of theirs. But when every person can be a writer, publisher, and distributor, everyone cannot be immune from these responsibilities. Granted, both private sector companies and government agencies have rules about what you can and cannot write about your job, and not everyone wants to participate. But many people have already chosen to opt-in to publishing blogs using WordPress, belonging to social networks like Facebook, and sharing real-time experiences on Twitter. The key question is, how do organizations channel such preexisting social communication talents of their workforce for better networking between government and citizens?

Social capital within large organizations should be harnessed, not punished. Such people engaged in communities of interest may very well be more in touch with grassroots conversations[12] than the public affairs office of an agency, which traditionally tend more towards unidirectional outward information flow. These employees may also already be trusted members of a community of interest, flush with knowledge and generous with assistance. It's difficult to think of good reasons to not use such pre-adapted social engagement to the government's advantage.

Government "social ambassadors" should be fully accessible, transparent, authentic, and collaborative leaders that inspire people to cooperate and engage with their government and with each other for the sake of common concerns. As part of their missions, government brand ambassadors should conduct community-based research to better understand the grassroots interests of the average person, which are sometimes misunderstood or overlooked. Listening to and participating in online conversations is quickly replacing polling as a way to understand what communities of interest are actually interested *in*.

With government social ambassadors using new media to more effectively reach out to communities of citizens, and with citizens using those same tools to lobby[13] their government, a two-way channel of information flow may slowly become a "government with the people". While governments certainly face challenges in using social technologies, experts estimate that the benefits of using these tools to engage the public outweigh the negatives.[14] Social technologies can make networking and engagement with the public simple and powerful, make informal research faster, identify influencers in useful micro-niches, provide mechanisms for combating negative publicity and measure public sentiment to help inform public policy and improve governance.

Dr. Mark Drapeau (@cheeky_geeky) is a scientist, consultant and writer who can be contacted through his website (http://markdrapeau.com), listing his publications and other activities. He has a Ph.D. in biological sciences from the University of California and held postdoctoral fellowships at New York University and the National Defense University.

[1] White House Memorandum For the Heads of Executive Departments and Agencies. Transparency and Open Government. Jan. 22, 2009. See: http://j.mp/DVta

[2] Government 2.0: The Rise of the Goverati, ReadWriteWeb, Feb. 5, 2009. See: http://j.mp/kmNG

[3] Ori Brafman and Rod Beckstrom, *Starfish and the Spider: The Unstoppable Power of Leaderless Organizations*, Penguin, 2006. Clay Shirky, *Here Comes Everybody: The Power of Organizing Without Organizations*, Penguin, 2008.

[4] Robert H. Waterman, Jr., *Adhocracy*, W.W. Norton & Co., 1993.

[5] Interestingly, this phenomenon may be responsible for the fast-growing influence of the Goverati. According to a new research paper (Hai-Tao Zhang et al., Effective Leadership in Competition, 2009 preprint: http://j.mp/pMijh), relatively few new leaders within a large group can shift the balance of power by distributing their ideas broadly and retaining allegiances well. Social media can facilitate exactly that when used well.

[6] Mark Drapeau, Celebrate the 'Summer of Gov' in Washington, DC and San Francisco, *Examiner.com*, July 10, 2009. See: http://j.mp/4v1r55

[7] BRIDGE was funded by the Deputy Director of National Intelligence for Analysis. Information about how BRIDGE is helping the U.S. Intelligence Community connect with outside subject matter experts who understand emerging technologies can be found here: http://about.bridge-ic.net/index.html

[8] Mark Drapeau, How Social Media Could Transform Government Public Relations, *PBS MediaShift*, Jan 2009. See: http://j.mp/Env1

[9] Tim O'Reilly, What Is Web 2.0: Design Patterns and Business Models for the Next Generation of Software, Sept. 30, 2005. See: http://j.mp/aa1sP

[10] Amanda Lenhart, Social Networks Grow: Friending Mom and Dad, Jan. 14, 2009. See: http://j.mp/I6kV

[11] The term "lethally generous" with regard to social media usage was coined by author Shel Israel and means that rather than adopting a command-and-control strategy, someone seeking to be a thought leader in a community should participate in its conversations and add the most value possible. See: http://j.mp/1usndH

[12] Good online community managers tend to have a unique combination of skills including those of a magazine editor, orchestra conductor, teacher, and parent. Simon Young, What do you need in a community manager? June 5, 2009. See: http://j.mp/kE5kw

[13] The recent White House experiment called the "Open Government Initiative" is a good example of how social technologies are empowering citizens to contribute to the government policymaking process. It was directed by the Office of Science and Technology Policy. See: http://j.mp/KXTBh

[14] Mark Drapeau and Linton Wells II, Social Software and National Security: An Initial Net Assessment, *Defense and Technology Papers*, National Defense University, April 2009. See: http://j.mp/TJLA4. James Jay Carafano, Social Networking and National Security: How to Harness Web 2.0 to Protect the Country, *Heritage Foundation Backgrounder*, May 18, 2009. See: http://j.mp/XKlee.

#4

THE EMERGENCE OF GOV 2.0: FROM GOVLOOP TO THE WHITE HOUSE

Steve Ressler
Founder, GovLoop.com

A revolution is happening in government as the result of a new generation of government employees, the rise of Web 2.0 technologies, and the Obama administration's focus on transparency, participation, and collaboration. Often called Gov 2.0, this next generation of government is marked by the principles of openness, transparency and collaboration, and the idea that the voices of the many are smarter than the voice of one.

While this movement has been brewing for a few years, Gov 2.0 tipped in late 2008 in the United States and has swept Washington, D.C. Excitement about the government's use of Web 2.0 technology begun as agencies saw the Obama campaign utilize web 2.0 technologies such as the social network myBarackObama, Facebook and Twitter, to bring together a community of millions of citizens towards a common goal.

This excitement continued during the Presidential Transition period as the various Transition teams continued to utilize new media, from YouTube videos from the various Transition teams, to the Google Moderator Open for Questions sessions to a modern change.gov website.

This continued as President Obama moved into his new role. One of President Obama's first acts in office was to issue a directive calling for a more transparent, collaborative and participatory government. Leaders from the Office of Management and Budget and Office of Science and Technology Policy solicited input to the memo from all federal employees through the OMB MAX wiki.

The first White House New Media team was formed headed by Macon Phillips from the Obama campaign team with details from government insiders such as Bev Godwin. They have been working through new challenges based on rules created decades ago, but have already launched the "Ask the President" contest where they received hundreds of thousands of suggestions from citizens. Additionally, new media directors are being put in place at the major cabinet agencies.

The General Services Administration has led a number of initiatives in the space. They have worked with web 2.0 providers such as YouTube, Facebook and MySpace to sign Terms of Service agreements allowing federal agencies to utilize these new tools. The Federal Web Manager Committee has formed the Social Media Subcouncil, co-chaired by Jeff Levy of US Environmental Protection Agency and Joyce Bounds of US Department of Veterans Affairs, focusing on sharing lessons learned via their blog, wiki and webinars with web 2.0 companies such as Facebook, YouTube and O'Reilly Media.

Government agencies have begun using social media tools for various events. For both the Peanut Butter Recall and the H1N1 virus, agencies such as HHS, CDC and DHS utilized Twitter, Facebook, blogs and widgets to ensure that government information reached the citizens where they interacted. There are many others examples including Hilary Clinton's Digital Townhall of the Americas.

At the grassroots level, a group of knowledgeable insiders is forming, connecting and spreading information across social networks such as GovLoop and Twitter. The Government 2.0 Club, modeled after the popular Social Media Club, was launched in March 2009 and provides further mechanism for branding events and sharing wisdom. They recently held the first Gov 2.0 Barcamp, where over 500 members of the government community met and shared ideas on making Gov 2.0 happen. And non-profit organizations like The Sunlight Foundation are developing applications and hosting events in an effort to make government more transparent and ultimately more accountable to the public.

Silicon Valley has started paying attention and moving into D.C. Tim O'Reilly (founder of O'Reilly Media and creator of the term Web 2.0) recently launched the Gov 2.0 Summit and has shifted focus on the importance of open government with the idea of "government as platform". Tim O'Reilly argues that government does not need to just serve as a vending machine serving up services, but instead should be set up as a platform much like Apple with the iPhone and allow non-profits, citizens and start-ups to build on-top of government core functions. Additionally, government Luminaries such as Craig Newmark (founder of Craigslist) have begun showing up at various government conferences and trying to connect the Geeks to Wonks.

One of the most successful examples of Government 2.0 is GovLoop.com, an online community created for and by government employees, which has brought together more than 17,500 members of the government community. Dubbed by some as a "Facebook for Government," GovLoop brings together government employees from the U.S. and other nations to discuss ideas, share best practices and create a community dedicated to the betterment of government.

In only a year, GovLoop has begun to smash the age-old silos that existed between federal agencies and facilitating dialogue that has never existed before between state, local and international government agencies. Members range from CIOs, White House political appointees, dozens of city managers to brilliant government innovators all across levels of government. Since its launch, GovLoop members have written over 1,500 blogs, started 1,200 discussions, posted over 450 events, shared 4,000+ photos and created over 200 videos.

The creation of a new way for government to connect and solve problems has caught fire, and GovLoop has been recognized by its peers, including, by winning the prestigious Federal 100 award.

Most importantly GovLoop members have started connecting in ways to improve government. The open, accelerated flow of information on GovLoop has led to the rapid replication of ideas and best practices across all levels of government, assisting in improved government operations and performance.

For example, a California City Attorney's Office was able to set up an official government social media presence in a matter of days instead of months, by leveraging the best practices and experiences of the state of Massachusetts, which was shared on GovLoop.

In another example, the Office of Personnel Management was looking for feedback in improving federal internship programs and reached out to the National Association of Schools of Public Affairs and Administration (NASPAA). NASPAA and GovLoop combined to host an online dialogue where they received over 40 ideas from current and former internship recipients with real concrete ways to improve the internship programs.

Additionally, GovLoop members have already:

- Developed a burgeoning "Acquisition 2.0" movement to employ innovative acquisition methods
- Been the leading source of government input into the Obama Administration's Open Government Memo
- Established a repository of best practices on items including Social Media Policies, Government Hiring and Government Twitter Use

- Brought together international government leaders from across the globe including Canada, United Kingdom, Brazil, and Australia
- Created the first-ever Tweetbook summarizing all the messages on Twitter at the Open Government and Innovations Conference into a concise e-book for readers worldwide
- Launched a top-rated podcast Gov20Radio.com with guests like Tim O'Reilly (founder of O'Reilly media) and Craig Newmark (founder of CraigsList.com).

Further, government agencies across the world have started collaborating at a peer-to-peer level that is rarely seen. On GovLoop, approximately 10% of the membership is international with hundreds of members from Canada, U.K., Australia, New Zealand, Brazil, Spain, among many other countries. It has been fascinating to connect with people like Stephen Collins of Australia who is a key part of the Australians Gov 2.0 Taskforce (see Stephen Collins' chapter), and Helio Leite Teixeira who is building the burgeoning Gov 2.0 movement in Brazil. Despite cultural differences, there are many similarities across the globe in the adoption curve of Gov 2.0 and it has been of great value to bring the thought leaders together. In traditional situations, best practices around e-government are shared at conferences where only a few select countries and a few representatives can attend. GovLoop has fostered peer-to-peer information sharing at the international level amongst both leaders and at the working level.

Personally, it has been amazing to watch the ecosystem of government develop at GovLoop. People that would have never met in real life based on geography, agency and type of work are really connecting and learning from each other. For example, in the Acquisition 2.0 GovLoop group some of the top participants range from a GSA employee, DOD IT program manager, CEO of a social networking platform and a USDA Graduate School trainer. Additionally, it has begun to bring government innovators together – when you see a green GovLoop "Bureaucrats Need Not Apply" lanyard in the hallway, you know a like-minded innovator is in your path.

The beauty of government is that we are all in it together and we are not competitors. If an international, federal, state or local agency is working on a problem, there is no doubt another agency has already researched the problem and found a solution. With the power of sites like GovLoop, employees can learn from each other rather than reinvent the wheel. In the end, they are learning and working together to create a faster, quicker, cheaper, and more effective government.

While the tipping point may have been reached, Gov 2.0 still has a long way to go. The current examples are mainly early adopters and many government agencies are still just dipping their toes into the space. Additionally, with these new technologies and new generation of government employees, there is a huge cultural shift that must take place moving from a hierarchical-based structure to a networked approach where good ideas rise and are implemented regardless of where they came from. However, it is clear that in solving government problems, we should leverage the wisdom of the millions of citizens, government employees, and their past experiences.

Steve Ressler (@govloop) is the founder of GovLoop.com, a "Facebook for Government" which connects and foster collaboration among over 11,000 members. In September 2009, GovLoop became an operating division within GovDelivery, a provider of government-to-citizen communication solutions. Steve is also the co-founder of Young Government Leaders, a professional organization of over 2,000 government employees across the U.S. Steve received the 2007 and 2009 Federal 100 Award for his service in the government IT community.

#5

STRUCTURED CROWDSOURCING: HARNESSING EXTERNAL EXPERTISE IN GOVERNMENT

Dan Doney

CTO, Strategic Enterprise Solutions,
US Office of the Director of National Intelligence

Web 2.0 technologies provide an environment where individuals can collaborate to create, share, organize, edit or comment on Web content. Through the network effect, where many (often small) individual contributions provide great collective value, technologies like wikis, blogs, social networking and media sharing applications have transformed the internet unleashing the creativity of the masses and facilitating the worldwide spread of ideas and experiences in an instant.

But, harnessing the network effect to support the mission of government agencies has proven a more elusive challenge. The complicated and unique nature of internal environments designed to support a mission can be difficult to blend with rapid evolution of technologies on the open web. Leveraging popular Web 2.0 technologies directly on the web can have mission benefits, but will add to "knowledge fragmentation", the condition where knowledge expressed by the users in an enterprise is spread across disconnected applications, which can result in loss of collective awareness and can create unacceptable security conditions. But when Web 2.0 technologies are brought "in house", the power of the network can be reduced, possibly changing the value of the tool fundamentally. Failure to integrate new tools with existing enterprise technologies developed to support an organization's specific mission, or unique workflows, can force a zero sum game forcing users to choose between collaboration and their "day job". Technologies with inconsistent security models can result in a similar tradeoff between security and openness.

New approaches are emerging to strike the balance between the coordination needed to support an enterprise mission and the openness required to tap into the network effect. More than just Web 2.0 tools, Gov 2.0 refers to ambitious, network effect-based efforts underway to boost public sector efficiency, make government more responsive and spur innovation in agencies. Successes of Peer-to-Patent[1] at the US Patent Office and elsewhere point to the potential for transformational impact on a government agency's mission by tapping into the power of the network.

To realize unleash this potential, agencies must address 4 fundamental challenges that are underscored by Gov 2.0 approaches. First, greater coordination between CIO, CFO, and mission managers is required to unfetter new Gov 2.0 paradigms for acquisition, governance, organizational structuring, human resources, etc. Second, inculcating pervasive change requires a platform of enterprise services that infuse existing tools designed for the mission with Gov 2.0 principles without wholesale replacement, while at the same time providing a mechanism to integrate new tools that change organizational paradigms. Most importantly, agencies need to propagate new standards and services that ensure that security and sharing complement rather than compete as goals enabling productivity gains without compromising security. Finally, agencies must adopt practices that enable them to rapidly adapt at the pace of technology change.

We'll take a close look at one Gov 2.0 initiative called BRIDGE[2] that enables the understandably insular US intelligence community to tap into innovation on the web without sacrificing enterprise security needs. This environment extends the Wiki model, which has enabled end users to easily contribute textual content en masse, to technology providers. This model enables innovators to contribute technologies that enhance the intelligence mission in a matter of days through a "virtual sandbox", where all players - academics, integrators, innovators and agencies - can interact on new applications while still protecting intellectual property.

It is important to emphasize BRIDGE is not a Web 2.0 tool. It is a process for discovering, leveraging, and transitioning tools. Often the biggest challenge for government agencies is to recognize that the process is more important than the tool.

To embrace Gov 2.0 is to avoid the temptation to attempt to build the killer app and instead focus on processes that provide a platform for disruptive technologies, the ones they didn't know to ask for or build, to thrive. When you let a thousand flowers bloom...

Efficient Discovery

Organizations struggle to remain aware of, let alone harness, the rapidly evolving state of the art in information technology. Large organizations often establish research elements to develop cutting edge technologies that meet their unique mission needs. But, no matter how well funded and staffed these elements may be, there are always more innovators outside an organization than inside. Failure to tap into outside sources can leave an organization at a competitive disadvantage.

One challenge for organizations is wading through a myriad of alternatives to find the best solution to mission challenges. Traditional acquisition processes often implement selection criteria that don't align with the actual need, employ judges who don't represent the needs of users or don't have the expertise required to filter potential solutions, and set requirements that unnecessarily constrain the set of potential solutions. The result is poor adoption rates and a decrease in the probability of discovering disruptive technologies, those that come from outside expected solution trajectories. Without reform, the process strictly regulates dialogue with vendors, prevents the dissemination of promising ideas and unnaturally separates the end user from the innovator.

In the past few years, a growing number of organizations have conceived of methods to overcome these limitations to more efficiently tap into the expertise of the wealth of innovators across the globe. There is an impressive list of "crowdsourcing" success stories as companies develop creative ways to tap external innovation. Some prominent examples: The Netflix Prize, the DARPA Grand Challenge, Apps for Democracy. In each case, the organization opened a channel to enable innovators to participate in solving important mission challenges. To succeed, the competition must be carefully designed and be open to a broad set of participants. Incentive structures drive participation but competitive forces result in self-selection with only innovators who believe they have a credible chance of recouping investment participating. No arbitrary measures of perceived value prevent unexpected approaches from competing or even winning. When the prize is properly set to account for the difficulty of the challenge and the risk taken by participants, the organizations hosting the prize have seen tremendous return on investment.

BRIDGE takes a similar approach to selection. Providers can offer solutions to challenges that are explicitly expressed or implied in the space. Participation is open to technology providers from across government, academia and industry. The "prize" for participants is the opportunity to deploy technologies that show promise to mission settings and reap the benefits of license revenue that ensues. To participate, technologies must meet a minimum set of specifications for enterprise deployment. They are designed to be easily met, so as not to constrain participation by resources or approach. But this minimum barrier is enough to discourage participants who do not believe their capability is likely to impact the intelligence mission, which helps to separate the wheat from the chaff in the solution landscape.

BRIDGE provides a direct connection between the end user and the technology provider. As with the internet, end users in the space ultimately decide which technologies "win" by "voting with their feet". This also creates a setting that minimizes government risk by enabling agency managers to evaluate technologies before acquisition in a "try before you buy" setting. The result is a meritocracy that reflects technology capability *and* usability with the best ideas for the mission rising to the top. Technologies that have higher adoption rates and greater impact on the mission are selected.

Creating a platform for innovation

But for many organizations, government agencies specifically, the complicated and unique nature of internal environments make it difficult to express needs in a way that lend themselves to crowdsourcing. The US intelligence community is no exception. Given the closed nature of the intelligence mission, tapping into external innovation is a difficult challenge. The need for secrecy results in high market friction separating the creative solution providers from national security challenges. In many cases, articulating a need publicly can signal vulnerability. Outside innovations may appear promising but may not conform to standards necessary for security, integrate with existing infrastructure or fit naturally with processes specific to the mission. This friction (the cost of technology discovery, evaluation, accreditation, and integration) results in a lag between the technologies available to agile adversaries and those that are available to an intelligence analyst in the workplace.

To minimize the barriers that stifle innovation, BRIDGE provides an unclassified access controlled environment accessible to users and technology providers via the internet. This framework enables application providers to host their own solutions while connecting to the "virtual platform" without third party involvement. It exposes core services that emulate intelligence community mission settings enabling providers to mash-up with one another and leverage existing services without being forced to "reinvent the wheel". Providers can develop against the service endpoints, get direct feedback from users resulting shorter development spirals and reduce the time it takes to transition to production. These endpoints instantiate security and sharing best practices, providing a forcing function that pushes technologies in directions that support enterprise goals. As a result, promising tools can be plucked from this environment and quickly integrated into classified mission environments.

This creates a technology pipeline which follows the iPhone App Store model by providing a low barrier-to-entry platform that enables tech providers to easily expose capabilities to users, so that they can discover/use next generation capabilities that have value to their mission even while the capabilities are still in beta. iPhone apps have proliferated explosively since its inception due to its accessibility, clear specifications for participation and an active user base (buyers). These conditions are necessary for crowdsourcing and have unleashed the creativity of thousands of innovators. BRIDGE is beginning to see the same effect.

At the intra-agency level, BRIDGE provides an App Store-like decentralized repository of big ideas and innovations. Through a SOA framework, this repository facilitates technology reuse, reducing duplication of effort while giving agency managers access to best practices.

Propagating Enterprise Standards

Perhaps the most important factor in harnessing the undirected power of the network effect is the careful selection and enforcement of enterprise standards. To meet enterprise goals, CIOs spend significant time and resources creating elegant enterprise architectures and extensive service guidelines. All too frequently, these guidelines are impractical, unclear or unenforceable. Forced to decide between compliance and mission imperatives, mission managers often ignore these guidelines, creating a "black market" for technologies which perpetuates fragmentation and prevents the spread of best practices. The promise and ease of enterprise deployment of Web2.0 technologies has exacerbated this problem in many cases by widening the gap between new technologies and legacy mission systems. The pace of technology change and the diversity of capabilities demand a more decentralized approach to enterprise IT governance. In a way that parallels governance in market economies, CIOs establish a small set of ground rules that facilitate informed choices of managers rather than mandating solutions.

The first step towards propagating enterprise best practices is to ensure that it is easy for mission managers (ultimately the decision maker who decides what technology to buy or implement) to identify technologies that conform. Many CIOs establish enterprise guidelines through reference architectures but stop short of establishing a mechanism to verify application conformance. A "rule" creates a mechanism to verify conformance to the guideline. To shape enterprise practices, a rule must be enforceable, practical and part of acquisition or implementation decisions. Guidelines without a rule are often ignored since they can be ambiguously interpreted, vendors claim compliance since there is no way to verify, and implementations may be incompatible, ultimately giving mission managers no mechanism to filter (and no benefit from filtering) potential solutions.

BRIDGE introduces the concept of a conformance endpoint, a web service interface that implements the rule. Applications that consume the service can be verified to conform in a standard way, making it easy for providers and evaluators to validate compliance. Mission managers are provided a conformance checklist for technologies enabling them to make informed decisions on a technology's implementation of standards and integratability with existing mission systems.

Establishing rules that shape acquisition decisions gives CIOs a powerful mechanism for driving technologies towards enterprise standards through a light touch. It is equivalent to steering with a canard, a small control surface toward the front of the airframe. In front, a canard has the same steering effect as a much larger surface near the rear. For IT governance, the effort required to shape technologies before acquisition and integration is much less than that required once they are implemented in mission systems. The mission critical nature of operations makes it almost impossible to reshape solutions once implemented. By enforcing standards as a barrier to entry, tech providers are more likely to embed them into core offerings reducing the likelihood that a third party integrator will need to make modifications to ensure conformance with each new release.

Rules drive down the cost of integration and coordination. But, they come at the expense of innovation. Additional rules increase the barrier to entry for new technologies and may create a barrier that keeps creative ideas out. Before establishing a rule, the organization should carefully consider the impact on innovation, the practicality of implementation, the scope of its enforcement and its permanence. Rules that can't be met practically, are not uniformly enforced or are frequently changed will be ignored. Too many rules will reduce agility and cause an organization to fall behind the state of the art. The optimal set of rules for an organization depends on the balance between the need for enterprise coordination and the value of agility. This balance will depend on the complexity of the organization, the diversity of the mission and other factors.

The Six Simple Rules

Since striking this balance for the intelligence mission is central to the BRIDGE approach, it would be worthwhile to explore the specific rules for BRIDGE in greater detail. Technology participation is governed by the 6 Simple Rules, a set of standards which ensure that technologies in the space work together – sharing information freely and securely across application boundaries.

As has been documented, intelligence analysis has suffered from an analytic environment that is very fragmented. A direct consequence has been that decision makers (and analysts) have found it difficult to know what is collectively known about a particular topic. The complexity of the mission requires hundreds of specialized tools to support a wide variety of analytic challenges and data sources. But the large number of tools - and the fact that insight expressed through analysis in a tool is difficult to leverage if you don't regularly use that tool - has created "tool chaos," an excessive fragmentation of insight. Additionally, most analytic insight (hunches, experience, processes and source assessments) is not captured and is entirely lost when an analyst leaves, retires or even changes roles. Web 2.0 tools have been implemented to increase knowledge worker productivity by capturing and reusing knowledge worker insight. But these techniques tools are disconnected from mission systems solving some problems while creating others. The 6 Simple Rules were established to create a framework that brings the network effect to all tools makes standalone tools collaborative, and collaborative tools better - creating a connected enterprise.

The rules do not specify *what* technologies will meet intelligence analysts' needs, but rather *how* technologies (existing and future) can be modified to enable integrated analysis. Establishment of these rules and proper governance enables many tools to work together in a radical new environment for sharing/linking/layering of insight consistent with the vision of the ODNI Analytic Transformation (AT) initiative. The 6 Simple Rules: 1) Web User Interface, 2) Unified Authentication, 3) Activity Logging in a Common Format to a Service, 4) Access Aware Applications, 5) Discoverable/Linkable Artifacts and 6) Core Capabilities Available via Web Services. These rules create a number of enterprise benefits:

Rapid transition of capabilities: Establishing the rules through accessible web service conformance endpoints provides technology providers clear specifications to create capabilities that are more easily integrated into existing intelligence community environments. Web service enabled capabilities in conformant tools are more accessible – providing an environment that supports new combinations of capabilities after stand-up. The Simple Rules reduce the cost of transition to the government and the risk associated with development to the technology provider.

Enhanced security: The Simple Rules provide for a more secure environment through common authentication, access aware applications and auditing of activity in a common format that can be mined to identify malicious behavior.

Enhanced sharing: Pulling group associations, communities of interest (COI) and social network data out of individual applications to use collectively through "access aware" applications enhances the utility of these groupings – since they may be expressed once and used frequently for trusted sharing of insight. Having a common service for exposing affiliations connects Web 2.0 "friends lists" with formally established groups enabling deeper awareness and sharing. An easy to use access control framework enables end users to draw their own boundaries for dissemination appropriate to their mission.

Broad availability of tools: Different mission needs result in a wide variety of IT infrastructures and desktop configurations. These differences limit the distribution of tools, increase accreditation costs, result in uneven analytic toolsets, prevent usage convergence towards best of breed technologies and add to the fragmentation of insight. The Simple Rules distill integration requirements to the essential components to give compliant applications the broadest distributability across the community. The rule which requires web user interfaces is an example. One of the few enterprise wide similarities is the availability of web browsers to analysts. Recent advances in the richness, speed, and interactivity of information presented in a browser have closed the gap in functionality between web and desktop applications. As a result, there is a growing list of capabilities presented via a web interface that have near enterprise-wide reach. There are very few desktop applications (Microsoft Office excepted) that can make this claim.

Context shared across tool boundaries: One tool can leverage the fact that an analyst has expressed interest in a specific target/topic in a different tool - without directly integrating with that tool. Through Simple Rule compliant applications that log activity in a common format, context can be shared across tool boundaries (without expensive app to app integration) alleviating the need for an analyst to restate needs, priorities and interests repeatedly for each application required to do his/her job.

More powerful technologies: Since Simple Rule compliant technologies can be more readily combined, technology providers can focus on extending core competencies while leveraging the strengths of other services resulting in quicker development cycles and lighter weight, recomposable applications that combine best of breed components.

The Simple Rules alleviate technology barriers to information sharing enabling more effective analysis: Fragmented Insight, Limited Discovery, Prohibitive Integration Costs, Bloated Tools and Reactive Security.

Supporting Perpetual Beta through Technology Availability Levels

Many technology companies have implemented development strategies that enable them to continuously upgrade their product even while deployed. Consumers are willing to accept reasonable risk in a "perpetual beta" model in exchange for rapidly adapting technologies that remain at the edge of the state of the art.

BRIDGE has adopted this model for technology development. The environment is open to technologies that are still maturing. Developers can leverage existing services, mash-up new combinations of services and get direct feedback from users enabling shorter development spirals. Users can try out these technologies, work directly with technologist on analytic challenges and shape the technologies of the future. Early interaction with end users is one of the biggest factors in successful deployment of technologies.

But supporting a variety of technologies at varying levels of maturity in the same environment comes with risks. If users don't have a means to distinguish between reliable tools and technologies that are unstable as they rapidly evolve, they can become frustrated. For this reason, BRIDGE assigns technologies in the space a *Technology Availability Level* (TAL) rating. TALs range from 1-4 (development, alpha, beta and core service. Technologies in the space are required to prominently display their TAL to users. This enables users to distinguish between developing technologies and applications that have been verified to be stable.

TALs are assigned by testing against 3 dimensions: conformance to the Simple Rules, stability as established by random availability tests, and commitment to remain in the space. To "graduate" from BRIDGE to mission settings, applications must progress to the highest TAL level.

Expertise Outreach

An access controlled but low barrier to entry environment that accepts risk is also well suited for expertise outreach. BRIDGE provides an environment for intelligence community analysts to reach out to expertise elsewhere in federal, state and local government, in academia, and industry. BRIDGE employs a "web of trust" access control model that enables users in the space to let others in by taking responsibility for them through sponsorship. These users can, in turn, let others into the space in the same way. In this way, all users in the space are part of a trust chain. This model enables communities to form and morph quickly – permitting cross organization, attributable conversations in an access controlled environment, providing access to minds outside traditional intelligence circles – an analytic force multiplier.

This complements the tool discovery and role of BRIDGE since evaluation (especially of Web 2.0 tools) requires a vibrant environment full of activity. Access to cutting edge technologies draws users. Active users create the conditions necessary to evaluate tools. This activity and the challenges represented draws innovators. This is network effect at work. The more users and technologists participate, the better the environment gets.

Instantiating Enterprise 2.0 or Gov 2.0 requires more than the standup of Web 2.0 tools. It requires processes that tap into rapidly developing innovations outside the organization while gently shaping them into capabilities that support the unique mission. New approaches to technology discovery, evaluation, integration and governance provide this mechanism giving CIOs the control needed to meet enterprise goals without providing an unnecessary barrier to innovation. These approaches unfetter innovators, provide a platform for them to connect, and facilitate interactions with end users resulting in technologies that can transform an agency's mission effectiveness.

Dan Doney is CTO at Strategic Enterprise Solutions in the US Office of the Director of National Intelligence, and a technical advisor to the intelligence community on information sharing, collaboration and enterprise architecture. He is leading a Gov 2.0 initiative called BRIDGE designed to overcome barriers in technology adoption through a new governance framework that enhances technology discovery and evaluation, while streamlining accreditation and integration. He comes from a research background where his focus has been on the application of network effect (Web 2.0) and complex adaptive system approaches to information foraging and sensemaking in support the intelligence community mission.

---

[1] Beth Simone Noveck (2009) *Wiki Government. How Technology Can Make Government Better, Democracy Stronger, and Citizens More Powerful.* Brookings Institution Press.

[2] For more about BRIDGE, see http://about.bridge-ic.net/

#6

GOVERNMENT IN THE 21ST CENTURY: A STATE'S PERSPECTIVE

David G. Fletcher
Chief Technology Officer, State of Utah

In government, we are currently on a bridge to a new future. Not only has the way that we are and can do things changed, but the very nature of what we do is also evolving at a rate never before experienced. Over the past 15 years, government has felt a series of waves that continue to impact what it does and, in fact, what it is. These impacts are reaching down into every level of government and providing new opportunities at the same time that old structures are beginning to erode and find themselves incapable of meeting new demands. State governments in the U.S. find themselves at the center of this surge, trying to respond to citizens, legislators, elected officials, businesses, the federal government, local government and education. This chapter will discuss these impacts and how the state of Utah has responded to them by understanding and leveraging technology to participate in this new era of government.

For those involved at a state level in promoting change, government 2.0 is both local and global. Technology creates an opportunity to provide new experiences and improved service for local constituents. At the same time government workers, including technologists, are able to participate in the much broader experiment of government, which is not only national, but global. Collaboration at this level has never happened to this degree. Managers in Utah are able to tap into the experiences of Europe, Asia and Latin America in real time, and learn from those experiences. Those who leverage the global evolution in e-government stand the most to benefit from it by applying its lessons on a daily basis.

There are many ways that local and state government can benefit from what is really a global revolution. In Utah, we have focused on how we can maximize these benefits. Some of the key areas where we have benefited include 1) Improved management, 2) More participation and better collaboration, 3) Integration of services for a better user experience and 4) More interest in the future and the opportunities it presents.

Using Technology to Manage

Although Utah has consistently been ranked as one of the best managed states in the U.S., it faces a growing number of complex issues just like most governments. These have included the recessions and consequent budget contractions of 2001-03 and 2007-09, leadership changes in governors and legislators, new demands from citizens and businesses, etc. Government 2.0 helps us view such changes as opportunities, and not just as problems or challenges. New online platforms are providing ways to manage government differently. In some cases, when new services or regulatory operations are being developed in Utah, they are being done entirely online, particularly when there is not an existing agency already performing the function. To be successful, personnel overseeing these new processes must understand not only how business can be performed online, but also what the ramifications are for stakeholders. Managers need to be careful to understand their constituents, what they are doing online and how government services and information can serve these constituents in a virtual environment that is increasingly complex and noisy.

Citizens are busy people. They have more distractions than ever before. There is a lot that government can do, not only to streamline their internal operations, but also to help citizens perform the functions that they may be required to perform. Government 2.0 requires interaction. It is no longer about providing information and static forms that can be printed off so the user can then mail it in or deliver it by hand. Throughout a lengthy transition, and particularly with new services, the government entity should consider facilitated interaction available 24x7. That means that there must be channels for feedback and response if government is really to improve and provide the greatest benefit. It also requires that government be agile at shifting resources to these new channels in order to respond in an acceptable way.

With mounting economic challenges, most political leaders are focusing on ways to make government more efficient. The second stage of e-government, which was transactional in nature and put government services online, can deliver efficiency, but in order to do so, it must be nurtured to ensure a high degree of utilization. When the online channel becomes the primary channel for delivering these services, or in some cases, the only channel, the economic impact is very significant. Collaborative government can help achieve the quantitative goals that government has for the adoption of services. When these goals are met and the metrics are shared with policy makers, digital government will move on to the next stage of maturity which is multi-dimensional in nature and will offer citizens more choice and more involvement, while maintaining a high level of fiscal responsibility. Collaborative government means that government is more personal and more direct, while also being more immediate and responsive. At the same time, today's tools make it possible to have a larger reach than ever before. As governments become more digitally mature in the way that they offer services, the most mundane of these services can become even easier to use and less intrusive in the lives of citizens.

Governments that are still fairly low on the e-government maturity curve and who wish to participate in the benefits of collaborative government should not try to bypass the benefits of transactional and service-oriented e-government[1]. Without a solid base of well-utilized e-services, it will be difficult for a government to sustain progress. However, collaborative government can provide creative mechanisms to support and build up a base of e-services as demonstrated by Washington D.C. with their Apps for Democracy contest. If government wants to achieve its greatest potential, it must understand the needs and desires of its citizens, which means that it needs constant collaboration and feedback. It must be agile and flexible in responding to that feedback.

Collaborating Like Never Before

Opportunities for government to interact with its citizenry now abound everywhere. Twitter, Facebook, MySpace, Slideshare, YouTube, Swivel, UStream, Vimeo, Google and Yahoo Groups, FriendFeed, SecondLife are all among a fast growing list of digital platforms where citizens are choosing to spend a growing percentage of their time. Many government entities are choosing to interact with their citizens within these virtual spaces and finding unexpected results. For example, in Salt Lake City, Utah, over 300,000 people had signed on to the local Facebook network by 2009. Public officials like Governor Gary Herbert and Attorney General Mark Shurtleff have discovered that having a presence on these sites is much like having an open door policy for citizens although it is easier to manage and quicker to respond to. Others, like state representatives Steve Urquhart and John Dougall, have discovered blogging as a way to share public opinions about the legal process and laws that they are proposing. Their blogs have become highly interactive public forums where citizens can register their views about important issues and generally receive a direct response for these public officials. Representative Urquhart even set up a public wiki called Politicopia as he was seeking a way to encourage greater political dialogue among Utah's constituents. The wiki became a new e-democracy initiative, serving as a continuous virtual town hall.

Perhaps the most ambitious experiments were undertaken by the Utah Senate majority, which established a blog-centric website, SenateSite.com, with the purpose of opening up government, particularly the law making and budget setting process. The website features a growing number of web 2.0 experiments, including a Senate Radio channel using GCast, live streaming video with UStream, a YouTube Channel, Facebook site and Twitter feeds along with photo sharing on Picasa. Even during the time when the Legislature is not in session (10 months out of the year), this site still receives thousands of monthly visits to hear the senators most recent comments and activities. As government becomes more open and makes more information available, corresponding activity in the private sector and from individual citizens has also increased. Many more people are realizing that they can have a direct channel to their legislators which has resulted in a proliferation of blogs, chats and websites involved in civic dialogue.

Although many government workers in Utah experimented with blogging in 2002, many were not willing to continue with an exercise that required a significant amount of effort to maintain and like elsewhere, many blogs went silent after a period of time. Participation in microblogging services, particularly Twitter, is less time consuming and more measurable. Agencies can see how many are following their posts and just as importantly, who is following. In the case of Utah, this has resulted in a significant increase in collaboration between government, the traditional media and the education community, as well as a more informed and involved public.

Integrating Service Across Government

The state of Utah has recognized that it does not have the budget that would be required to do everything it is asked to do or would like to do through traditional means. Web 2.0 offers the opportunity to begin looking at government differently and accomplish some of these things in new ways. What has resulted is that the doors of government have been thrown wide open. People are realizing that they no longer have to be content to be impacted by government agencies, but that they can have their own impact on the social compact known as government.

In order to facilitate use by citizens, governments have been discussing ways to deliver services based on the user perspective such as life events or communities of interest for many years. This has resulted in the creation of "cross agency portals", especially by state and federal governmental organizations.

Utah has created an architecture that leverages both local and global infrastructure. Local infrastructure provides stability for large scale data management. Global infrastructure provides flexibility and collaborative capabilities. Combined effectively, the organization can move forward in a dynamic way that supports growth of knowledge, service capabilities and innovation.

Looking Forward to the Future

The future provides many opportunities for changing the face of government. New technologies are emerging every day, even before we can implement many of those that are becoming mainstream. Government needs a way to sift through the multitude of technologies, programs, widgets and ideas to identify those which really matter and can be implemented within their structure and environment in a way that will make an impact. Becoming part of a global discussion about government effectiveness and innovation has helped Utah move forward.

Many technologies are very exciting and relevant, but the cost structure to implement them may be prohibitive within the time frame when they could really make a difference. Sometimes, the cost may be acceptable, but the complexity and ability of the organization to implement them may mean that the organization will lose other opportunities which may be equally great or greater. In Utah, a governance structure was implemented that allowed for agility and flexibility. Strategic planning has become a daily process as we evolve and incorporate new opportunities presented by technological advances. Social networks enhance the organization's ability to identify the best of these opportunities.

Government 2.0 is now an integrated part of governmental operations for many state and federal governments. Others are just getting started. Those who are at the leading edge are ready to move forward to an increasingly multidimensional form of online government, which will likely involve the semantic web, virtual worlds, augmented reality and increased social participation.

David Fletcher (@dfletcher) is the Chief Technology Officer for the State of Utah. He oversees the state's digital government initiatives which resulted in the state being named as the #1 digital state in the United States in 2008 by the Center for Digital Government, and the state's portal, Utah.gov, was named as the #1 state portal in both 2007 and 2009. David maintains a blog on e-government at http://davidfletcher.blogspot.com.

---

[1] eGovernment Maturity, Phillip J. Windley, Ph.D., http://j.mp/Lq3DB

#7

Looking to the Future by Learning from the Past

Steve Radick

Associate, Booz Allen Hamilton

Webster's Dictionary defines democracy as "government by the people". For more than 200 years, it's the one word that has defined the United States government. Starting as early as 1775 with colonial assemblies and Committees of Correspondence, the philosophy of a "government of the people, by the people" has been reinvigorated by a new era of technologies designed to facilitate openness, transparency and public participation—Government 2.0.

While the principles have remained the same, the methods of communication have and will continue to evolve. Newspaper and television changed the way we *receive information*, email and the Internet changed the way we *communicate*, and social media is changing the way we *build communities*, both online and off. "Government 2.0" has become the latest and greatest buzzword, with thousands of evangelists gathering in grassroots events[1], high-profile conferences[2], and full-scale social networks[3]. Agencies and departments from across the government are eager to realize the benefits, starting blogs, creating YouTube channels and establishing

Twitter accounts. Government 2.0 has also been grabbing headlines in traditional media, including the New York Times[4] and Wall Street Journal[5].

But is the concept of Government 2.0 really all that new, or is it just the next step toward realizing a vision first laid out more than 200 years ago?

Take a look at the following headlines:

> **"Talking to Clinton, Via Computer"**
>
> Call it a town meeting in cyberspace.
>
> That's what President Clinton is trying to hold, in cooperation with CompuServe, one of the country's largest computerized information services.
>
> *The Bergen County Record, Neil Reisner, July 29, 1993*

> **"White House Correspondence is Shifting to Electronic Mail"**
>
> Want a full transcript of President Clinton's latest speech on housing or welfare? Just tap in a command on your home computer.
>
> Want the White House to know instantly what you think of Mr. Clinton's economic plan? Call the "White House comments line" and punch in a response on your touch-tone phone.
>
> *The Dallas Morning News*, Richard Berke, April 18, 1993

"Government Expands its Claim on the Web"

In the brave new world imagined by the visionaries on Vice President Gore's "Reinventing Government" team, one day students will apply for and receive college loans online, police officers at crime scenes will tap into computerized fingerprint files and travelers will submit passport applications from the comfort of their living rooms.

Washington Post, Barbara J. Saffir, March 18, 1997

"Servicing Citizens with the Internet"

One thing emerged clearly from a federal webmaster conference Northern Virginia this year: World Wide Web sites are becoming an important part of the government's strategy to shed its bureaucratic image and provide faster public service.

Washington Post, Gabriel Margasak, April 21, 1997

"Understanding the IT Revolution"

Among the more profound effects of the revolution in information technology and, with it, the World Wide Web, are the global interest and effort in reinventing government and the pursuit of business process re-engineering activities at the national level.

Washington Technology, John Makulowich, May 7, 1997

Sound familiar? Today's stories about Government 2.0 sound very similar to the stories told 10-to-15 years ago when the government first started using the Internet.

In reading through these and other articles from Internet archives, I was reminded that the challenges the government is facing in implementing social media are the same challenges we faced in implementing email, Web sites, and even the telephone. While the tools and technology will always change, the fundamental challenges of changing government culture are remarkably consistent over time.

Government 2.0 (circa 1995)	**Government 2.0 (present day)**
People will spend all day on email not doing any work	People will spend all day on Facebook not doing any work
Viruses will infect our systems so we have to block the Internet	Viruses and spyware will infect our systems so we have to block social networks
People can't program a VCR, but we expect them to know how to log into CompuServe?	This social media stuff is for Generation Y – we can't expect Baby Boomers to log into Twitter
The public can send us electronic mail	The public can comment directly on our blog and Facebook page
Government agencies are creating Web sites but blocking employee access to the Internet	Government agencies are creating profiles and channels but blocking employee access to social networks
The National Science Foundation promotes government-wide Internet development and hosts "webmaster workshops"	Members of GovLoop organize tweetups and attend Social Media Club events
Government agencies hire Web programmers by the truckload to create Web sites	Government agencies are creating entire teams dedicated to social media
Government will be able track the sites I visit	Government will be able to tell exactly who I am and collect information on my private life

It is easy to get so caught up in the vision of President Obama's *Transparency and Open Government* that we forget the mistakes (and successes) of the past. We can all benefit from looking at the experiences of our innovation predecessors to avoid the same pitfalls, take advantage of missed opportunities, and set realistic expectations for ourselves.

I recently went back in time myself and re-read the *Cluetrain Manifesto*[6], a fantastic, ground-breaking book published 10 years ago. In the technology world, a decade is a lifetime. Ten years ago, there was no Facebook, no Twitter and no YouTube. Ten years ago, email and the Internet were transforming the government. Ten years later, the principles and concepts laid out in the Cluetrain Manifesto continue to not only be relevant, but almost prophetic in their application to today's government.

The Cluetrain laid out 95 theses that described the new global conversation taking place via the Internet. Here are my 20 theses[7] (I'm not nearly as ambitious as the Cluetrain authors) for carpetbaggers, gurus, civil servants, contractors and anyone else interested in today's Government 2.0.

1. The risks of social media are greatly outweighed by the risks of NOT doing social media.

2. Your Government agency/organization/group/branch is not unique. You do not work in a place that just can't just use social media because your data is too sensitive[8]. You do not work in an environment where social media will never work. Your challenges, while unique to you, are not unique to the government.

3. You will work with skeptics and other people who want to see social media fail because the transparency and authenticity will expose their weaknesses.

4. You will work with people who want to get involved with social media for all the wrong reasons. They will see it as an opportunity to advance their own their careers, to make more money, or to show off. These people will be more dangerous to your efforts than the biggest skeptic.

5. Younger employees are not necessarily any more knowledgeable about social media than older employees. Stop assuming that they are.

6. Before going out and hiring any social media "consultants", assume that there is already someone within your organization who is actively using social media and who is very passionate about it. Find them, use them, engage them. These are the people who will make or break your foray into social media.

7. Mistakes can and will be made (a lot). Stop trying to create safeguards to eliminate the possibility of mistakes and instead concentrate on how to deal with them when they are made.

8. Information security is a very real and valid concern. Do NOT take this lightly.

9. Policies are not written in stone. With justification, passion and knowledge, policies and rules can and should be changed. Sometimes it's as easy as asking, but other times will require a knockdown, drag-out fight. Both are important.

10. Be humble. You don't know everything so stop trying to pretend that you do. It's ok to be wrong.

11. But be confident. Know what you know and don't back down. You will be challenged by skeptics and others who do

not care and/or understand social media. Do not let them discourage you.

12. There are true social media champions throughout the government. Find them. Talk to them. Learn from them.

13. Government 2.0 is not a new concept. It's getting so much attention now because social media has given a voice to the ambitious, the innovative and the creative people within the government.

14. Social media is not about the technology but what the technology enables.

15. Social media is not driven by the position, the title or the department; it's driven by the person[9]. Stop trying to pigeon-hole into one team or department and instead think of a way to bring together people from across your organization.

16. Instead of marketing your social media capabilities, skills, experience, platforms, software, etc. to the government, why don't you try talking with them? An honest conversation will be remembered for far longer than a PowerPoint presentation.

17. Today's employees will probably spend five minutes during the workday talking to their friends on Facebook or watching the latest YouTube video. Today's employees will also probably spend an hour at 10:00 at night answering emails or responding to a work-related blog post. Assume that your employees are good people who want to do the right thing and who take pride in their work.

18. Agency Secretaries and Department Heads are big boys and girls. They should be able to have direct conversations with

their workforce without having to jump through hoops to do so.

19. Transparency, participatory, collaborative - these terms do not refer only to the end state; they refer to the process used to get there as well. It's ok to have debates, arguments and disagreements about the best way to go about achieving "Government 2.0." Diverse perspectives, opinions and beliefs should be embraced and talked about openly.

20. It's not enough to just *allow* negative feedback on your blog or website; you also have to *do* something about it. This might mean engaging in a conversation about why person X feels this way or (gasp!) making a change to an outdated policy. Don't just listen to what the public has to say, you have to also care about it too.

When the Continental Congress appointed Benjamin Franklin as the nation's first Postmaster General in 1775, it could take up to 14 days to carry a letter from New York to Philadelphia. When President Obama appointed Aneesh Chopra as the nation's first Chief Technology Officer more than 200 years later, people across the world could have real-time conversations via wireless phone, microblogs or videoconferences. While the technology supporting our government can and will evolve, the principles of participation, transparency and collaboration are timeless. Today's technology may make it easier to realize these principles, the people and the processes behind the technology will truly determine if this will be a revolutionary phase in our history, or just an evolutionary step.

**thanks to Rick Levine, Christopher Locke, Doc Searls and David Weinberger for inspiring me and many others with their book,* The Cluetrain Manifesto.

Steve Radick (@sradick) is Associate at Booz Allen Hamilton. As one of Booz Allen's social media and Government 2.0 leads, Steve works with the federal government to integrate social media strategies and tactics into organizational strategies. He blogs about his approach to social media and his experiences working with his government clients on his blog, "Social Media Strategery," located at www.steveradick.com.

---

[1] Government 2.0 Camp was an unconference about using social media tools and Web 2.0 technologies to create a more effective, efficient and collaborative U.S. government on all levels (local, state, and federal). It was attended by more than 500 government employees, contractors and media. http://j.mp/troW

[2] Gov 2.0 Summit, a new government technology conference co-produced by O'Reilly Media and TechWeb, was held in September 2009 in Washington, DC. http://www.gov2summit.com/

[3] Launched in June 2008, GovLoop is the "Facebook" for Government, and boasts more than 14,000 members as of September 2009. http://www.govloop.com/

[4] "Government 2.0 Meets Catch 22," by Saul Hansell, The New York Times, March 17, 2009. http://j.mp/19tzVJ

[5] "WTF? Military Web 2.0 Report Actually Making Sense", by Noah Shachtman, Wired, April 10, 2009. http://bit.ly/AmYyq

[6] The Cluetrain Manifesto, written by Rick Levine, Christopher Locke, Doc Searls and David Weinberger, was first published in 1999.

[7] "Twenty Theses for Government 2.0, Cluetrain Style", by Steve Radick, Social Media Strategery, February 15, 2009. http://j.mp/PSLAq

[8] Intellipedia is a secure wiki built on the MediaWiki platform available to employees of the 16 agencies in the Intelligence Community and other national-security related organizations. It was created to enable open communication and collaboration across firewalls and individual agencies. http://j.mp/3ckFU

[9] "Social Media is Driven by the Person, Not the Position", by Steve Radick, Social Media Strategery, January 18, 2009. http://j.mp/rpY3

#8

Government 2.0, e-Government and Culture

Stephen Collins
Founder, AcidLabs

> *"Every dystopia is a utopia turned inside out... The problem isn't in the basic idea, it's in the arrogance of implementation. It's in the idea that we will get it right the first time."*
> - *Steven Lloyd Wilson*[1]

Government 2.0 is more than just e-Government with a new name. e-Government in Australia has largely focused on delivery of services and programs via online or connected means — an admirable agenda that has in large part been successful in the 10 or so years it has been a priority. But online delivery is just a part of what Government 2.0 offers.

My personal view is that Government 2.0 is an unhelpful term. As with Enterprise 2.0 and Web 2.0 before it, it somewhat unintentionally puts technology in people's minds and creates visions of something large, expensive and complex that will be done to government rather than by government and misses the point about the groundswell culture and practice change supported by technology that is arguably the more substantial and world-changing aspect of the thing.

Tim O'Reilly, one of the co-creators of the term Web 2.0[2], and now passionate Government 2.0 advocate, describes[3] Government 2.0 as requiring a shift to platform thinking, where government provides the platform for amazing things to happen — think highways, the Internet, GPS (all originally created by government) — and builds services on it, but also opens it up in order for citizens and business to build their own applications, products and services. Ones not considered or even dreamed of by government, but using the infrastructure and data provided by government.

Still, this description focuses on the tools and technology. I think the end game Tim is moving towards is systems thinking — considering government and all the things it does as a part of much larger, contextual puzzle. If we focus on the tools and technology, we risk becoming obsessed with minutiae that hide the real possibilities.

To my mind, the tools and technology are the scaffolding upon which Government 2.0 can be built — a critical part of the whole, but not the answer in and of itself. Rather, for Government 2.0 to succeed, we should focus on the models delivered by 2.0 thinking — lightweight, agile, responsive over reactive, prepared to make small mistakes, open, collaborative — and the fact that at its heart, it's about people.

So, let's begin with a useful definition, the definition used by the very active Australian Government 2.0 community[4] that has gathered on Google Groups to discuss the subject. I've chosen this definition not just because I had a hand in making it, but also because I think it's one of the most balanced out there:

> *Government 2.0 is not specifically about social networking or technology based approaches to anything. It represents a fundamental shift in the implementation of government —*

> *toward an open, collaborative, cooperative arrangement where there is (wherever possible) open consultation, open data, shared knowledge, mutual acknowledgment of expertise, mutual respect for shared values and an understanding of how to agree to disagree. Technology and social tools are an important part of this change but are essentially an enabler in this process.*

You will see from the definition that there's a significantly larger picture that needs to be understood, explored, experimented with and ultimately implemented to make Government 2.0 the reality it can be.

Government 2.0 makes a deliberate effort to break down what can seem impenetrable barriers of bureaucracy and introduce a more human face to the executive arm of government. Public servants are encouraged to engage with each other and with the public where possible, within their own spheres of expertise.

Rather than outbound communication from agencies to the public, the discourse becomes conversation — amongst the public sector, between the public sector and the community, and amongst the various parts of the community itself. This conversational approach offers many benefits — the public sector is kept constantly attuned to the needs and wants of the public, the public is less baffled by bureaucracy as they are in more frequent touch.

Borrowing heavily from the culture of Open Source, Government 2.0 assumes that publicly open, multiple and rapid iterations of policy, of programs and of ideas is a good thing. Not necessarily for everything government does, but as and where appropriate. Adopting this practice allows for a more agile approach to policy development and program delivery. The big bang approaches of the past where services delivered by the public sector are found to not be suitable for some reason, but are unchangeable and therefore an expensive waste of funds and effort due to the implementation model, can be replaced with an approach that sees things tested in public and subject to change as shifting priorities and needs are identified.

The Government 2.0 Taskforce[5] created by the Australian government to address issues and report on needed changes to implement the cultural, practice and technological changes necessary in Australia to adopt this new model, is itself using the model to help identify the priorities the public want to see returned to the government in its report. So too are events such as Labor Senator, closet geek and strong ICT advocate, Kate Lundy's Public Sphere[6], which have proved measurably successful and have cast the net wide for input and expertise. Efforts in other jurisdictions too, have seen significant success in prioritizing policy, funding and human resource needs. Just last week several announcements here and overseas moved the conversation along.

New Zealand's State Services Commission has announced NZGOAL[7], an experiment in licensing Public Sector Information with an appropriate license in order to adopt, as they say in the announcement[8], "principles which embrace, among other things, the notions of open access, open licensing, creativity, authenticity, non- discrimination and open formats." They very deliberately state it is an experiment, designed to be iterated and improved over time through input from many sources. This announcement and what it means has been noticed here and as far away as the UK by senior members of the Parliament[9], as well as by advocates of more open licensing of PSI.

In Australia, we have moves in this direction too. The reform agenda[10] around Freedom of Information and publication status of government and public sector information will necessarily see a change in licensing for some material, it's a change that has already been adopted by some organizations and there is help available from the Government Information Licensing Framework[11] for agencies unsure how they should more permissively license their data for reuse.

In September 2009, NSW Premier, Nathan Rees announced[12] at the first NSW Sphere event[13] that not only would the NSW Government be sponsoring a $100,000 competition[14] for development of applications that made innovative use of public sector data, but also that "Governments have to overcome old habits of secrecy and control. We've got to be interactive. The old one- way street style of politics has to go."

This announcement bore more than a passing resemblance to the Prime Minister's words[15] in his John Paterson Oration at the 2009 Australia New Zealand School of Government Annual Conference[16], where he emphasized the need for an innovative, open, outward-looking Australian public sector and a culture within the Australian public sector that supports these things. It also echoed the words of outgoing Commissioner Lynelle Briggs who has more than once stated[17] the need for a citizen-centric public sector and the need to look outside the boundaries of agencies to academia, to business and to the public themselves by using systems thinking to solve "wicked problems"[18].

The solving of wicked problems and a truly citizen-centric approach to government will mean that the ability for the public sector and the legislature to connect closely and collaborate with those outside government must be enhanced. Amongst other things, approaches like this support and enhance the government's Social Inclusion agenda[19].

Moving our public sector to a culture, set of practices and technologies that actively embraces Government 2.0 is high on the agenda of the current government with the Taskforce due to report on its findings at the end of 2009, the Prime Minister expressing his desire to see these types of changes and Minister Lindsay Tanner strong in his support[20] for culture, practice and technological change that will support this agenda. I have no doubt that it presents a significant challenge for public servants of every generation, but the promise it holds can deliver better evidence-based policy, more targeted programs and an open environment where the public sector is no longer an inscrutable mystery to large parts of the community but is something made up of real, approachable human beings with names and who really care about us — it's not that these things aren't already the case, but by adoption of Government 2.0 they become a given.

Government 2.0 is so much more than just e-Government with a new name.

> *"We need to connect citizens with each other to engage them more fully and directly in solving the problems that face us. We must use all available technologies and methods to open up the federal government, creating a new level of transparency to change the way business is conducted ... giving [people] the chance to participate in government deliberations and decision- making in ways that were not possible only a few years ago."*
>
> *- Obama campaign policy statement*[21]

Culture Change for Government 2.0

In our modern democracies, the ability for members of society to participate in some way is a fundamental and accepted right. Indeed, we use the term participatory democracy to describe one in which constituents are empowered to engage in the political decision-making process.

There has until recent times, been a burden of activity and wherewithal required that has meant only those with a singular desire to engage with the process of democracy - either at the legislative or executive level - have truly been empowered to do so. Whether that has meant by lobbying, protest or civil unrest, letter-writing or even the burdensome process of being elected to some form of legislature, it has been a task that took real effort.

How things have changed.

In the 21st Century the old, largely broadcast model has been broken. The ability for people, anywhere, to participate has shifted thanks to a medium, the Internet, that is ever more ubiquitous, more social, and relatively cheap.

We really are all a part of a huge melting pot possessed of the capability to participate. One-to-one and one-to-many communications are no longer the optimum modalities. We are now the inhabitants of a many-to-many world.

In recent times, as we have seen in the near-instant distribution of news in China after the Sichuan earthquake and in the coordination of political action in Moldova[22], Egypt[23] and most recently, Iran, the capability for production and participation has been bolstered by the easy availability of networks where each participant is both broadcaster and receiver.

A desire to participate, an increase in real or sought-after freedoms, relative ease and low cost of connectedness and the ever-accelerating power of tools that connect people online now means that there is a massive supply-side surplus to the ability of people everywhere to engage actively and meaningfully in the political process.

The power of networks is such that for every new node - each new person - the power of the network increases exponentially. We are hyperconnected[6] and there is no going back. In fact, we are leaping ahead at pace.

It is more than time for our social institutions - for government - to join in. They are no longer the broadcasters, *apart* from the conversation. They, and we, are part *of the conversation*.

But there is a problem. Governments are largely used to mostly talking *at* the constituency rather than *with* the constituency. It's not their fault. It's simply the way things have always been.

So why is it a problem?

It's a problem because in today's hyperconnected world, a legislature and an executive that isn't engaged in a close, many-way conversation with the public it serves is *no longer fit for purpose.* Both risk rapidly increasing irrelevance if they fail to adapt to the new world; one in which the public can, will and has done for itself where bureaucracies are too slow to respond to emergent needs and changes in opinion. In a hyperconnected world, to invoke Gilmore's Law[24] is easy – the connected community *will route around the damage* and do what needs to be done without the help of government.

In my country, Australia, as in nations across the globe, there are several organizations that are living, breathing examples of this very action – GetUp![25], which is arguably the most powerful movement for social and cultural change in Australia, OpenAustralia[26], which emulates the TheyWorkForYou model from the UK, the Centre for Policy Development[27], which is actively engaged in the progressive policymaking process and TweetMP[28] that tracks and analyses politicians' engagement using Twitter. The number of individuals and groups willing to participate in democracy in some for and to take action is growing. We're all empowered to do more than we could be in the past by our communities and our connectedness.

The Public Sphere is the title of a series of increasingly important and popular events created by Labor Party Senator and technology advocate, Kate Lundy. Senator Lundy is using the events to canvass, online and off, sentiment and opinion with respect to issues affecting Australia and its use of technology as a society. The events have proven so successful popular that the model has been adopted by several others and implemented equally successfully. The term Public Sphere, coined by German philosopher and sociologist, Jürgen Habermas, defines a place, physical or virtual, where open discussion of issues prevalent in society can take place and political action to remedy those issues can be formed. A strong, civil public sphere is a fundamental underpinning for a functional and successful liberal democracy.

Members of governments in Australia, in the UK, in New Zealand and most particularly and publicly in the US, say many of the right things about participatory government underpinned by a connected and engaged society. This is a much needed first move. But it is only the first. It is far from the end game.

In a society as connected as Australia, where according to recent research from Forrester[29], 3/4 of Australian adults online use social tools and 1/4 create their own content, around half are members of social networks and government needs to be present in online communities, listening and responding and sometimes talking.

A public service that is disconnected from the public it serves through the government of the day is no public service at all. Rather, it is a bureaucracy. Impenetrable. Byzantine. Inscrutable.

The legislature and the public service need to take action to participate online in a more sophisticated way than previously. This will require a fundamental shift in views on openness, risk, conversation, community, collaboration. A shift in the "who", the "what" and the "where". This will be a difficult task. But it is one that we must do soon if Australia is to be truly the clever country we have claimed to be for so long. There are well-evidenced benefits to innovation and creativity from collaboration of all kinds.

It is a misquotation to use it here, Churchill will no doubt spin in his grave, but it seems apt. A public service not engaged in active, ongoing conversation with the public "is a riddle, wrapped in a mystery, inside an enigma; but perhaps there is a key."

That key is a change in culture.

Australia is arguably a few steps off the pace with respect to the public sector being comfortable, and often, even prepared to engage with the community in a conversation aimed at collaborating on making our democracy better.

In this case, one of two things happen, and occasionally both. First, the public sector risks being inadequately informed of the needs and wants of the public and risks giving bad advice to government resulting in bad policy, programs and legislation. And second, the public may grow increasingly frustrated with the public sector, and through it, the government, for not heeding their mood.

I doubt anyone considers either of those outcomes desirable.

The right moves are being made at high level. But too slowly and not publicly enough. That said, we are beginning to see significant progress being made in setting the new agenda by the federally appointed Government 2.0 Taskforce after what appeared to be a slow start.

The Australian Public Service Commission has had a document in draft, Circular 2008/8[30], since December 2008 that lays out a largely workable set of guidelines for online engagement of public servants. But why is it still a draft in late 2009? The APS Commissioner recently gave a speech[31] to the John Curtin Institute of Public Policy that laid a framework for a much richer engagement with the public that squarely places the citizen at the center of government. And the most recent State of the Service Report[32] makes specific mention of the need for government and the public to engage more closely. So too, the Prime Minister[33] and several other senior Ministers[34] have made specific mention of much needed public sector reform addressing openness and innovation as key issues. The concern is, however, that these are largely words and may not be borne out in reality.

When I speak with public servants as I often do, too few of them *at any level*, are aware of these documents, the policies they embody, and the strong push for this new openness and engagement. In conversation, I hear many arguments against open engagement between government and the public. Too hard. No skills. Management resistance. Not allowed. It's not the way we do things.

We need to take action to remove whatever it is that causes these blocks.

There are many public servants at all levels of government who stand ready, willing and able to engage directly with the public if only you will let them. They are knowledgeable and capable and proud of their work. They will help you govern and help you develop and deliver better government by being deeply connected into the communities they serve. By being a trusted, real and human part of those communities. If only you will let them.

We need to actively encourage change within our parliaments and our public sector that removes the resistance to this engagement. It is far easier to point out the size of the chasm than to start building a bridge over it.

As politicians, as public servants and as citizens we should ensure our colleagues, our staff and our political representatives *at all levels* are empowered to participate and provided with the skills they need to engage with the public openly and on an as-needed basis within their spheres of expertise.

And we need to do it urgently. Urgency does not imply haste, it simply implies rapidity. And this culture change *is* urgent. Of this have no doubt.

As a former public servant, as someone who works with the public service today and as a member of the public, I, and others like me, believe this is a matter of national importance and that we must act soon and decisively.

And, as people who understand how both the public sector and the online world work, we want to help.

Together we must reboot the model for engagement between government and the public to make it more open, more human, more frequent, more of a regular conversation focused on listening. And we must empower public servants at all levels and not just official communicators to be those that engage.

If we make that change, our governments and our public sector can be more relevant to the people; enacting policy and programs and delivering services that *really matter* and working hand-in-hand with an engaged, informed public participating in government.

Not only Yes We Can[35], but Yes We Must.

Culture in the New Order[36]

> *"There is nothing more difficult to take in hand, more perilous to conduct, or more uncertain in its success, than to take the lead in the introduction of a new order of things."*
> *- Niccolo Machiavelli, The Prince (1532)*

One of the biggest hurdles for the public sector and legislators tasked with fulfilling the promise of Government 2.0 will be the cultural change involved.

Culture change is tough in any organization, let alone in huge, distributed, diverse and largely conservative organizations such as federal and state public services. Yet it is this change that will be the make-or-break factor in the transformation that the Government 2.0 Taskforce will advise the Federal government on and that other levels of government (and other governments across the world) are also seeking to.

Change is an uncertain thing. How do we convince others of the need for the change? How will we be successful? How do we define success? How do we measure that success when we don't even know where the journey of change might take us? And how do we go about making change happen despite this uncertainty?

The Government 2.0 Taskforce is moving ahead fairly well in defining the issue for its audience and incorporating input from the Gov 2.0 community of interest. There are some significant issues that the Taskforce will need to address when it delivers its report:

- a lack of a cohesive 'whole of government' approach at any level of government
- a view of accountability that inadequately rewards those responsible for success and innovation
- inadequate trust and permission models across public sector management
- a need to shift to openness as a default, including removing the reticence to participate and obstruction of participation
- a negatively- colored perception of risk

Of course, these issues are not problems for all individuals, nor even their agencies, in the Australian public sector. They are, however, representative of the public sector generally, based on my experience as a public servant and my time working with the public sector as an outsider. My conversations and reading of similar material from across the globe suggests that the issues are similar in most modern democracies.

In New Zealand[37], the US and the UK[38], the public sector has been equipped with well-publicized rules of engagement for workers that permit them to actively engage with the public in online communities. These rules are ably backed up by existing codes of behavior that govern overall public sector employee conduct. In Australia, such rules exist[39], but the weight attached to them, their currency, the level of publicity and explicit, high- profile support for them from either Ministers or the most senior levels of the public service is largely missing or unclear.

No wonder both individuals and agencies are largely confused or indeed, oblivious, to what the position is on the engagement of public servants online.

Other nations have appointed both Ministers for Digital Engagement and, in the case of both the US and the UK, senior public servants whose ambits include digital engagement. In the US, we have seen the young, vibrant and demonstrably engaged, Vivek Kundra, the United States Chief Information Officer, driving change from the top. In the UK, Andrew Stott is the Director of Digital Engagement, and is also leading the way, connecting directly with the public and public servants. These people understand the online environment and its importance to the advancement of the Government 2.0 agenda, and also visibly live and breathe the culture it requires.

In Australia, we have neither a Minister nor a senior public servant with carriage of digital engagement as a specific responsibility. Some Ministers even seem at cross-purposes. The Internet censorship agenda being advanced by Senator Stephen Conroy is in fact anathema to the Government 2.0 model. Yet, as mentioned, Finance Minister Lindsay Tanner is strong in his support for a reform agenda that can hardly be enhanced by a filtered and potentially slower Internet.

In my time as a public servant, and in my experience since, the model of accountability that we see in the public sector is largely tied to responsibility for action and carriage of blame should something go wrong. Again, this is not true of the entire public sector, but it does represent the perception you get from the whole.

Taskforce member, Martin Stewart-Weeks of Cisco, noted recently that, "*We need a theory of 'accountability 2.0' to match the instincts and values of gov2. Any ideas?*"[40] My response[41] to Martin argued that it was not just accountability that was needed, but also new models of authorship, trust and permission. In order to achieve the cultural change needed with the least possible resistance, several things must happen.

First, I believe a mandate to implement these reforms and to behave and implement in the required way is needed from the highest levels. The Prime Minister and the Secretary of the Department of Prime Minister and Cabinet should be the ones that deliver this mandate to the Australian Public Service (APS), to remove any possible doubt about whether agencies and individual public servants are acting in accordance with the wishes of the elected government. They should be supported by the APS Commissioner, the Finance Minister in his capacity as the Minister responsible for the Australian Government Information Management Office (AGIMO), and the Special Minister of State.

And, second, the sometimes closed culture of the public sector must be shifted to one in which:

- the creators of innovative programs and thinking are identified for their good work, publicly and often
- openness and publication of material is the default (it should be noted that the FOI reform agenda of the current government is moving this way)
- all public servants are explicitly and implicitly permitted to engage with the public online (and offline) where they have the necessary expertise to do so, and
- public servants are trusted by their senior executive and Ministers to not just do their job, but to do it in the public eye and in concert with an engaged, contributing public.

An example of the need for this is alive and kicking now in the work of the Government 2.0 Taskforce. As noted[42] by Matthew Landauer of OpenAustralia, few of the public servant members of the Taskforce have seen fit to engage via the online channels the Taskforce is using, whereas almost all of the non- public servant members of the same have engaged in some way. This is unfortunate.

Very few of the many public servants who participate in the Australian Government 2.0 community on Google Groups do so officially. Many of them have explicitly stated that they are unsure or afraid of the consequences of doing so. They use personal email addresses and are sometimes reticent to discuss not only what agencies they work for but what projects they are involved in. That this approach is viewed as necessary by so many is disappointing.

Third, and finally, there needs to be a change in the negative perception of risk in the public sector. It is not often that you encounter a public servant whose perception of risk encompasses risk as an opportunity to innovate. You more often encounter a fearful perception of risk that imagines how an adverse outcome might be difficult to explain for the member of the Senior Executive who will be questioned in Senate Estimates. You can hardly blame public servants for being risk- averse in these circumstances – so the circumstances must change.

All these changes must be supported by relevant and ongoing education and mentoring to ensure that the public sector is equipped with the skills to manage this transformation with the greatest opportunity for success.

I'm under no illusion that the change needed in the public sector at all levels of government will be easy. So, what to do? I do not have all or even many of the answers. But I have many ideas. As do others. It is when these ideas are allowed to come forward, treated seriously and acted on equally seriously that we will have the most opportunity to bring about this much needed change.

So, public sector, let's act. Let's "take the lead in the introduction of a new order of things".

Stephen Collins (@trib) is an Australian thinker and doer in social media and user experience. He is recognized internationally as an innovator, community builder and engaging public speaker. Having worked for many years in the Australian public sector and consulting industries, Stephen founded acidlabs in late 2006 to help bring his philosophy of a more open, collaborative and hyperconnected world to his clients. This chapter is a compilation and update of a number of his previous pieces.

[1] http://j.mp/WOnyg
[2] http://j.mp/aa1sP
[3] See O'Reilly's chapter in this book. Also, see http://j.mp/gtydY.
[4] http://j.mp/mCVuE
[5] http://gov2.net.au/
[6] http://j.mp/12AMyZ
[7] http://j.mp/nSwZ5
[8] http://j.mp/Ipy8h
[9] http://j.mp/2VByiE
[10] http://j.mp/CazFA
[11] http://www.gilf.gov.au/
[12] http://j.mp/rxc3A
[13] http://pennysharpe.com/live
[14] http://j.mp/3Jk7IF
[15] http://j.mp/z5Qkh
[16] http://j.mp/DScr8
[17] http://j.mp/hA1cg
[18] http://j.mp/cXR78
[19] http://www.socialinclusion.gov.au/
[20] http://j.mp/2Z2T5A
[21] http://j.mp/3K8dBJ
[22] http://j.mp/cA14y
[23] http://j.mp/2TiROs
[24] http://j.mp/hgEhj
[25] http://www.getup.org.au/
[26] http://www.openaustralia.org/
[27] http://cpd.org.au/
[28] http://tweetmp.org.au/
[29] http://j.mp/nHxHE
[30] http://j.mp/7QHYa
[31] http://j.mp/LCQiG
[32] http://j.mp/qjcEW
[33] http://j.mp/z5Qkh
[34] http://j.mp/2Z2T5A
[35] http://j.mp/2jA3GA
[36] This section is a slightly edited version of my contribution to the Centre for Policy Development's Insight: Upgrading Democracy, which consists of several pieces from well- known thinkers and doers in the Government 2.0 sector and was CPD's submission to the Government 2.0 Taskforce. See http://j.mp/gYFSQ
[37] http://j.mp/4QXTW
[38] http://j.mp/SoAY1
[39] http://j.mp/FWAcN
[40] http://j.mp/fMY5m
[41] http://j.mp/ahXSp
[42] http://j.mp/19oFVF

#9

A Short History of Government 2.0: From Cool Projects to Policy Impact

David Osimo
Director, Tech4i2 Ltd

This chapter aims to provide an overview of the progressive structuring of web 2.0 in government. The early phase was characterized by spontaneous bottom-up project, such as those of MySociety.org. More recently, several meso-level initiatives were launched, which proactively support and facilitate bottom-up projects. Finally, a new (macro) policy vision is now emerging and being embraced by some governments. This is a logical framework (micro-meso-macro), but reflects also a chronological development.

The figure below illustrates this (chrono)logical framework, although it is obviously a strong simplification. It illustrates how government 2.0 initiatives were born since the early days of web 2.0 – indeed sometimes before. While bottom-up project continue to grow, they were then accompanied by meso-level initiatives and finally by macro-level visions and government policies. The three levels co-exist and co-evolve, and are not to be considered as successive phases, but as additional layers.

Gov 2.0	Macro-level							
	Meso-level							
	Micro-level							
Web 2.0								
		2003	2004	2005	2006	2007	2008	2009

User-driven innovation in public services

The emergence of web 2.0 applications such as blogs and social networking appeared to many as the apogee of ego, vanity and navel-gazing. This perspective has now clearly been dismissed by the wide emergence of collaborative applications pursuing social goals, which create collective value and bring societal benefits from the users' perspective – the prime example being Wikipedia.

In the government context, projects such as PatientOpinion.org, FarmSubsidy.org and TheyWorkForYou.com seek to challenge, disrupt and improve traditional models of public service delivery from the outside, building on the web 2.0 principles of openness, transparency and sharing. Several studies[1] have started collecting and analyzing the innumerable initiatives in this field, but it was the election of Barack Obama and his first policy choices as president that placed web 2.0 at the centre of policy debate. The recent call from web 2.0 guru Tim O'Reilly to work on "stuff that matters" reflects this growing importance of the social dimension of web 2.0, especially in times of crisis[2].

These bottom-up web 2.0 projects share common characteristics. They emerge spontaneously, out of a problem-solving attitude or for the simple pleasure of a challenge. They tend to address one simple goal, like in the case of PatientOpinion.org in the UK, which allows citizens to comment and rate the UK hospitals. The websites are often developed in a very short time, with very little resources, and generally using open source software. Famously, the citizens-generated government portal DirectionLessGov.com in the UK was developed in one morning at zero cost, as stated on the website: "*We got so fed up with the general uselessness of the multi-million pound shambles otherwise known as the Direct.gov.uk portal, that we decided to build something better in under an hour. Sadly, we ran catastrophically behind schedule, but we still finished before lunch*". They strongly focus on usability; with very simple design and clear communication they manage to make public data more meaningful and useful. Another good example is FarmSubsidy.org, which extracts data from unusable government database and makes them meaningful through visualizations and rankings. Finally, they are flexibly adapted after their release, based on the feedback of users. For example, the Petitions site of the UK government, run by developers from Mysociety.org, had 50 changes in the first day.

All this is obviously very much at odds with current government practice in managing IT projects. We lack the exact amount of money invested on making public services available online, but suffice to say that Italy alone invested 6 billion Euros in the years 2000-2006. The results are not impressive: take-up of these services does not grow up from 10% of EU population.[3]

The logical conclusion from this paradox would be to stop government from building interfaces and services, and let the "thousand flowers" bloom. Because of the low cost of technology, the barriers to entry are now dramatically lowered. Yet it is also clear that these bottom-up initiatives are not only spontaneous. In the last 2/3 years, several initiatives have been launched, which aim at proactively support and stimulate this kind of bottom-up innovation: we call it "the meso-level."[4]

The emergence of a meso-level government 2.0

One of the key questions stemming from analyzing the wide array of bottom-up projects described in the previous chapter, and the public value they create, is: is this simply an organic spontaneous growth, or can appropriate measures be put in place to encourage their development?

We here describe a set of initiatives, which try to stimulate these bottom-up projects:

- Social Innovation camp[5]: a two day workshop bringing together developers and social activists to create new applications for solving collective problems
- Kublai project: a network project to bring together creative people to launch local development projects in southern Italy, where traditional regional development projects appear ineffective
- Rewired State: a 8 hours day meeting of hackers who built 26 working applications on top of government data, with the only reward of personal satisfaction, fun, beer and attention from government
- IBBT Inca award: a competition for applications with social purpose, built on purpose in one month. 20.000 Euros of reward will be distributed among the best applications.

These initiatives have several common points, revolving around the issues of money, people and how (not) to manage both.

The originating assumption is that traditional policy tools to stimulate public innovation do not work very well in the context of public services 2.0. First, in these initiatives public money is not the main tool to stimulate innovation. Money is the outcome, rather than the pre-condition of the initiative. The availability of funding attracts the wrong kind of participants, the opportunists, and the consultants "able to building any kind of project by paying lip service to the right buzzwords," as Alberto Cottica put it in his presentation at the public services 2.0 workshop[6]. The inability to attract the right kind of people is indeed a crucial problem of funding mechanisms; for example, the panel evaluation of the EU ICT research program admits[7] that "there are major barriers to involving the most innovative and growth-oriented SMEs." In many cases, traditional government funding mechanisms are at odds with the values of creative people and companies.

Instead of focusing on money, these initiatives focus on attracting the right kind of people. The absence of money as the main motivator ensures that participants are mainly involved because of enthusiasm, commitment and passion. With little money and lots of passion you can achieve dramatically better results than with lots of money and little passion. Sometimes, money is a risk, rather than an asset, as it sends the "wrong signals to the wrong kind of people" (quoting from Alberto Cottica presentation). Creative people look for meaning before money.

But what is new today is the scale of the possibility, as made possible by the dramatic reduction in the cost of collective action, as described by Clay Shirky[8]. Technology tools are much less expensive, due to overall reduction in prices, open source software and software as a service. Technology diffusion makes it much easier to ensure collaboration without the need for formal organization. Barriers to entry in organizing and designing collaborative effort are now very low.

The reduced costs means that it is now possible to start up project without public funding, in order to demonstrate what can be done. Funding is then necessary to make the project stand on its feet and ensure up scaling, full deployment and sustainability. This is why in many of the presented cases, the final result is a "working and fundable project" submitted to the attention of the funders. The community acts as a producer of the project, and as a filter to improve and select the best projects. Only at the end of this process comes the funding possibility. Money follows results, not the opposite: it is the public policy equivalent of the new "publish then filter" model, versus the traditional "filter then publish": create-then-fund. RewiredState, at the end of the development cycle, presents the projects to the government for purchase. Social Innovation Camp delivers the award at the end of the weekend of work, looking at the best working projects. Kublai acts as a collective platform to improve projects proposals from ideas to fully-fledged business plan, which can be presented to different funders. INCA rewards the best applications after they have been developed, not the best project ideas. This create-then-fund approach is effective in this context because it crowds away the experts in proposal-writing, and attracts the "doers". Secondly, it is more open to unpredictable outcomes, which is more in line with the nature of bottom-up projects, which often take unexpected turns following the behavior of users. Thirdly, such an approach accepts failure as a normal part of the learning and innovation process.

The meso-level initiatives are necessary new interfaces that bring together different people who would not meet in existing structures. Innovation generally stems from cross-fertilization of different communities and expertise: government and developers (Rewired State); social innovators and developers (Social Innovation Camp), creative people and structural funds officers (Kublai), researchers and hackers (INCA).

Another important lesson learnt is that these initiatives grow in an organic, not planned fashion. There is no structured management approach. These social processes are successful when viral, and it is impossible to rigidly plan ex-ante and top-down. A different approach is necessary. The "right people" are mainly attracted informally, through word of mouth, and reputation mechanisms are crucial to make it work. This is why these initiatives are seldom managed directly by government, but rather by trusted third parties and individuals. Government has to learn to act indirectly, by leveraging networks. Secondly, while a control approach does not work, a great deal of work goes into the careful preparation of a favorable context for innovation to happen. All the resources that are not spent in technology and in attracting people are dedicated to organizing the event. Rewired State collected a great list of public data; Social Innovation Camp works for months before and after the event to make it effective; Kublai developed a wide array of synchronous and asynchronous tools to leverage creativity. These meso-level events share a feeling of enthusiasm, community and energy which is greatly enhanced by the synchronicity of events: intense one day gathering, short term development times such as the one month given for the INCA award.

These viral and creative activities cannot be artificially induced, but are not totally spontaneous either: they have to be carefully designed and implemented. In other words, public policy has to evolve from a planning to a design approach, focusing on setting the favorable context for innovation to happen rather than defining the innovation path ex-ante.

These initiatives are therefore more the result of craftsmanship than of industrial planning: it is therefore not clear if and how they can be up scaled and achieve large-scale impact. Yet they are already very much able to show a radical difference in results from traditional government-led initiatives.

Should government just make data available online?

Slowly, a new policy vision is taking shape on e-government. The sharp contrast between the low cost, fast development and high usability of user-generated applications, and the poor track record of government IT spending, has obviously generated the conclusion that government should refrain from building services online, and simply expose its data and web services for reuse by (more tech-savvy) third parties. This perspective is very much visible in bottom-up initiatives such as RewiredState.org, which claims on its homepage: "*Government isn't very good at computers. They spend millions to produce mediocre websites, hide away really useful public information and generally get it wrong. Which is a shame. Calling all people who make things. We're going to show them how it's done.*"

Sunlight Foundation, the organization running some of the finest government 2.0 projects in the US, argues in a blog post[9] that government should not provide visualization of its data, but simply expose them for other people to make those visualizations. The reason? "*Because other people will do that and probably do it better.*"

These thoughts have then been consolidated in more articulated visions. Robinson et al. argue that government "rather than struggling, as it currently does, to design sites that meet end-user needs, it should focus on creating a simple, reliable and publicly accessible infrastructure that "exposes" the underlying data."[10] Gartner's VP Andrea DiMaio[11] called for a "no government" vision, where services to citizens are provided by private intermediaries, while government simply exposes machine readable data (e.g. RDFa) and web services (e.g. REST).

Transparency and publication of reusable data is certainly key to enable user-led innovation. It is still the case that the bottom-up initiatives above described are implemented without the awareness, and in many cases with passive resistance from government to provide the data. Most of the time and resources is dedicated to scrapping the data and making them usable and machine-readable. Releasing government data would bring about several key benefits, such as better government accountability, more engaged citizens, more citizens-oriented services and new opportunities for technological innovation. In this sense, the 8 principles of Open Government Data[12] and the W3C note on making government data accessible[13] remain key references. It is clear that the new US administration is also setting a new standard by launching the data.gov catalogue of government data; by placing transparency at the centre of its e-government policy, as expressed in the President Memorandum on transparency which was the first act signed by President Obama; and by mandating agencies to release funding data linked to the recovery bill in fully reusable format.

But we believe that having government to simply make data available online is certainly the most urgent thing, it is necessary – but it is far from sufficient. The large majority of the excellent government 2.0 initiatives are from the US and UK: other countries lack the spontaneous bottom-up initiatives, and arguably need proactive stimulus guaranteed by the meso-level. Furthermore, most of the users of government 2.0 initiatives are affluent and cultivated – as well as digitally savvy: market and civil society are unlikely to fully cover the needs of all citizens. Government still has a subsidiary role to play to ensure that all citizens benefit from public services. In other words, it should intervene in cases of market or civil society failure: and as it is the case today, there are lots of market failures. We therefore proposed[14], rather than the approach of the no-government scenario, a more subtle scenario: the e-Subsidiarity scenario, where government and civil society are both investing in providing services and continuously collaborating to innovate and provide better services and to address the complex societal challenges of our times.

This e-Subsidiarity scenario is best visualized through the metaphor of Tao. This Chinese symbol, vaguely similar to our visualization of the e-Subsidiarity scenario, represents two opposite forces, the Yin and Yang, which are necessary to one another, and fully compenetrated. It is a dynamic principle, permanently changing.

The metaphor aims to highlight the main criticism to the No Government scenario: it points to a static, wall-against-wall, zero-sum game where the prevailing role is either the state or the market/society. Instead, the e-Subsidiarity scenario is flexibly adapted to different user profiles, and it is dynamic across time. Most of all, it rejects the zero-sum paradigm but rather aims at a positive-sum situation, arguing that government and markets are complementary, fully compenetrated and necessary to one another. In doing so, the idea refers to the fact that positive-sum games are a typical connotation of network economies, and in particular of the Internet economy. History shows that public and private initiatives are not a zero-sum game: in the late 19th century, the welfare grew parallel to the development of the voluntary sector. It is not by accident that the UK and the US lead the world in both bottom-up civil society initiatives and government understanding of government 2.0.

From visions to policy design

We need therefore not to discuss if government should provide services, build interfaces and visualization, promote innovation: but when and how it should do it.

This is the rationale behind the building of the "Open Declaration on Public Services 2.0"[15]: to make a positive contribution towards the organic integration of web 2.0 in service delivery, and go beyond stereotypes and contrapositions between government and civil society.

The open declaration is collaboratively built and endorsed by EU citizens who share the view that the web is transforming our society and our governments. We feel e-government policies in Europe could learn from the open, meritocratic, transparent and user-driven culture of the web. We also feel that current web citizens should engage more positively with government to help designing a strategy, which is genuinely difficult to adopt in the traditional culture of public administration.

In the first phase of this initiative, we sought to tap the collective intelligence through an open process that aimed to answer the question: How should governments use the web to improve public services and deliver greater public value for citizens? The second phase of the project was about trying to turn these sparse ideas into an impactful message for ministers. The Mixedink.com collaborative writing tool was used so that anyone could co-create the manifesto. Finally, the initiative looks for large-scale endorsement of the manifesto[16].

In conclusion, it appears clear that web 2.0 in public services is becoming more structured, from bottom-up to meso and macro-level initiatives, and is moving from the periphery to the centre of policy debate. Yet it is also clear that web 2.0 initiatives are still exceptional and marginal in the government context, and that progress is too slow so that the gap with web-based innovation is widening, rather than closing up.

2009 is an important year for the EU ICT policy. A new ICT strategy will be put in place and a new e-government action plan. Citizens have to assume a shared responsibility to push the public services

2.0 agenda forward. It is a window of opportunity to accelerate change, and the Open Declaration aims at taking advantage of this opportunity.

Dr David Osimo (@osimod) is managing partner in Tech4i[2] and has 15 years experience of EU policies and projects. He worked three years in the Joint Research Centre of the European Commission, where he was coordinating research activities on e-government, with a particular focus on the future impact of emerging technologies such as web2.0. Previously he worked as policy advisor and project manager on the information society strategy of the Italian Emilia-Romagna region.

---

[1] See e.g. Osimo, D. (2008a). Web 2.0 for government: why and how? Technical Report. DG JRC; IPTS. Seville JRC. http://j.mp/pvcul

[2] http://j.mp/iE6T

[3] See Eurostat data 2008 available at http://j.mp/GC3jA

[4] http://j.mp/10Nflb

[5] http://www.sicamp.org

[6] http://j.mp/VY5EL

[7] Information Society Research and Innovation: Delivering results with sustained impact Evaluation of the effectiveness of Information Society Research in the 6th Framework Programme 2003-2006. May 2008. http://j.mp/ejzCo

[8] Shirky, C. (2008). Here Comes Everybody: The Power of Organizing Without Organizations. Penguin

[9] http://j.mp/jFQbK

[10] Robinson et al. (2009) "Government Data and the Invisible Hand " Yale Journal of Law & Technology, Vol. 11, p. 160, 2009 available at http://j.mp/hRSz

[11] http://j.mp/tkGXc

[12] http://j.mp/bXpmm

[13] http://j.mp/UnUqe

[14] Codagnone, C. and Osimo D. (2009) Future Technologies for Future eGovernment Services: Services Platform Analysis, Report for the European Commission, Brussels: Information Society and Media Directorate. http://j.mp/4r13Gj

[15] http://eups20.wordpress.com/

[16] http://www.endorsetheopendeclaration.eu/

#10

WAITING FOR GOVERNMENT 2.0: WHY DO PUBLIC AGENCIES TAKE SO LONG TO EMBRACE SOCIAL MEDIA?

Alexandra Samuel
CEO, Social Signal

When the EU held its first ministerial conference on e-Government in 2001, Lombardy's Roberto Formigoni framed the challenge of e-government in terms of government's role as the "guarantor of the democratic participation of all citizens". Looking back even further to the early 1990s, when we saw the birth of academic and political interest in e-democracy, 2001 looks like roughly the halfway mark between the birth of aspirations for digitally-enabled grassroots participation, and the state of the art today. But when you step back to look at the larger picture of life online, the past eight years encompass a far broader and more transformative period of online engagement: since the first ministerial e-Government meeting, the web has exploded with ordinary citizen engagement as people around the world take to their new roles as bloggers, citizen journalists, social networkers and digital videographers.

What has not accelerated is the pace of online, grassroots engagement with government decision-making. For all that we spent the nineties dreaming of large-scale democratic engagement through the Internet - dreams that the birth of Web 2.0 promised to make real - government has been very slow to embrace the tools that now make that kind of engagement not just feasible but familiar to anyone who engages in conversation online. True, there have been pilot projects and scattered initiatives - some of them with high profiles and public fanfare - but on the whole, there has been little sign that genuine online engagement is becoming the norm, and not merely a remarkable exception.

Like many who worked in the e-democracy field throughout the Web 1.0 era, I've found government reticence on Web 2.0 to be occasionally frustrating and disappointing, but rarely surprising; governments face an array of constraints in engaging with the public, and my work experience in government has given me a personal vantage point on those limits.

In this chapter, I look at the opportunity for democratic engagement that governments have been offered by social media, and identify the institutional and cultural factors that have moved government from the forefront of online engagement to nearly the back of the pack. In the conclusion, I outline principles that governments will have to embrace if they are to overcome their limitations in embracing social media in order to realize their aspirations for the democratization of political participation.

Early promise, high hopes

The first ministerial conference roughly coincided with the conclusion of the Governance in the Digital Economy research program that Don Tapscott and I launched in 1998. The consortium of governments who were part of the Governance program included a couple of EU members, who like their colleagues in Asia and North America had expressed particular interest in the question of how e-Government offered new opportunities for citizen engagement with government, and perhaps even a fundamental transformation in the relationship between governments and their citizens. In our 2001 paper[1] on the topic, which reflected the input of our public sector participants, we mapped out the hope for a transformation in how governments engaged with their citizens as both stakeholders and customers:

> *Citizens are no longer just the "end users" of government services; they are also decision-makers, contributors, and partners in service design and delivery. But who are these new partners? At the same time that citizens are assuming new and expanded roles in government service, citizens themselves are changing. Today's citizens are much more informed and involved than were their parents or grandparents. These citizens expect new levels of service efficiency and quality from government, and they expect more accountability, too. We refer to this transformation in citizen perspectives as the "e-citizen effect."*
> *- from "Serving e-Citizens," Governance in the Digital Economy program, June 2001*

No wonder that the advent of Web 2.0 – what we'd now call social media – elicited such high hopes. After all, Web 2.0 tools seemed to deliver on so many of the aspirations for online political participation and government accountability, hopes that governments had previously tried to meet with a mishmash of well-intentioned but cumbersome tools for online dialogue. At the 2005 e-deliberation conference in Stanford, which coincided with the early days of social media, the various software tools and pilot projects that were demonstrated mostly reflected technology approaches that tried to translate best practices and principles for offline participation into online form. That included tools like wikis, immersive virtual environments and blogs, as well as more established tools such as email.

I was part of the throng that engaged in those earnest, literal-minded efforts. In early 2005 I worked with Angus Reid, best known as one of Canada's foremost public opinion researchers, to develop an e-consultation toolkit. I drew on examples like Viewpoint Learning's terrific workbook-driven methodology[2] for informed citizen dialogues to create virtual workbooks, and AmericaSpeaks' large-scale citizen townhalls to plot out the large-scale aggregation of citizen input.

As e-consultation professionals like me beavered away on our well-theorized online engagement plans, a spontaneous online revolution was unfolding. The principles and visions espoused by e-democracy geeks were being realized in a new generation of web technologies that were driven not by democratic theory, but by the pragmatic needs and market opportunities spotted by software developers. Many of the folks laboring in the e-democracy trenches saw these emergent tools as the answer to our hopes. Andrea Kavanaugh, for example, wrote:

> *In our own thinking about modifying blogs for citizen deliberation, we have been building on software toolkits and an evolving suite of components to support synchronous and asynchronous collaborative authoring and data manipulation ... Basic Resources for Integrated Distributed Group Environments tools can be composed into sets that produce web-viewable documents, annotated images, and interactive collaborative environments. This integration of editing functionality into standard web tools removes a significant barrier to information production and maintenance by minimizing the overhead of switching between viewing and editing. Automated tracking of web accesses, comments, and queries also provides data that can be used to generate summaries of active, recent, and popular artifacts in the library. For example, citizens may be able to link comments directly from posted Town agendas that might be aggregated as a separate file for viewing by other citizens and government. Specific requirements for individual tool capabilities and configurations varied widely among previous de-*

ployments, so we expect modifications will be necessary for civic participation and deliberation purposes, and government integration of citizen feedback[3].

David Wilcox wrote:

I suspect a lot of e-democracy is just going to be old-style participation online, without much impact on the cultural and organization problems that need to be challenged. ...So where can we look for new models, new methods – and new attitudes to match?...the current buzz around what's known as Web 2.0 may offer some insights, if mixed with thinking around "openness"...new web tools have the potential for shifting the way that knowledge is organized from top-down to bottom-up....Instead of trying to get people to contribute to one place, why not enable them to create their own places and then join them up. The can be done by people producing blog items instead of email, adding tags to label the content, and then being able to select what they want to read from others by filtering using the tags... Participation version 1.x can be a bit like the old top-down ways of organizing knowledge: "you can join in, but only on the terms that we set. If we don't deliver what you want, I'm afraid there's not much you can do about it."....The Web, linked with a new approach to events and collaboration, is starting to change that – and particularly the new tools and ethos of what's being called Web 2.0[4].

Stephen Coleman wrote:

The main political value of blogging is not to be found in politicians presenting themselves to an audience of potential voters, but in the dense networks of intellectual and symbolic intercourse involving millions of private-public bloggers. The blogosphere is characterized by three democratizing characteristics. Firstly, it provides a bridge between the private, subjective sphere of self-expression and the socially-fragile civic sphere in which publics can form and

> *act.....Secondly, blogs allow people – indeed, expect them – to express incomplete thoughts. This terrain of intellectual evolution, vulnerability and search for confirmation or refutation from wider sources is in marked contrast to the crude certainties that dominate so much of political discourse....Thirdly, blogs lower the threshold of entry to the global debate for traditionally unheard or marginalised voices, particularly from poorer parts of the world which are too often represented by others, without being given a chance to present their own accounts....It is as channels of honest self-presentation that blogs make their greatest contribution to democracy*[5].

We had good reason to feel hopeful. There was a remarkable correspondence between the e-democracy visions expressed in the Web 1.0 era, and the dynamics of emergent Web 2.0 tools and communities.

In the OECD's 2003 publication[6], "Promise and problems of e-democracy," Stephen Coleman argued that an effective representative democracy requires a five-way information flow: Government to Citizen (G2C); Citizen to Government (C2G); Representative to Citizen (R2C); Citizen to Representative (C2R); and Citizen to Citizen (C2C).

As he then noted, "*[w]ithin the existing model of democratic representation, these flows are somewhat restricted or clogged.*" Web 2.0 tools promised to address many of these clogs:

2003 assessment from Coleman	Web 2.0 promise
Government to Citizen G2C takes place largely via the mass media, principally television and the press. Government distrusts the mediating interpretations of the media; citizens distrust the extent and quality of Government information and tend to switch off when presented with it.	Public servants can communicate directly to citizens via websites, blogs and social networks.

Citizen to Government C2G is limited. Government runs many consultations, but few citizens participate in these and there is much skepticism about Government responsiveness to public input. Most citizens believe that whatever views or expertise they possess will have little influence upon Government.	Citizens can blog or comment about policy issues, or contribute to online forums, without waiting for an official government invitation for input.
Representative to Citizen R2C is limited outside of election campaigning. Representatives work hard to win citizens' votes, and make strenuous efforts to use local media to inform their constituents about how well they are being represented, but there are few opportunities to hear what their constituents think about specific policy issues.	Elected officials can maintain blogs (or more recently, Twitter feeds and Facebook pages) to keep constituents up-to-date on their activities and considerations.
Citizen to Representative C2R is very limited. Citizens can raise issues with their representatives in local surgeries or by mail - in some case by email. But, outside of traditional lobbying, there are few opportunities to feed in to the legislative process by raising new information or perspectives. Few citizens are active members of political parties or lobby groups, so few voices tend to be heard by representatives when policies are being evaluated.	Citizens can blog or comment about their elected representatives, creating public pressure for a response. More recently, Tweets and Facebook updates have emerged as quick ways to share thoughts with public officials. The onus is on representatives to do effective social media monitoring so they know what is being said about and to them.
Citizen to Citizen C2C is the basis of a healthy civil society, but it is in decline, consistent with a broader decline in "social capital". In general, citizens do not discuss policy issues with one another - even when those issues matter to them. It is not easy to find places or networks for such discussion. The media provide some opportunities, but these rarely enable citizens to develop communication with other citizens.	Citizen-journalist coverage of government policy issues, issue blogs, citizen-driven wikis and online conversations via forums and status updates give citizens ample (and widely used) opportunities for citizen-to-citizen policy discussion.

It seemed like the era of e-democracy was finally upon us: a world in which the decentralized, self-organizing conversations of the social web could be applied to the policy questions of the day. It seemed as though we were moving from engagement as the tightly-controlled exception, to engagement as the norm, with citizens as full partners in setting the agenda – as well as deciding when, where and how those conversations would occur.

Constraints and roadblocks

The technologies of online conversation have indeed advanced at a blistering pace. The public, in turn, has adopted those technologies widely and rapidly. But governments – with a few high-profile exceptions, most recently and notably the incoming Obama administration – have not. Instead, while public figures talk about the transformative potential of the Internet, the governments they lead usually restrict their online engagements to small-scale projects and one-off pilots.

As reported last year in *Government Technology*[7]:

> *The adoption curve for Web 2.0 applications currently has a trickle-down pattern. While 67 percent of large businesses have already implemented some form of Web 2.0 applications or tools, IT decision makers in medium-sized businesses fall slightly behind with 53 percent currently using Web 2.0. Only 27 percent of small businesses and 30 percent of government organizations have adopted Web 2.0.*

Although disappointing, nobody should have been surprised by governments' slow tempo in adopting Web 2.0 tools. They face serious constraints that other actors do not, or do not face to the same degree.

Those constraints include:

> *Legacy systems:* Many government agencies rely on an aging IT infrastructure, coupled with budget restrictions and pri-

orities that impede upgrades. That infrastructure often does not support Web 2.0 technologies, or can only do so with a substantial software or programming investment.

Organizational risk aversion: Effective social media engagement demands that the sponsoring organization relinquish a large degree of control over the content and nature of the conversation – an approach directly at odds with the risk-minimizing culture typical of bureaucracies (public and, to be clear, private alike).

Those bureaucracies must answer to elected officials who govern in an adversarial world – one where openness to criticism carries heavy political risks (perceived or real). And because conversations cannot easily be compartmentalized, one department's social media initiative can impose risks on another department, giving them a strong motivation to block or restrict that project.

Finally, the social media world relies heavily on third-party applications, services and sites. Governments that incorporate such services into their social media offerings take on substantial risk, ranging from service outages to security breaches.

Personal risk aversion: Advocating the use of resources for an unproven approach carries a double risk for public servants: wasting time and energy on an unsuccessful proposal, or gaining approval for the proposal and then seeing it fail publicly. That's especially true in the restricted fiscal environment where most governments have spent the past two decades.

And let's be honest: the kind of people who are drawn to public service tend not to have a high degree of personal risk tolerance. One of the attractions of working for a big, stable employer – whether it's a government agency or a large blue-chip company – is the relatively high degree of job security. If you're the kind of person who craves novelty, and you have a high degree of risk tolerance, you're more likely to land in a start-up or an edgy NGO – no wonder that's where we see a lot of social media innovation! Of course, there are exceptions to this generalization, and indeed it's those exceptions – the folks who go into public service not because of its stability but in spite of it – who can often be found in the front lines of online innovation.

Policy limitations: Public agencies must often work within the boundaries of inflexible constraints governing such areas as design standards (often expressed as a "common look and feel") and content approval. Those constraints inhibit innovation and dampen the free flow of conversation necessary for successful engagement.

Governments must also grapple with their role as custodians of private and personal information. Many jurisdictions have policies and procedures that privilege the protection of privacy over information disclosure – voluntary and involuntary – by participants in Web 2.0-enabled conversations. Bring third-party services such as Facebook into the mix, with their contentious privacy and terms-of-use agreements, and the sea of conflicting priorities becomes even harder to navigate.

What's working?

Yet some governments have succeeded in moving into Web 2.0, and with the rapidly accelerating embrace of social media among businesses, NGOs and citizen-consumers, more and more public sector organizations are making serious efforts to incorporate online community and social media tools into their repertoire of public engagement and communications approaches. This includes examples like:

- The British Prime Minister's e-petition site, which has garnered more than 4,600 petitions and hundreds of thousands of signatures, and the blogs maintained.
- The Barack Obama administration's array of social media initiatives, such as the use of YouTube for weekly addresses, online user submission and voting for townhall questions, an open data repository and a broader, far-reaching open government initiative under the management of a Chief Technology Officer.
- Northern Ireland's Department for Employment and Learning's Facebook page, geared to encouraging immigration to the country.
- The City of Melbourne's "Future Melbourne" wiki, where residents could collaborate on a strategy document shaping the city's future.
- Certain individual political leaders. Mayors of Canadian municipalities such as Vancouver and Toronto not only maintain Twitter presences but engage actively with followers. (Toronto actually held a Web 2.0 summit in late 2008, brainstorming ideas for implementing social media across the municipal government). And Margot Wallström, EU Vice President in charge of Institutional Relations and Communication, has maintained her blog – complete with comments – for several years.

From these and other examples we can distill the emergent opportunities and best practices for governments seeking to tap the power of social media:

Focus on small wins: Look for projects that minimize risk while demonstrating measurable results, building the case for more ambitious initiatives to come. Such projects can not only avoid failures that poison the well for future endeavors; they help to change internal culture, and identify potential policy issues, internal bottlenecks and unforeseen challenges while their impact is still small. And planned as part of a larger strategy, they can build not just support, but the software and social infrastructure - such as a community of users - that can make larger projects a success.

Go where the public is: Even an agency with the budget of the White House relies on YouTube as a video channel. As a rule, it is easier and less costly to engage people where they are currently participating, than to convince them to visit a new and unfamiliar web presence and learn a new and unfamiliar interface (not to mention creating yet another online profile, and monitoring yet another conversation platform). Moreover, you gain from network effects as users' participation is mirrored in their activity feeds to their social networks. And perhaps most important, engagement on users' terms rather than governments' can help to build trust and encourage citizens to lend a civic dimension to their existing modes of participation.

Focus on tangible benefits and problem-solving: Particularly in a culture of caution, support for a project can be difficult to come by if its benefits to the organization aren't explicit or direct. Identifying a pain point and proposing a credible solution, on the other hand, can be a powerful way of mobilizing internal support (and maintaining it in the face of a budget cut). For example, the U.S. Navy's online community allowing moms of serving sailors to talk with anxious or skeptical mothers of new recruits helped the armed service deal with a serious obstacle to recruitment.

Import success stories: Governments are not known for their avid pursuit of first-mover advantage; favoring more proven approaches over cutting-edge innovation can allow governments to avoid risks, learn from others' mistakes and successes, and set realistic benchmarks based on past experience. Thus an array of e-petition sites begat Number 10's online version, and Dell's IdeaStorm begat President Obama's user-selected townhall questions.

However, perhaps the best advice to anyone who wishes to advance the use of social media in citizen engagement by governments is to manage expectations: inside government, with the public and with themselves.

Government communicators and leaders need to be ready for the certainty that they will hear things they don't want to, that they will be unable to control the conversation, and that it will veer from time to time into unexpected territory. (For an extreme case, look to the short-lived takeover of the White House question-submission application by supporters of the "birther" movement.) They need to be prepared to respond to attempts to hijack conversations for partisan or malicious purposes without stifling legitimate voices. And they need to recognize that, as with any emergent field, successful projects will not come without accompanying failures.

The public needs to know just what the parameters of engagement are: what's on the table and what isn't; which kinds of participation are welcome, which are merely tolerated and which are discouraged; and what the outcome of the conversation will yield. They need an explicit and accurate picture of the extent *and limits* of their government's openness. And they need a clear and compelling understanding of the value of their participation – to themselves as well as to their community.

And those of us who would evangelize social media as a tool of government engagement with the public would do well to temper our own expectations with the hard-won knowledge that, in government, change is nearly always evolutionary rather than revolutionary. We are dealing with large organizations, entrenched cultures and a massive set of formal and informal rules, and turning that apparatus around takes patience and time.

But it's important work nonetheless. Governments – democratically-elected ones, at any rate – *do* wear the mantle of guarantors of democratic participation. They are in a headlong race for the online attention of their citizens, competing with commercial entertainment and online shopping on one side and grassroots self-organizing on the other. A growing number of political leaders, along with the newest generation of public servants, recognize the urgency of that race and are doing their best to pick up the pace.

Alexandra Samuel (@awsamuel) is the CEO of Social Signal, a Vancouver-based social media agency. Alexandra has helped to conceive and build online communities like NetSquared.org, ChangeEverything.ca and Tyze.com. Alexandra holds a Ph.D. in political science from Harvard University. She currently blogs for Harvard Business Online and on SocialSignal.com.

---

[1] http://www.alexandrasamuel.com/researchwriting.html

[2] Viewpoint Learning, ChoiceDialogue Methodology, http://www.viewpointlearning.com/offer/methodology.shtml

[3] Kavanagh, A. et al. (2005) Detecting and Facilitating Deliberation at the Local Level. Paper presented at the 2nd Conference on Online Deliberation: Design, Research, and Practice / DIAC-2005. http://www.online-deliberation.net/conf2005/viewpaper.php?id=38

[4] David Wilcox, If Participation 1.x isn't working, let's develop Engagement 2.0, October 1 2005. http://j.mp/h2fSX

[5] Stephen Coleman, Afterword: Blogs as listening posts rather than soapboxes in Blogs: Craze or Convention, UK Hansard Society, 2004

[6] http://www.oecd.org/dataoecd/9/11/35176328.pdf

[7] "IT Decision Makers Cautious in Adopting Web 2.0 in the Workplace", Government Technology, June 18 2008. http://j.mp/37Dfjz

#11

3 Reasons Government Isn't Ready for 2.0 Yet

Ariel Waldman
Founder, Spacehack.org

On July 16, 2009, a congressional hearing in the US Congress Subcommittee on Space & Aeronautics took place on Enhancing the Relevance of Space[1]. Miles O'Brien[2] carried a powerful message to NASA and similar government agencies, as he responded to a question:

Olson asked:

> *"How do we communicate how beneficial NASA has been to our society from a technological, from a national security perspective, and from an inspirational perspective? ... Mr. O'Brien, I'd like to give you the first crack at that. What can we tell our constituents? What can they do to make a difference?"*

O'Brien responded:

> *"You know I think the irony is that 40 years after the launch of Apollo 11 NASA suffers from a bit of timidity when it comes to unleashing the message. Now they have a natural*

legion of foot soldiers, evangelizers. Everyone I meet who is involved in space is deeply passionate about what they do; love what they do. They are committed to their jobs in ways most people are not. And unfortunately if they attempt to blog about it or tweet about it they get shut down. This happens all the time because the concern is that they'll be off message.

It's important to empower the agency and thus its foot soldiers to know that they can — they can be a part of this. If — if a flight controller wants to tweet and let her social network in on what's going on inside mission control, assuming we're not you know in some sort of mission critical situation that would cause danger to somebody, why not empower her to do that? But instead the message is you can't.

So I think what Congress can do is to the extent they can streamline the rules for NASA and make it easier for them to do marketing, but also to the extent that they can avoid the tendency to get on the phone every time something comes across the bow that might — might offend somebody in somebody's constituency. Because what that does is it cows the agency. And they need to be empowered too because if you unleashed the power of that workforce and allowed them to spread the word we could just stand by and watch them win the country over."

Relearn the phrase "don't burn bridges"

The quote above comes at a time where I still to this day receive emails from people inside NASA who tell me about how they were forced to shut down their personal blog for fear of being fired. Even worse, I still receive stories about people being forced by their managers to unblock people who are harassing them from their *personal* social networking accounts. The social web is a bridge between personal and professional lives and should be respected as such. Learning how to navigate this isn't easy. Scrambling to put together a "digital policy" for employees might sound like the right solution, however, digital policies are equally dangerous due to their inability to evolve as the digital environment does. Starting off with general guidelines like "play nice" that encourage the use of social networks and respect privacy is a better first step.

Eliminate "the public"

The mindset of people in government is deeply rooted in using the term "the public" when referring to anyone who doesn't also work in government. Not only does this term massively inhibit their ability to communicate effectively and connect with anyone, but it also frames their view for using the social web - something that "the public" uses and thus they should use as an extension of their job (instead of having a personal AND professional interest in it). This is a hard term to tackle, as I started saying it shortly after joining NASA as well. I recommend stepping down from using the term by saying things like "people will be able to better access this" or "this program allows people to get involved with XYZ."

We need a "Freedom of Information, Except for Jerks" Act

The title of this section was joked about while conversing about this issue over dinner. The government has no standards or process[3] in place for blocking abusive, harassing and/or all-around trolling people (see Tantek's Troll Taxonomy[4]). In fact, the government is so terrified of being called out for denying conversational access to someone, that they often pander to the poisonous person over protecting their own employees. As a result, "super villains" are created to feed off of the fear culture - a term Heather Champ[5], the community manager at Flickr, uses to describe someone who keeps coming back to haunt you forever. As Heather stated in a talk about Shepherding Passionate Users, "Sometimes you have to make difficult decisions and take actions that won't be appreciated."[6]

Ariel Waldman (@arielwaldman) is a digital anthropologist and the founder of Spacehack.org, a directory of ways to participate in space exploration and encourage citizen science. She is also a sci-fi movie gadget columnist for Engadget and the founder of CupcakeCamp, based off of the BarCamp model. Previously, she was a CoLab program coordinator at NASA, and the community manager for Pownce, a P2P sharing social network.

---

[1] http://j.mp/ditAn
[2] http://j.mp/44490F
[3] http://j.mp/bGVB
[4] http://j.mp/yvILG
[5] http://hchamp.com
[6] http://j.mp/SwUe4

Section II

OPENING GOVERNMENT

#12

Data Triggers Transformation

W. David Stephenson
CEO, Stephenson Strategies

When many of us go to Washington D.C., we like to visit historic landmarks.

We *don't* necessarily like carrying maps and guidebooks, especially since most try to be comprehensive, while you might be particularly interested in one aspect, such as Lincoln, so the other material would be irrelevant to you. Now you can use the *D.C. Historic Tours* application on your iPhone[1]. Just type in "Lincoln," and it instantly creates a walking tour only of Lincoln-related places, then guides your actual path block-by-block. As for the content of that tour? Willing volunteers located the places to include in the tour and uploaded the data and photos about them to the Web for use in the application.

In New Zealand, Auckland drivers use an application that uses real-time data from the government's InfoConnect program[2] to show where there are traffic jams & then zero in on a local traffic cam. They can change their routes to steer around the jams.

In the Netherlands, companies have the option of filing a single set of numbers instead of the multiple reports to multiple agencies that they formerly had to file. Participating companies can save up to 25% on their reporting costs, and the agencies can actually do a better job regulating the companies.[3]

What makes these innovations work? *Free, real-time access to unfiltered, valuable data.*

Data pervades our lives.[4]

Government agencies and companies collect data around the clock about our births, deaths, education, jobs (or lack thereof), our race and gender, our spending and saving, our health. Then they use that data to make decisions affecting our incomes, our buying options, even whether we qualify for special benefits.

Data determines how much governmental assistance our communities receive.

Data determines where roads will be built, then our GPS devices process data from government satellites to guide us down those roads and help us find services.

Data is the basis of medical and scientific research.

Yet, for all of data's influence on our lives, you and I have surprisingly little direct access to it ourselves to use as *we* might like. That's particularly true with the most valuable type, real-time data. Because it is made available as it is gathered, this data can be used to automate equipment and services and/or help us make decisions, rather than simply analyze the past, as can be done with historical data.

Despite those benefits, this data is more likely to remain buried in data warehouses and be costly and/or difficult to obtain. When we do get it, it's often in a form that is difficult to use.

That's outrageous.

If we *did* have access to that data, we could do our work more efficiently and cheaply, engage in more productive political debates, and even contribute directly to new ways to deal with some of our era's most pressing problems, such as global warming or health care cost containment.

Yet, there's little sense of public concern, and even less outrage, about our relative lack of unfettered access to critical information.

Frank DiGiammarino, former vice-president of strategic initiatives at the National Academy for Public Administration and now the Obama Administration's deputy coordinator for Recovery Implementation, says that's a major problem in the United States (and worldwide, for that matter):

> *"We as a country need to treat data as a national asset and resource. It is a valuable commodity but we don't treat it that way. We don't think in terms of where it is. In current structures, it is stovepiped but, needs to be moved fluidly ... The default question has to be why can't we share it? Data has to become a core component of how government works and how leaders think of dealing with issues."*[5]

Similarly, Sara Wood, a leader in the nascent movement to make data both available and understandable to the general public, says that:

> *"It may not be obvious to everyone, but there exists an important problem of data apathy. No one cares about data. And by no one, we mean in the democratic sense.... Good data should affect policy – but politicians don't care because they know their voters don't care. People who vote don't care because data is not engaging, not to mention accessible, usable, and relevant to their lives."*[6]

Data apathy is no longer tolerable. Data is so important to our lives that we must all care about data and demand access to it.

The transformation triggered by democratizing data

The time has come to make data freely available – and usable. Take some simple steps to transform your government's raw data into a more versatile and usable form, place that data at the center of your government's operations, make it accessible to everyone who really needs it, and everything changes.

Data that has been "processed, organized, structured or presented in a given context so as to make [it] useful" is elevated to the status of *information.*[7]

A handful of tools, none of them radically innovative by themselves but revolutionary when combined, make it simple and economical for governments to make valuable information available to those who need it, when and where they need it, to improve their decision-making and actions. Since that was never possible before, the potential for change in every aspect of how we work and live is profound and pervasive. The results, as demonstrated by the limited examples from around the world where democratizing data has already taken hold, are astonishing.

Let us call this transformation democratizing data:

> *Democratizing data makes it automatically available to those who need it (based on their roles and responsibilities), when and where they need it, in forms they can use, and with freedom to use as they choose – while simultaneously protecting security and privacy.*

Five principles guide the process of democratizing data:

1. *Data should be free*

   That is meant in both an economic and figurative sense. Our tax dollars paid for collection and processing of most public data, and the costs of commercial goods and services, include similar services, so we have already paid for the data and shouldn't have to pay again to obtain it. Similarly, data should not be kept locked in data warehouses: to be valuable it needs to be freely available.

2. *Data should be distributed in real-time*

   Data is more helpful when it is available on a data-in, data-out basis. It can provide "situational awareness", and information on fast-changing factors such as traffic, health conditions, or weather that we need to consider in decision-making, as well as allow automation of many processes that can be triggered and governed by real-time information.

3. *Data should be available to all who need it*

   In the past, it was so expensive and time-consuming to collect, process, release and provide tools to work with data that it made sense to only give access to senior management or salespeople. Those barriers have now been eliminated or significantly reduced, so relevant data (based on individuals' roles and factors such as their security clearances) should be made available to all who need it, in order to help them make better decisions and/or improve their ability to manage and live their own lives.

4. *Data should be shared*

   When formal or even informal groups of people jointly access and can discuss and analyze data together, the resulting analysis is fundamentally richer and more nuanced, while ramifications, or need for additional data, are better explored than when any individual works in isolation. Equally important, shared data can be acted upon simultaneously, rather than sequentially.

5. *Data should be made useful*

   Numbers are enriched and become useful information when they are put in context. Equally important, tools that allow us to manipulate and analyze data in a variety of ways, as well as to share data, also make it more useful.

It seems audacious to claim that an act as modest as modifying the way you treat your government's raw data can lead to sweeping economic, governmental and social change.

That is precisely what democratizing data will do.

For far too long, we have been more concerned with creating data warehouses in which to store data than we have been with actually using that data to its full potential. In fact, it's rather astonishing that governments have prospered to the extent they have, considering how limited access to real-time, actionable information has been.

This remained true even recently, when we have had powerful computers to gather, accumulate and disseminate data. It still remained costly and difficult to deal with data, so access to it was typically limited to management, analysts and other elites. Even these power users rarely had access to the most important data, in *real-time, non-aggregated* form, which allows the user the most freedom and makes its ability to affect current actions most powerful.

Putting data squarely at the center of everything we do, and making it usable – and shareable – by everyone, not just those with statistical skills, is a dramatically different approach from how we've regarded data in the past.

Democratizing data sparks wide range of change

Making data automatically available when and where it is needed triggers widespread and fundamental changes.

Because this data is machine-readable, i.e. encoded in a way that a computer or machine can automatically scan or process, it can provide the real-time information necessary to operate a wide range of devices, which has both economic and quality-of-life benefits.

Perhaps the most common example today of real-time data spawning an entirely new industry would be global positioning systems (GPS). Location-based services (LBS), just one component of the range of businesses made possible by GPS, are expected to grow by 104% through 2011.[8] Can you imagine the potential economic development and quality-of-life opportunities if all of the non-confidential geospatial data compiled by government agencies was routinely released on a real-time basis?

In the political realm, debate and disagreement will always be with us, so one should not over-estimate the benefits of access to data. However, beginning debate on proposed legislation from a pool of data that was accessible to all on a simultaneous basis *might* increase the chances of reaching consensus, or at least isolating the most extreme positions that were clearly not supported by data. The more data is analyzed and debated before passage of legislation, the less likely it will be that critical data that only comes to light after passage would undermine the law itself, or significantly alter public opinion.

Similarly, when data on government operations, campaign finance and "earmarks" are made public, it is much harder to conceal corruption or unjustified disbursements. For example, making campaign contributions public allows watchdog groups and the media to create visualizations that explore possible correlations between contributions and votes that might favor a particular contributor.

Equally important, although few governments have tried it so far, making real-time, actionable data available to your entire workforce (with the exact amount and type available filtered depending on your role: this is not a one-size-fits-all approach) can elevate all workers to the status of "knowledge workers". That will help workers increase their efficiency and reduce costs. They will be able to see which other employees have access to the same data and therefore are likely to share tasks, responsibilities and oversight and interests, engage in the kind of collaborative data analysis mentioned above. They can see potential synergies, overlaps and gaps between programs that must be addressed.

Democratizing data essential today

The lack of widespread access to real-time data was regrettable in the past. Given the unprecedented worldwide organizational and social changes facing government, the global economy, and our personal lives today as a result of the global crisis that began in 2008, it is intolerable.

We need *every* potential tool and piece of information at our disposal to deal with these conditions and to improve our own lives.

For government agencies, it is essential that workers who remain after layoffs be able to be as efficient and effective as possible. As mentioned above, democratizing data will make it possible for the first time to give your entire workforce the raw, *real-time* information needed for them to work more efficiently, new tools to help them better analyze that information, and to collaborate as never before.

Data will give us usable information on everything from traffic, to our personal carbon footprints, to our health conditions in applications and devices that will allow us to act on that data and improve our lives.

In the United States, the regulatory system, in shambles after revelations of lax enforcement in the past decade, was at least in part to blame for the sub-prime mortgage scandal and its cascading effects on the overall economy. Regulation can be reinvigorated through a shift to "smart" regulation, which substitutes a single data file for countless traditional forms. All of the agencies responsible for reviewing a company's operations will be able to share data simultaneously, allowing coordinated review and enforcement for the first time. This should improve the quality of regulatory review and uncover suspicious activities sooner. The same single-business reporting approach will allow companies to reduce their regulatory compliance costs, perhaps as much as 25%.[9] By introducing parallel, integrated regulatory systems worldwide, based on innovations pioneered by the Netherlands and Australia, we will be able to facilitate world trade while protecting the environment and workers.

In the past, effective regulation would inevitably have driven *up* corporate reporting costs, because the only way to increase scrutiny would have been to require filing more forms. Now a radically simplified, but more informative and integrated, system can benefit government, the public and corporations.

Equally important, government agencies must rebuild public confidence. They will be able to do so through democratizing data.

Demeaning, "trust us" platitudes are no longer enough in the face of voter outrage. Instead, by releasing large amounts of unedited data directly to media, voters and watchdogs, they can take a "don't trust us, track us" approach, inviting unfettered scrutiny.

In the United States, the soaring federal budget and deficit have united the political spectrum in demands to cut out waste and inefficiency, and to open up the legislative process so that the public can be heard.

Vivek Kundra, the former District of Columbia chief technology officer, named by President Obama as the first chief information officer of the United States, refers to this approach as the "digital public square".[10]

> "... *technological advances now allow people from around the world unfettered access to their government. Through these advances, constituents can hold their government accountable from the privacy of their own homes. The District of Columbia is bringing people closer to government through collaborative technologies like wikis, data feeds, videos and dashboards. We're throwing open DC's warehouse of public data so that everyone—constituents, policymakers, and businesses—can meet in a new digital public square.*"[11]

Finally, and perhaps most exciting, democratizing data can lead to innovation.

It is now possible, by allowing free access to real-time data streams, to unleash "crowdsourcing" of new services for government and industry alike, better serving diverse groups' needs at low or no cost.

Crowdsourcing, as explained in the book by the same name by Jeff Howe,[12] is the phenomenon in which communities, whether intentional or *ad hoc* ones, come together using Internet resources, especially open-source software, to accomplish a task collaboratively, by each providing a small portion of the overall solution.[13]

Even better, as more governments embrace this revolution, the more the benefits will multiply, because democratized data inherently fosters linkages and synergies between programs and services that share the same data, and open source solutions that all can share and improve upon. Because these programs use global standards, free to everyone, the revolution can and must be global in nature, benefitting nations of all sizes and development status.

This is not just a vision of possible transformation in the future. True, the amount of innovation is severely limited by the lack of freely-available structured data that is the underpinning of democratizing data. Despite those limits, pioneers in government worldwide are already realizing tangible results with innovative datacentric strategies that would have been impossible only a few years ago.

In the United States, Nevada's innovative Controller, Kim Wallen, has taken the lead by designing a portal system for businesses, which provides them with a single, simplified point-of-entry and coordinates regulatory reviews by all state agencies.[14]

In the District of Columbia, Aki Damme, director of the District of Columbia's IT ServUs team, had to manage a project to buy and install 6,000 computers in city classrooms for a high-visibility new program. The original estimate was that the project would take an entire year to complete. However, an expedited purchasing program and his ability to plan the installations using a Google Maps mashup cut the total length to only 7 weeks, and saved thousands of dollars in costs.[15]

Agencies responsible for disaster preparedness and response in Alabama can now access "Virtual Alabama," a comprehensive, integrated array of real-time geospatial information – right down to the layout of individual classrooms – that helps them change emergency evacuation routes, know instantly where response vehicles are located, and monitor real-time sensors locating chemical releases and their plumes.[16]

The US Patent Office now allows individuals outside its staff to participate in the review of patent applications under the trial "Peer to Patent system," designed in part by NYU Law Professor Beth Noveck, now an Obama Administration official. The project promises to reduce the "patent thicket" that slows innovation.[17]

Since, as mentioned above, these pioneering examples are made possible by international, open-source standards for handling data, it becomes increasingly easy for other agencies to launch their own democratizing data programs, building on the experience of the pioneers and adding to the "library" of data-based solutions to complex problems.

That will mean that those who begin democratizing data now can directly benefit from this library. The benefits, should other government agencies move quickly to take the basic steps required, should increase exponentially because of the synergies between initiatives worldwide.

Keys to the strategic shift

Effective democratizing data initiatives require a paradigm shift from past ways of regarding data:

> **Make your government data-centric.**
> In the past, because the tools to distribute and use data were primitive, it was understandable that access to data was primarily second-hand. It was usually warehoused, embedded in proprietary software, and/or interpreted by an elite group of analysts and executives. Today, open source software, metadata and other tools allow the data to remain independent, accessible to all whose jobs require access to it. Truly, data must be thought of as at the heart of everything the government does.
>
> **Treat all workers as knowledge workers**.
> When data was hard to access and the software to interpret it costly, limiting access to real-time data to a relative few was justifiable. Now it isn't. Every worker's job performance and satisfaction can be increased by direct access to data (the exact mix of data delivered to individual workers will be determined on the basis of his or her role.)

When appropriate, release real-time data for outside use and scrutiny.
Government agencies accumulate vast amounts of data that could be used externally, not only to earn public trust through transparency, but also (especially with real-time and geo-spatial information) to create valuable new services that can complement what the agencies do themselves, or, in its machine-readable form, to drive embedded devices in a wide range of products. That data is also more valuable when it is released in the original, granular form in which it was collected, rather than as interpreted and aggregated by others. Today the default must be *to* release data. Exceptions to that rule must be justified.

In no way does a democratizing data strategy justify breaches in personal privacy and/or security standards.
In fact, as we will see, establishing the right access standards can mean people ranging from those with no security clearance at all to top-secret clearance may all access portions of the same data set based on the situation and their roles, but with widely-differing specific levels of access. A comprehensive democratizing data strategy should in fact help uncover security and privacy breaches rather than encourage them.

Above all, adopt a new collaborative attitude toward data.
In the past, if data was shared at all, it was usually sequentially, because data was effectively captured and altered by various proprietary programs. Now, with open-source, open-access programs and structured data, data can be more effectively analyzed and used if it is shared on a real-time basis. Collaborative data analysis is fundamentally different than analysis by individuals, harnessing different perspectives and expertise to yield a richer, more comprehensive picture that benefits from all of these perspectives and is more nuanced and balanced.

Democratizing data is both a process and an attitude. The more people who can access data and use it, the more valuable the data will become, the more workers will be able to improve their performance, governments will become more accountable and transparent, and average people will become both better consumers of data and be able to use it to become active participants in creation of goods and services.

W. David Stephenson (@DavidStephenson) is a leading Gov./Enterprise 2.0 strategist and theorist. He particularly focuses on homeland security and disaster management and ways to directly involve the public in policy and services debate and delivery. He is completing a book, Democratizing Data to transform government, business and daily life, *on strategies for automated structured data feeds and their use to improve worker efficiency, transparency, and to stimulate mass collaboration.*

---

[1] Boalt Interactive, "DC Historic Tours", http://www.dchistorictours.com

[2] NZ Transit Agency, InfoConnect, http://j.mp/rLEYv

[3] Bob Schneider. "Dutch Taxonomy Project Cuts Red Tape", *Hitachi Interactive*. http://j.mp/9HSqL

[4] Strict grammarians remind us that data is the plural of datum in Latin. However, it has become common practice to use a singular verb with data, so that will be the practice observed here. In case you're interested, here's the argument: "The word data is the plural of Latin datum, "something given", but does that mean you should treat it as a plural noun in English? Not always. The plural usage is still common enough. Sometimes scientists think of data as plural, as in These data do not support the conclusions. But more often, scientists and researchers think of data as a singular mass entity like information, and most people now follow this in general usage." The American Heritage® Book of English Usage. A Practical and Authoritative Guide to Contemporary English. New York: Random, 1996.

[5] Frank DiGiammarino. Interview with author, December 05, 2008.

[6] Sara Wood. "Breaking the Vicious Cycle", Tasty Data Goodies blog, July 14, 2007. http://j.mp/U4r2X

[7] "Data vs. Information". *Diffen*. http://j.mp/3LgiTQ

[8] "World GPS Market Forecast To 2012". GPS News, http://j.mp/2ITWdq

[9] Schneider, *op cit.*

[10] Vivek Kundra. "Building the Digital Public Square", Oct. 15, 2008. http://j.mp/GoKE

[11] *ibid.*

[12] Jeff Howe. *Crowdsourcing: why the power of the crowd is driving the future of business.* New York: Crown Business, 2008 310 pps.

[13] Michael Arrington. "Search for Steve Fawcett Extends to Amazon's Mechanical Turk". *TechCrunch*, Sept. 8, 2007. http://j.mp/NblKJ

[14] Kim Wallen, "The State Business Portal," whitepaper. Mumbai: IRIS Business, 2009. http://j.mp/oVywY

[15] "OCTO Delivers Computers to Every DCPS Classroom", News Release, District of Columbia Office of the Chief Technology Officer, Jan 31, 2008. http://j.mp/NKHnG

[16] Alabama Department of Homeland Security, "Virtual Alabama Fact Sheet", http://j.mp/iJK22

[17] Nancy Scola. "Better Patents Through Crowdsourcing", Science Progress, http://j.mp/MkuPk. President Obama appointed Beth Noveck as deputy director of open government in the Office of Science and Technology Policy.

#13

THE POWER OF GOVERNMENT INFORMATION

Richard Allan
Director of Policy, EU, Facebook

The phrase *Power of Information* was coined to cover a range of issues related to public sector information and user-generated content, as well as to talk about innovation in public service delivery using Web 2.0 technologies.

There have been several phases in the development and delivery of this Power of Information agenda in the UK.

The *Power of Information Review* by Ed Mayo and Tom Steinberg set out the agenda comprehensively in June 2007. The Review had been commissioned by the Cabinet Office in April 2007[1] with a particular emphasis on the growing phenomenon of websites where citizens could share advice with each other.

> *"This is an unusual review in that it is a story of opportunities rather than problems. It takes a practical look at the use and development of citizen and state-generated information in the UK. For example, information produced by*

the government (often referred to as 'public sector information') includes maps, heart surgery mortality statistics and timetables, while information from citizens includes advice, product reviews or even recipes."
Power of Information Review, Executive Summary[2].

The recommendations in the Review were accepted by the UK Government and their response was given extra impetus with the appointment of Tom Watson MP as a Minister in the Cabinet Office in January 2008. Tom, who has since left the government, was strongly influenced by his own experience of technology as an early and prolific blogger[3], and by his appreciation of the work of key thinkers in the area of mass collaboration, especially Clay Shirky's 'Here Comes Everybody'[4].

Tom decided that the best way to speed up progress on the Review's agenda was to establish a Taskforce[5] bringing together people from industry, government and the voluntary sector with a shared interest in opening up government information. This group was set the task of developing further the proposals in the Review and of acting as champions for these across government.

The Taskforce was chaired by the author of this article and worked from the spring of 2008 until producing its final report[6] in February 2009.

With the acceptance of the Taskforce's further recommendations, the UK Government is now moving into a phase of mainstream government delivery of the Power of Information agenda. This has been a key objective – to attempt to move the agenda around public sector information and the use of it from being a fringe activity for the more technically minded to being something which is part of core government activity.

In order to deliver that agenda, the Government has set up a Directorate of Digital Engagement with the Cabinet Office and appointed

Andrew Stott[7] as the UK's first Director of Digital Engagement from May 2009.

Their job now is to deliver this as a mainstream policy agenda.

This thinking has already started to surface in the mainstream policy agenda with the following section in a public service reform paper "Working Together: Public Services On Your Side"[8] from March 2009:

- *"Open information – to have an effective voice, people need to be able to understand what is going on in their public services. Government will publish information about public services in ways that are easy to find, use, and re-use.*
- *Open feedback – the public should have a fair say about their services. We need more services like NHS Choices or PublicExperience.com to provide direct feedback to the Innovation Council.*
- *Open conversation – we will promote greater engagement with the public through more interactive online consultation and collaboration. We will also empower professionals to be active on online peer-support networks in their area of work.*
- *Open innovation – we will promote innovation in online public services to respond to changing expectations – bringing the concepts behind Show Us A Better Way into mainstream government practice."*

This message was reinforced by Tom Watson MP in his foreword to the Government's response to the Taskforce report, stating that –

> *"The Power of Information principles are no longer just recommendations in a report but will be core to the future development and implementation of government policy."*

It is also important to recognize that before these phases of activity were gathered under the "Power of Information" banner, several strands of work had been developing which were crucial to its development.

One was the large amount of activity that took place by web activists building websites and services that met needs they felt were not being met by the official channels. Much of this activity was itself triggered by Government proposals to introduce new powers to monitor internet communications in the year 2000.

This inspired activists to create a series of websites that aimed to make politics and politicians more accessible, such as the self-explanatory faxyourmp.com, which has since evolved into writetothem.com. This DIY activity remains very influential in the UK, much of it organized through an NGO called mysociety.org, and their flagship site has become theyworkforyou.com, which takes Parliament's own data and repurposes it to make it more intelligible.

Theyworkforyou.com had a significant impact on policy makers when they saw their own work taken and repurposed through open access to public sector information. The access to the Parliamentary record may not have been technically legal when the data was first taken, but since then licenses have been developed to allow people to use it. And MPs have moved from a position of, in some cases, concern about the service, to one of generally liking it and in many cases linking to it from their own websites.

The other strand of activity that was very significant was on the legislative front with the development of the EU Directive on Public Sector Information[9] in 2003, which was brought into UK law in 2005.

The introduction of the Directive led to the creation of the Advisory Panel on Public Sector Information[10], which brings together leading experts to advise government and to deal with complaints about access to public sector information. It also led to the development of the Office of Public Sector Information[11] as a piece of government with a specific focus in this area.

Both of these organizations, while not widely-known at the time of their creation, have been building expertise over several years which has been of real value and significance as this became a more high profile political issue over recent times.

The other major changes were at the technology level. We have seen how broadband penetration has expanded massively, so that it is now the norm to have fast home access in most developed countries. And we have seen the development of the simple software tools and packages of code, commonly labeled as Web 2.0 tools that allow us to build very complex systems without having to code from scratch. The level of technical expertise required to do something like a Google Maps mash-up can be very low indeed.

These technology changes and the spread of technology have also been very important in creating the climate for talking about the "Power of Information" as being relevant to most citizens rather than just as an issue for the highly technically-literate minority.

The Taskforce approached its work by deciding to develop 'exemplars' and 'enablers' for the "Power of Information" agenda. The exemplars were aimed at demonstrating possibilities to people across government for whom this may be very unfamiliar territory. The enablers were aimed at identifying what would be required to do this in a more consistent fashion across government.

A key component of the exemplars work was the creation of a competition for ideas for using public sector data called ShowUsABetterWay.com. This is along the lines of other competitions such as AppsForDemocracy.org in the US and many private sector examples.

These competitions are gaining some traction because they bring to life for people who may not fully understand what it is you could do if you encouraged innovation and made data available. The allocation of small budgets for prizes also has the beneficial effect of requiring the competition organizers to secure buy-in from the government organizations who are putting up the funding.

As well as generating good examples for use across government, the competition also highlighted some of the issues that need to be tackled within the enablers' strand of work.

It was already apparent that there were issues with access to some public sector data where activists had reported difficulties in obtaining the information they needed.

For example, we had a community of parents who wanted to access simple data about schools – their addresses – so they could organize parents into local groups around their local schools. They could not get hold of that dataset freely or easily due to a historic commercial arrangement, which could be dealt with once it came to light as it was contrary to current government policy.

The Office of Public Sector Information developed a data-unlocking service[12] in 2008, to allow the public to flag datasets of interest like this which they would then investigate.

But the competition also brought out a number of structural issues around datasets where they were either prohibitively expensive, or for which the licensing conditions were inappropriate, or which were simply not available in a usable form.

A lot of the data that was of interest was that generated by local government. But local government typically has its data stored across different local systems which are not necessarily consistent across regions or the country as a whole. They have had no reason in the past to do anything else, so this is quite a natural place to be.

But this becomes a barrier when you want to set up a new service such as the Loofinder[13] service that was proposed in the competition.

This was a service to allow people to find public toilets wherever they are, based on a service called SatLav developed by Westminster City Council. With SatLav you can text the word TOILET to a particular text number and it will text you back with the location of the nearest public convenience.

That would clearly be a service that would be useful at a national level, but when you are in those circumstances you don't want to have to know which local authority boundary you are in before sending your request off.

Your reasonable expectation these days is that you can send the request off and that somewhere behind the scenes the data would be aggregated from all the relevant local authorities and then presented to you in an accessible form.

Given the extent of this data, which has to be aggregated from local systems, there is a need to develop awareness of this issue in local government and for consequent changes to systems and data structures.

There is other data, which is simply not collected in a usable form at present.

An example of this from the competition was school catchment areas[14] – the boundaries which define eligibility to send your children to a particular school in the UK. The school catchment area may be defined by a paper map that sits in a drawer in the school office, and there may be no electronic or otherwise easily accessible version of that map.

A project has therefore been set up to try and put in place easily licensable and freely usable school catchment data. This will support people in building systems to help parents navigate the schools admissions process, perhaps mashing up the school catchment areas with user-generated experiences of access to those schools, and with the inspection data and other data about their performance.

The other issue of concern was the datasets which are currently not available in a form which is accessible for small-scale innovators, and this very much focused on spatial data in the UK.

Around a third of our competition entries wanted to take public sector data and present it spatially, typically using maps for display and using postcodes to locate public sector data items and service users.

Both of these data sets – maps and postcodes – present problems for the small innovator working from a limited or non-existent budget.

The official source of mapping data in the UK is an organization called the Ordnance Survey, which is expected to generate a commercial return on its activities in a model called a 'Trading Fund,' while postcode data is tied up in a commercial service offered by the Royal Mail.

The Power of Information Review in 2007 asked the Ordnance Survey to create a simple, free, product along the lines of Google Maps, and it had done so with a product called OpenSpace. While OpenSpace is useful, we found that the restrictions on it meant it was not the right product for many developers. The core mapping products that Ordnance Survey offers, for valid reasons around competition policy and fairness in the market, are also only available on terms where small innovators found it prohibitive to use that data.

We found that developers would therefore typically turn to a product like Google Maps instead. But this also creates some additional problems around what is called 'derived data'. For example, crime mapping is of current interest, but if you derived the boundaries for the local crime statistical areas from Ordnance Survey maps and displayed these on a Google Map, then Ordnance Survey believed that there was a conflict between the licensing terms for the two systems and has warned people accordingly.

The Taskforce recognized that there are some major commercial issues at stake here, including an ecosystem of people who work with the data at present, and that Ordnance Survey itself needs to have a reliable supply of funding for the future. But we did want to emphasize the point that improving access to spatial data was a priority from the innovators' point of view, which government should also prioritize.

There are alternative services developing like OpenStreetMap, which would avoid some of these commercial and licensing issues, but these would also benefit from freeing up the official government spatial data sources.

As a result of this activity, Ordnance Survey has been asked to look again at their strategy and have published a consultation that is now being considered. Their proposals for their future strategy include a major expansion of the data available through OpenSpace, as well as other changes to make their data more accessible. The robust online discussion about the Ordnance Survey and their strategy provides an interesting illustration of the contrasting positions on commercial exploitation versus free access to government data.

We also found that postcode data was of great importance to developers to allow them to link data to political or administrative boundary of relevance to citizens. The UK postcode dataset is held in a product called the Postcode Address File, which is part of Royal Mail's commercial business.

There are some issues around the fitness of that dataset itself for our purposes, as it is a record of delivery points designed to enable the post office to deliver mail rather than a comprehensive address database as such. It has been enhanced over time to include other address information to support direct marketing and other business applications.

There are other datasets which support addressing applications in the UK, but all of them are commercial and have their own licensing terms which can act as a barrier to innovators. Royal Mail did provide a copy of the Postcode Address File for the purposes of the ShowUsABetterWay competition, but this was a one-off exercise for those limited purposes.

There are now some drivers towards resolving the issue of an addressing database to support public service applications.

One of these drivers is the 2011 census where a full address database of all individuals in the UK is required and a team is looking at how to support this. They are evaluating the different address databases trying to evaluate their accuracy and considering how to pull all the sources together into a single comprehensive database for the UK.

This leaves open the question of what to do when the census is over and whether there is some attempt through this process at creating an ongoing comprehensive address database. These policy questions remain on the table providing a fresh point of focus on postcode-address lookup.

The other source of pressure is from some web activists. They have created a site called ErnestMarples.com which offers postcode-to-coordinate lookup and deliberately sets out to challenge what is permissible under license conditions.

> *"Post codes are really useful, but the powers that be keep them closed unless you have loads of money to pay for them. Which makes it hard to build useful websites (and that makes Ernest sad)."*

> *"So we are setting them free and using them to run PlanningAlerts.com and Jobcentre Pro Plus. We're doing the same as everyone's being doing for years, but just being open about it."*
> *Home page at ernestmarples.com.*

The site takes a number of different freely available sources for postcode lookup, for example you can do this on most of the common mapping sites, and offers a single interface to these for lookups. It doesn't hold the data itself but creates access to it.

As described by themselves above, the activists, Harry Metcalfe and Richard Pope, have done this to make the point that this kind of service should be freely available and can support a number of valuable public information services including ones they themselves have built.

A further area that has emerged as being of particular interest is transport data.

Transport data in the UK is typically not public sector information, but is generated and held by the private sector providers of transport services. This includes information about infrastructure, timetabling and service performance.

The development of apps for the iPhone has brought this issue to light in a number of places, including one with New South Wales CityRail[15] in Australia, as well as with National Rail in the UK[16].

The Taskforce recommended that government should not in the future sign up to deals with third parties, including transport operators, where the information is regarded as a commercial asset to be held externally and used to fund the service. Rather, the information asset should revert to government wherever possible, and this should be built into the contracts so that government can decide whether or not to freely distribute the data.

In the case of something like public transport information, if the public policy objective is to get more people using more public transport more efficiently, then there is a clear interest in making datasets like timetable information freely available. This creates conditions for innovative developments such as the creation of many iPhone apps competing on their own added value. It would also allow for valuable experimentation such as isochrone mapping to show travel times between places using different modes.

The Power of Information case is that a broad range of innovative activity can and will take place if the data is made available. If it is restricted on the other hand, then we will see a much lower level of innovation to the detriment of citizens and of those charged with delivering public services.

As well as these issues, which were drawn from our work on exemplars, the Taskforce looked at the shifts in thinking that would be required to enable government to act as a platform for innovation.

A key element in this was to consider a shift from the traditional model where the government website was the only end product and seen as the single correct way of presenting data, to thinking of government information as existing in three distinct layers which should be separated out – Presentation, Analysis and Data. The model also called for the insertion of Access layers, offering up the Analysis and Data content for re-use.

This model was described graphically in the Taskforce report and in the following terms –

> *"The emphasis of much web development to date has been on the presentation of the data to the public.*
>
> *The assumption was that a particular website would be the unique interface to a particular set of data.*

This meant that little or no thought might have been given to how anyone else would use the data set in question.

Sometimes the data and any analysis of it could be unpicked from such a site but in many instances this would be extremely difficult.

Thinking has moved on over recent years with a developing understanding of the importance of separating data from its presentation. If nothing else, this allows for simpler changes to the presentation layer as, for example, websites are redesigned.

PRESENTATION LAYER – the public-facing front end, typically a set of web pages

ANALYSIS LAYER – any form of interpretation of the raw data, typically for summary presentation

ACCESS LAYER – all the information needed to access the data, including technical, legal and commercial aspects

DATA LAYER – the raw data sets."

Power of Information Task Force Report, February 2009.

For some people they will want to access raw data, for others the analysis, and for many users they will simply want to access the fully-finished presentation layer product.

The Taskforce also found the paper 'Government Data and the Invisible Hand'[17] very helpful in developing its thinking in this area. And while their view was, that official government websites would remain important, websites need to be seen as part of an overall ecosystem in which innovators can create alternatives and those alternatives may have significant value.

The Taskforce also looked at measures that government might take actively to support open innovation.

A key recommendation in this area related to the development of innovation platforms within the government web estate. Such a platform would support the kind of innovation proposed by the ShowUsABetterWay competition entrants on an ongoing basis. This thinking was strongly influenced by the experience of BBC Backstage[18], which opened up BBC data sets for innovators and provided them with a space to come together.

As well as providing technical tools, this requires a cultural shift. There is a need to move from a mindset where government builds websites and services, and feels that if citizens try to do this, then this is some kind of threat, to one in which coproduction is seen as a positive benefit and opportunity for government.

Sometimes government services will gain directly, as external innovations are rolled back into their core services. This may be a common scenario as people create new services that they cannot sustain themselves.

On many other occasions, new services will remain free-standing and will provide complementary or alternative to existing formal channels to the benefit of their users.

Some services will be offered on a not-for-profit basis, others will be commercial, and many will have no formal business model at all, as they are simply the brainchild of one or more innovators who are wholly focused on producing a good solution. The Taskforce considered it important that government is able to work with this rich variety of innovation models and be creative in its response to working with them.

In order to deliver this 'backstage' capability, the core UK government website that is there to deliver most public sector information, DirectGov, was asked to create an innovation space. This is now live at innovate.direct.gov.uk. It will have a dual purpose: trying to create this community of co-producers and trying to stimulate demand for datasets to be released for re-use.

A further barrier to innovation can occur when government datasets are not well described or easily locatable. The US Government has recently provided a model for tackling this situation with their data.gov portal.

Work is now being carried out in the UK to deal with the same challenge of providing accurate and effective data signposting. This will draw on the US experience as well as the existing infrastructure of Information Asset Registers within government and of the Comprehensive Knowledge Archive Network outside government.

The final area of ongoing work is around licensing models. What is key for innovators, is that they do not need to have a team of lawyers on hand before starting to produce interesting services using public data.

This means that the licensing has to be simple and straightforward. The Taskforce was impressed with work in Australia on government data licensing, especially by Prof Brian Fitzgerald around Creative Commons and the Queensland Government's Government Information Licensing Framework[19].

The current position is one of anticipating that the existing open licenses of Crown Copyright will be maintained as these are highly permissive and well-developed. Crown Copyright together with the Click-use licensing service from the Office of Public Sector Information already provides a sound framework for many innovators. But work will continue on how any lessons from Creative Commons and other open licensing schemes can be applied also to UK public data.

It is also important to continue to work on compatibility between the licenses that apply to different forms of data. Innovative services typically combine a range of public and commercial datasets, which has the potential to generate conflicts as was seen in the Ordnance Survey and Google Maps case.

The UK agenda of offering data and other support for innovative web services has developed considerably over the last few years.

There is now a broader understanding of the value that can be generated by opening up data and encouraging innovation rather than seeking to place barriers in the way of this activity.

The debate has moved from being on the technical fringes to incorporation in mainstream government policy within a broader theme of openness and transparency.

There remain some tensions around particular datasets, especially spatial data due to the particular models the UK has developed for creation and maintenance of this data.

Finally, the Taskforce itself was a model for a different way of working within government. All of its deliberations were shared online, including a commendable beta version[20] of its final report. This is part of a current of internal innovation that is now running through parts of the UK administration and may also prove highly influential over time.

Richard Allan (@ricallan) joined Facebook in June 2009 to lead the company's public policy work in Europe. He was previously European Government Affairs Director for Cisco. From April 2008 to May 2009, Richard was Chair of the Cabinet Office's Power of Information Task Force. Richard was elected as Member of Parliament for Sheffield Hallam in 1997 and re-elected in 2001 before giving up his seat in 2005. Between 1991 and 1997, Richard worked as an IT professional in the NHS.

---

[1] Press notice announcing Power of Information Review. http://j.mp/18m4NH

[2] Power of Information Review, Ed Mayo and Tom Steinberg, June 2007. http://j.mp/1EfhGW

[3] Tom Watson's blog – http://www.tom-watson.co.uk/

[4] http://j.mp/dSCuU

[5] Press notice of Taskforce establishment. http://j.mp/1Va7RM

[6] Final report of Taskforce – http://poit.cabinetoffice.gov.uk/poit/

[7] Press notice of appointment. http://j.mp/1ac546

[8] http://www.hmg.gov.uk/workingtogether.aspx

[9] EU Directive on Public Sector Information. http://j.mp/oXof5

[10] http://www.appsi.gov.uk/

[11] http://www.opsi.gov.uk/

[12] OPSI Data Unlocking Service – http://www.opsi.gov.uk/unlocking-service

[13] Loofinder competition entry. http://j.mp/rnRXp

[14] School catchment areas competition entry. http://j.mp/2DoBHh

[15] New South Wales iPhone app story. http://j.mp/YM6ZY

[16] UK National Rails iPhone app story. http://j.mp/192FjC

[17] Robinson, David G., Yu, Harlan, Zeller, William P. and Felten, Edward W., Government Data and the Invisible Hand (2009). Yale Journal of Law & Technology, Vol. 11, p. 160, 2009. Available at SSRN: http://ssrn.com/abstract=1138083

[18] BBC Backstage – http://welcomebackstage.com/

[19] Queensland Government Licensing. http://j.mp/EblYI

[20] Beta version is still available for comparison with final version at http://poit.cabinetoffice.gov.uk/poit/

#14

THE EMPEROR'S NEW NAKEDNESS *OR* HOW TRUE TRANSPARENCY WILL SAVE GOVERNMENTAL PROJECTS FROM UTTER FAILURE

Tommy Dejbjerg Pedersen
CEO, Geekhouse

The internal systems of Twitter were recently attacked by a hacker. The hacker gained access to a lot of internal documents such as business plans, minutes of board meetings and other vital and sensitive internal information. The unintended transparency this suddenly created around the internal workings of Twitter had a huge marketing effect. Suddenly, Twitter and their roadmap, their potential exit strategies and much more was on everybody's lips. And anyone who had good ideas could now openly suggest these to the Twitter guys and co-create the future of Twitter.

Full transparency, participation and open collaboration in the extreme, and perhaps - unintended...

Unintended transparency may not be every public sector manager's dream.

But take a minute to think about what would happen if a large government project decided to release their entire code base, documentation and more to public display, in order to tap the support of the community.

Now close your eyes, and think of the consequences of this and then resume reading.

All done? Welcome back.

What did you see when contemplating the outcome of such an action? Was it bad for the project to suddenly be on public display? Or did it actually increase the chance of the project's success?

I will argue that transparency in all aspects of a project is an exercise we should seriously consider if we are to become truly aware of the advantages of transparency in governmental projects. Why not throw in a paragraph in the next major tender material that the customer reserves the right to publish *all* information, code and documentation in their project? I believe that would truly drive the quality and raise attention to performance in the project.

Attempts have already been made to go some of the way in a few government projects in Denmark. The government portal for information about standardization in the public sector, called Digitaliser.dk (translates to digitalize.dk), developed by the National IT and Telecom Agency (NITA), is one such project. Digitaliser.dk was developed as an agile project with (assumed) transparency between the supplier and the customer. Project plans were published along the way, but detailed project information on sprint planning was not made completely public, so the process itself was not made transparent. An issue tracking system was used to enable participatory collaboration with users, but the level of feedback to the users reporting the issues has been very poor. The code for Digitaliser.dk was said to be available as open source but, although the platform went live in spring 2009, the site for hosting governmental open source projects (softwareboersen.dk) does not yet contain any code releases. The head of NITA's infrastructural department recently reported[1] that the source will soon be available at a public Subversion site.

The mission statement for Digitaliser.dk seemed promising, but somewhere along the line, good intentions were not combined with appropriate action. A one-way issue tracking system and the failure to release the source code add up to no real difference in the transparency of governmental projects. Source code and milestone releases should be made widely available *during* the project to create the transparency that stimulates collaboration with the community. On the other hand, the wise decision to focus on transparency in this project, in both the source base and the project model, should serve as inspiration for other government institutions.

Another project called NemHandel (EasyTrade), also by NITA, is a framework to enable the digital interchange of business documents. The project was initially founded to enable digital interchange of business documents in Denmark and, in their own words: "Make the digital interchange of business documents as easy as sending email". Now the efforts continue in a ambitious project under the EC in a project called PEPPOL, Pan European Procurement Online[2], which targets the whole procurement process from tender, to bid, to offer and so on. This project has made all source code releases available on the government software exchange (Softwareboersen.dk). After the final release, source code is still available in a subversion repository for all to retrieve. During the pilot phase of the project, a number of software integrators actually retrieved the source from Subversion and worked on it to make it run with their own system. As a result, supporting the system integrators became part of the pilot project. This enabled the system integrators to build the system and change the parts they needed to fit it to their solution.

Transparency is fully achieved here, also with regards to very active issue tracking. But the outcome of such an undertaking clearly depends on active participation of software integrators.

As an example, NemHandel has had to face the fact that vendors of application servers had a very hard time understanding the business case, and thus put very little effort into integrating the NemHandel framework into their software.

The last example is a project called DKAL, which aims to build a central distribution platform for all sorts of messages from government systems, i.e. SMS and e-mails. On this project, NITA have begun to "open source" a document made in the project by the supplier, in order to get input on the way the supplier proposes to solve certain aspects of a solution. All these efforts are good signs of a government institution that aims for transparency and aims at community participation.

Why do governmental projects fail?

The Danish IT organization *Dansk IT* – a non-commercial interest organization for the IT sector in Denmark – recently published a report[3] called "5 statements on IT-supported government business projects" citing some of the reasons that government projects fail. The report was put together by a panel of experienced people with a long track record in large government and private IT-projects.

One of the key factors for success, according to the report, was to have a clear project goal which would be kept in focus during the entire course of the project. To paraphrase the report: "Too often the focus is on what goes wrong and what does not work, instead of the long term goal of the project." There are bound to be failures along the way, but these must be weighed against the overall advantages of the final project.

The report also points to another aspect as the source of project failure: Too often, the overall project goal is defined by top-management on both the customer and supplier side. But top management does not stay on the project after it has begun. It is important to keep these people close to the project all the time, to keep focus on the goal and ensure that this it is clear to all project members and external parties.

Another major reason for failure, according to the report, is that quality is still very poor in many projects, "even" if the IT suppliers have made dozens of government projects before. Quality is hard to achieve, and poor quality leads to slipping deadlines, budget overruns and many challenges in maintaining the project after final delivery, thus reducing the lifetime of the system.

Open source equals quality?

Many companies today[4] naturally view open source as a label to stick on their products, to sell something as a high quality solution to their customers. Public sector solutions are also often focused on building on open source, to get the best possible building blocks for as many solutions as possible. But does open source always equate quality and the flexibility we need, or what are the apparent characteristics that we associate with the label "open source"?

The answer may well be found in the many commercial business cases based on open source software. A large number of vendors have adopted open source projects with an intent to build commercial solutions on top. Vendors find open source projects to be great platforms for new solutions because open source projects are based on best practices and are typically of a very high quality.

These open source building blocks are usually framework components and thus isolated blocks that target an isolated purpose, rather than a full solution aimed at a full vertical process in a company. The goal of the company is to provide a business-focused layer around the components to ensure turnkey solutions aimed at creating business value for their customers. Customers generally support the choice of commercializing open source components, as it gives them a sense of freedom of choice with regard to their vendor.

Zooming in on these building block types of open source components, the level of quality achieved most certainly stems from two specific reasons.

Firstly, the code is implemented to solve a very specific isolated purpose. It aims at doing a few things and doing them very well, in contrast to large ERP solutions that also need to incorporate reporting facilities, activity monitoring as well as both administrative and client interfaces. The huge advantage of keeping the purpose simple and isolated is that you can envision the whole solution and carry out the design and development of it within the same frame of mind. Or to put it another way: You can pick up the ball, walk onto the court and just concentrate on playing basketball. Solving more challenges at one time can easily be compared to playing many different games at one time, which is very complicated and should be left for 6 year old kids playing Calvinball, the favorite game of cartoon characters Calvin and Hobbes, which has many rules but the most important is: "Any player may declare a new rule at any point in the game". Needless to say this game is highly complicated and doesn't fit well into rigid structures such as large IT project teams.

The point is: Quality in terms of solving a problem in the best possible way comes from the single-tasking effort of developing something that's limited to solving an isolated problem. Keeping the problem isolated does not in any way guarantee that the components will fit nicely together, nor does it ensure that the characteristics of the components adhere to the high standards needed in software components. The components naturally need to be flexible, open, secure and adaptable to the system or process in which they will be applied.

This leads us to the second reason that open source is a guarantee of high quality. Open sourced projects are usually initiated and maintained by highly motivated and skilled developers who are not afraid to exhibit the code they write for constructive criticism by the community. Thus the transparency achieved in open source projects drives the constant measuring of quality in every single aspect of the code. Developers, who want to achieve the status of committers on an open source project, need to prove to the project owners that their commitment to the project and that their skills live up to the high standards of the project. When you have made it onto the team, the pressure to keep your status pushes the standard of your contributions. The awareness that you are working on a project where every single contribution is openly visible to team members, as well as to the whole community, creates a drive to perform well.

Transparency leads to high quality projects and gives good velocity on projects in general, as seen when using agile methods. These methods have built-in transparency through the use of visible sprint plans. Sprint plans can be placed online for all to see along, with voting options to prioritize the sprint planning in a participatory way.

The two reasons described in the above are, when combined, a solid starting point for any healthy project focusing on quality and on delivering on time, within budget. We need to focus less on simply making everything open source per se, and instead focus on taking the characteristics, such as transparency, from open source projects and applying them to the whole process of developing and controlling the development of government systems.

I hope that, someday, a hacker will break in to a server containing all files in a large governmental project, and put all these files online for everyone to see. Alternatively, I would urge governments to consider a fully transparent approach to the next major project, in order to reap the benefits of transparency and true participation of the community.

Tommy Dejbjerg Pedersen (@tpedersen) is the founder of Geekhouse, the first geek-only incubator in Denmark and a division of the Danish IT-company Miracle. Geekhouse hosts "traditional" entrepreneurs but has also specialized in hosting unemployed people who want to start their own business. Tommy is a serial entrepreneur, leading specialist in Web 2.0 technology and has worked in the tough dot com business. He has also done a lot of advisory work on large governmental projects both on the supplier and the customer side.

---

[1] http://j.mp/3V8SBO

[2] http://www.peppol.eu

[3] http://j.mp/2XMVgq

[4] http://j.mp/3GfpKl

#15

AGAINST TRANSPARENCY: THE PERILS OF OPENNESS IN GOVERNMENT[1]

Lawrence Lessig
Professor, Harvard Law School

In 2006, the Sunlight Foundation launched a campaign to get members of the US Congress to post their daily calendars on the Internet. "The Punch-Clock Campaign" collected pledges from ninety-two candidates for Congress, and one of them was elected. I remember when the project was described to me by one of its developers. She assumed that I would be struck by its brilliance. I was not. It seemed to me that there were too many legitimate reasons why someone might not want his or her "daily official work schedule" available to anyone with an Internet connection. Still, I didn't challenge her. I was just coming into the "transparency movement". Surely these things would become clearer, so to speak, later on.

In any case, the momentum was on her side. The "transparency movement" was about to achieve an extraordinary victory in the election of Barack Obama. Indeed, practically nobody any longer questions the wisdom in Brandeis's famous remark – it has become one of the reigning clichés of the transparency movement – that "sunlight is ... the best of disinfectants." Like the decision to go to war in Iraq, transparency has become an unquestionable bipartisan value.

And not just in politics. If health care reform ever emerges from Congress, it is certain to spread nationally a project to require doctors to reveal to an Internet-linked database any financial interests they may have in any drug company or device manufacturer. Type the name of any doctor into the database, and a long list of consulting contracts, stock ownership and paid speaking arrangements will be returned to you, presumably to help you avoid doctors with too many conflicting loyalties, and to steer you to doctors who have themselves steered clear of conflicts.

How could anyone be against transparency? Its virtues and its utilities seem so crushingly obvious. But I have increasingly come to worry that there is an error at the core of this unquestioned goodness. We are not thinking critically enough about where and when transparency works, and where and when it may lead to confusion, or to worse. And I fear that the inevitable success of this movement – if pursued alone, without any sensitivity to the full complexity of the idea of perfect openness – will inspire not reform, but disgust. The "naked transparency movement", as I will call it here, is not going to inspire change. It will simply push any faith in our political system over the cliff.

The naked transparency movement marries the power of network technology to the radical decline in the cost of collecting, storing, and distributing data. Its aim is to liberate that data, especially government data, so as to enable the public to process it and understand it better, or at least differently.

The most obvious examples of this new responsibility for disclosure are data about the legislative process: the demand, now backed by the White House, that bills be posted to the Internet at least twenty-four hours before they are voted upon, or that video of legislative hearings and floor debate be freed from the proprietary control of one (easily disciplined) entity such as C-SPAN. The most dramatic examples so far are public data from executive agencies: the website Data.gov is just beginning to assemble an extraordinary collection of "high-value datasets" from the executive branch, all available in standard open formats, and free for the taking.

Without a doubt, the vast majority of these transparency projects make sense. In particular, management transparency, which is designed to make the performance of government agencies more measurable, will radically improve how government works. And making government data available for others to build upon has historically produced enormous value – from weather data, which produces more than $800 billion in economic value to the United States, to GPS data, liberated originally by Ronald Reagan, which now allows cell phones to instantly report (among other essential facts) whether Peets or Starbucks is closer.

But that is not the whole transparency story. There is a type of transparency project that should raise more questions than it has – in particular, projects that are intended to reveal potentially improper influence, or outright corruption. Projects such as the one that the health care bill would launch – building a massive database of doctors who got money from private interests; or projects such as the ones (these are the really sexy innovations for the movement) to make it trivially easy to track every possible source of influence on a member of Congress, mapped against every single vote that the member has made. These projects assume that they are seeking an obvious good. No doubt they will have a profound effect. But will the effect of these projects – at least on their own, unqualified or unrestrained by other considerations – really be for the good? Do we really want the world that they righteously envisage?

With respect to data about campaign contributions, the history of transparency is long. Disclosure requirements for federal elections are a century old next year. For more than three decades, we have known the names of everyone who gives significant amounts to a federal campaign. Or at least we have "known" them in the sense that if you hustled yourself to a government file cabinet, you could discover who contributed what – often months after the election, and often with the cabinet located far from any convenient place. To this day, practical matters work against practical access. In the Senate, for example, those names are reported to the Federal Election Commission (FEC) the old-fashioned way – on paper. Staffers for senators collect the data in sophisticated computer programs that make it simple to manage efficiently the most valuable data for any political campaign. When it comes time to report the data that they have collected, however, they print the data on paper, forcing FEC staffers to re-enter it into FEC databases. This process takes time, giving senators a comfortable window at the end of any campaign to secure last-minute funding to avoid defeat with minimal scrutiny.

The hope of the naked transparency movement is to change this. Through better code – in better legislative rules and in better technology – its aim is to make it trivially easy to get access to records suggesting influence, and then link those records automatically to the possible influence that they suggest. Consider, for example, an early instance of this work, presented in a recent report by Maplight.org, analyzing the House vote on the cap-and-trade bill. Titled "How Money Watered Down the Climate Bill," the report enumerates a long list of correlations between money given and results produced. In a section labeled "Amendment to gut the whole bill," for example, the report states: "Each legislator voting Yes ... received an average of $37,700 from the Oil & Gas, Coal Mining and Nuclear Energy industries between 2003 and 2008, more than three times as much as the $11,304 received by each legislator voting No." In a section labeled "Oil and gas giveaway," describing an amendment to "increase eligibility for industrial polluters like oil and gas refiners to receive carbon allowances," the report states that "the Oil & Gas industry gave an average of $72,119 to Energy & Commerce Committee members from 2003 [to] 2008." And in a section labeled "Redefining renewable biomass," the report describes an amendment "to broaden the definition of renewable biomass [which the League of Conservation Voters said] would have removed critical safeguards that prevent habitat on our nation's public and private forests from being plowed up": "Energy & Commerce Committee members who voted Yes on the Walden amendment received an average of $25,745 each from the Forestry and Paper Products industry, ten times as much as the $2,541 received, on average, by each member voting No."

This is a crude but powerful beginning. It points to an obvious future. Even this clarity took an enormous effort to produce, and there are obviously a million other ways in which the data might be inspired to speak. As Congress complies with the clear demands of transparency, and as coders devise better and more efficient ways to mash-up the data that Congress provides, we will see a future more and more inundated with claims about the links between money and results. Every step will have a plausible tie to troubling influence. Every tie will be reported. We will know everything there is to know about at least the publicly recordable events that might be influencing those who regulate us. The panopticon will have been turned upon the rulers.

What could possibly be wrong with such civic omniscience? How could any democracy live without it? Finally America can really know just who squeezed the sausage and when, and hold accountable anyone with an improper touch. Imagine how much Brandeis, the lover of sunlight, would have loved a server rack crunching terabytes of data. As a political disinfectant, silicon beats sunlight hands down.

Brandeis coined his famous phrase in 1914, in a book called *Other People's Money*, an extraordinary progressive screed directed against that generation's bankers. (He wrote the book when he was still practicing law. It is the sort of book that no Supreme Court nominee today could survive having written.) In the context of the then-frenzied demand for financial reform, Brandeis called for "publicity" – the idea that "bankers when issuing securities ... make public the commissions or profits they are receiving."

This publicity was designed to serve two very different purposes. First, Brandeis thought that the numbers would shame bankers into offering terms that were more reasonable – a strategy that has been tried with executive compensation by the Securities and Exchange Commission, with the result not of shame, but jealousy, leading to even higher pay. Second, and more significantly, Brandeis believed that publicity would make the market function more efficiently. The "law," Brandeis counseled, "should not undertake ... to fix bankers' profits. And it should not seek to prevent investors from making bad bargains." But the law should require, he emphatically declared, "full disclosure," to help the buyer judge quality, and thus better judge the "real value of a security." Transparency could thus make a market work better, and should be encouraged as a more efficient way to regulate this potentially dangerous market.

In this simple insight, Brandeis described what has become a school of regulatory theory – what Archon Fung, Mary Graham and David Weil describe in *Full Disclosure: The Perils and Promise of Transparency* as *"targeted transparency."* As they define it, targeted transparency "represents a distinctive category of public policies that, at their most basic level, mandate disclosure ... of standardized, comparable, and disaggregated information regarding specific products or practices to a broad audience in order to achieve a public policy purpose."

Its "ingeniousness," as Brandeis had promised, "lies in its mobilization of individual choice, market forces and participatory democracy through relatively light-handed government action." Moreover, this "ingeniousness" has now been copied, and ever more frequently. Fung and his colleagues have catalogued fifteen targeted transparency programs in their study, ten of them created since 1986, all with substantial bipartisan support, and all with a common mechanism: give the consumer data he or she can use, and he or she will use it to "regulate" the market better.

This mobilization works when the system gives consumers information that they can use, and in a way that they can use it. Think about the requirement that car manufacturers publish average mile-per-gallon statistics for all new cars. We all can compare 36 mpg to 21 mpg. We all understand what that comparison means. That "targeted transparency" rule simplifies the data and presents it in a way that conveys meaningful information. Once simplified and standardized, it makes it possible for consumers to change the way the market works.

The problem, however, is that not all data satisfies the simple requirement that they be information that consumers can use, presented in a way they can use it. "More information," as Fung and his colleagues put it, "does not always produce markets that are more efficient." Instead, "responses to information are inseparable from their interests, desires, resources, cognitive capacities, and social contexts. Owing to these and other factors, people may ignore information, or misunderstand it, or misuse it. Whether and how new information is used to further public objectives depends upon its incorporation into complex chains of comprehension, action, and response."

To know whether a particular transparency rule works, then, we need to trace just how the information will enter these "complex chains of comprehension." We need to see what comparisons the data will enable, and whether those comparisons reveal something real. And it is this that the naked transparency movement has not done. For there are overwhelming reasons why the data about influence that this movement would produce will not enable comparisons that are meaningful. This is not to say the data will not have an effect. It will. But the effect, I fear, is not one that anybody in the "naked transparency movement," or any other thoughtful citizen, would want.

What does the fact of a contribution to a member of Congress mean? Does a contribution cause a member to take a position? Does a member's position cause the contribution? Does the prospect of a contribution make a member more sensitive to a position? Does it secure access? Does it assure a better hearing? Do members compete for positions based upon the contributions they might expect? Do they covet committee assignments based upon the contributions that the committee will inspire? Does Congress regulate with an eye to whether its regulation might induce more contributions?

There is little doubt that the answer to each of these questions is, in some sense and at some time – remember those qualifiers! – yes. In a series titled *Speaking Freely,* published by the Center for Responsive Politics, you can find testimony from many former members from both parties to support each of those assertions. Everyone inside the system knows that claims about influence are, to some degree, true. It is the nature of the system, as we all know.

But there is also little doubt that it is impossible to know whether any particular contribution or contributions brought about a particular vote, or was inspired by a particular vote. Put differently, if there are benign as well as malign contributions, it is impossible to know for any particular contribution which of the two it is. Even if we had all the data in the world and a month of Google coders, we could not begin to sort corrupting contributions from innocent contributions.

Or at least "corrupting" in a certain sense. All the data in the world will not tell us whether a particular contribution bent a result by securing a vote or an act that otherwise would not have occurred. The most we could say – though this is still a very significant thing to say – is that the contributions are corrupting the reputation of Congress, because they raise the question of whether the member acted to track good sense or campaign dollars. Where a member of Congress acts in a way inconsistent with his principles or his constituents, but consistent with a significant contribution, that act at least raises a question about the integrity of the decision. But beyond a question, the data says little else.

But then, so what? If the data does not tell us anything, what is the harm in producing it? Even if it does not prove, it suggests. And if it suggests something false, then let the offended legislator rebut it. The public will weigh the truth against the charge. Enter another Brandeisean cliché: "If there be time to expose through discussion the falsehood and fallacies ... the remedy to be applied is more speech, not enforced silence." This sounds right.

But would such a remedy work? Would more speech really help to uncover the falsehoods? In answering this question, it helps to think concretely. How, actually, does this sort of dialogue proceed? Consider an example. In the waning days of the Clinton administration, friends of the credit-card industry were trying to get what would become the Bankruptcy Abuse Prevention and Consumer Protection Act of 2005 enacted into law. President Clinton was originally in favor of the bill. But in 2000, first lady Hillary Clinton read an op-ed piece in *The New York Times* detailing the harm that the bill would do to lower-middle-class Americans. She began referring to "that awful bill" - lower case "b" - and took on the mission of stopping her husband from making it law. He apparently acquiesced, letting the bill die in a pocket veto.

Two years later, First Lady Clinton was Senator Clinton. And two years later, she had received over $140,000 in campaign contributions from credit-card and financial-services companies. Two years later, the bill came up for a vote. But by now, Senator Clinton apparently saw things differently from how First Lady Clinton had seen them. In 2001, she voted for "that awful bill" twice. (In 2005, she switched her position again, opposing its final passage.)

Objectively speaking, there are any number of reasons why Senator Clinton would view the financial-services sector differently from how First Lady Clinton would view it. She was, after all, a senator from New York. New York has a special relationship to financial-services companies. (Put aside for a moment that it also has a special relationship to lower-middle-class credit-card holders.) There are many reasons why these differences would have an effect on her support for an "awful bill." But whatever objectivity might teach, we all know something undeniable about this fact of $140,000 being attached to any sentence about switching support in a political context. Everyone learning the fact now "knows" just why she switched, don't they? Whether true or not, money is the reason for the switch in this case. Even supporters of Senator Clinton found it hard to see things differently.

The point is salience, and the assumptions of our political culture. At this time, the judgment that Washington is all about money is so wide and so deep that among all the possible reasons to explain something puzzling, money is the first, and most likely the last, explanation that will be given. It sets the default against which anything different must fight. And this default, this unexamined assumption of causality, will only be reinforced by the naked transparency movement and its correlations. What we believe will be confirmed, again and again.

But will not this supposed salience of money – the faithful disciple of Brandeis asks – simply inspire more debate about whether in fact money buys results in Congress? Won't more people enter to negate the default? Like a rash of flat-earth defenders, won't the attention cause round-earth truth to spread? Again, we must keep our intuitions guided by the concrete. No doubt false claims will sometimes inspire more truth. But what about when the claims are neither true nor false? Or worse, when the claims actually require more than the 140 characters in a tweet?

This is the problem of attention-span. To understand something – an essay, an argument, a proof of innocence – requires a certain amount of attention. But on many issues, the average, or even rational, amount of attention given to understand many of these correlations, and their defamatory implications, is almost always less than the amount of time required. The result is a systemic misunderstanding – at least if the story is reported in a context, or in a manner, that does not neutralize such misunderstanding. The listing and correlating of data hardly qualifies as such a context. Understanding how and why some stories will be understood, or not understood, provides the key to grasping what is wrong with the tyranny of transparency.

Once we have named it, you will begin to see the attention-span problem everywhere, in public and private life. Think of politics, increasingly the art of exploiting attention-span problems – tagging your opponent with barbs that no one has time to understand, let alone analyze. Think of any complex public policy issue, from the economy to debates about levels of foreign aid.

Even the increased demand for "privacy" in acts that one commits in public – activities on the Internet, for example – might best be explained by the attention span problem. Consider, for example, a story by Peter Lewis in *The New York Times in 1998:*

> *Surveillance cameras followed the attractive young blond woman through the lobby of the midtown Manhattan hotel, kept a glassy eye on her as she rode the elevator up to the 23rd floor and peered discreetly down the hall as she knocked at the door to my room. I have not seen the videotapes, but I can imagine the digital readout superimposed on the scenes, noting the exact time of the encounter. That would come in handy if someone were to question later why this woman, who is not my wife, was visiting my hotel room during a recent business trip. The cameras later saw us heading off to dinner and to the theater – a middle-aged, married man from Texas with his arm around a pretty East Village woman young enough to be his daughter.... As a matter of fact, she is my daughter.*

"Privacy" here would hardly be invoked for the purpose of hiding embarrassing facts. Quite the contrary: the hidden facts here are the most innocent or loving. Yet it would hide these facts because we may be certain that few would take the time to understand them enough to see them as innocent.

The point in such cases is not that the public isn't smart enough to figure out what the truth is. The point is the opposite. The public is too smart to waste its time focusing on matters that are not important for it to understand. The ignorance here is rational, not pathological. It is what we would hope everyone would do, if everyone were rational about how best to deploy their time. Yet even if rational, this ignorance produces predictable and huge misunderstandings. A mature response to these inevitable misunderstandings are policies that strive not to exacerbate them.

So are there ways to respond? Can we get the good of transparency without the bad? The *Journal of the American Medical Association* (JAMA) thought that it had found a way to do so. JAMA has long had policies designed to ferret out conflicts of interest between JAMA-published authors and the medical industry. Like most journals in medicine, JAMA required disclosure, and was among the most aggressive in the extent and the reach of the disclosures required.

But as attention to disclosure grew in the medical field, the failure to disclose adequately has become a serious charge. Omission is now a serious commission. Indeed, the mere charge of failing to disclose is enough to stain a reputation. As with a charge of sexual harassment, the establishment of innocence does not really erase its harm.

In response to this sensitivity, JAMA instituted a policy that was designed to avoid the costs of wrongful charges of conflicts of interest. As described in *The Wall Street Journal,* JAMA required that anyone filing a complaint with JAMA that a conflict had not been disclosed must remain silent about the charge until it was investigated. The motivations behind this "gag order" (as it was referred to by those who opposed it) are not hard to see. While JAMA has a strong institutional interest in avoiding publications that hide conflicts, it also has an interest in avoiding charges that will do harm whether or not they are proven to be true. Recognizing both the salience problem and the attention-span problem, JAMA sought a way to avoid the bad in a regime of disclosure (misunderstanding), while preserving the good (verifiable conflicts).

The rule was inspired earlier this year by Professor Jonathan Leo of Lincoln Memorial University. At the beginning of the year, he filed a complaint with JAMA about the failure of one researcher to disclose a conflict. JAMA sat on the complaint for five months. In frustration, Leo published his charge in the *British Medical Journal*. As reported by the *The Wall Street Journal*, JAMA responded angrily, demanding that he stop his campaign until JAMA's investigation was complete, and formally requiring anyone making a similar charge to remain silent until JAMA has responded.

But, once the story of JAMA's effort to silence a critic had been made public, that "gag rule" was of course doomed. After an internal review, the journal reversed its policy. Any effort to protect the accused against unjustified criticism was abandoned. Unfair complaints would have to be tolerated - as they would have to be in any similar context. The age of transparency is upon us. The need to protect the whistleblower is unquestionable - driving off even modest efforts to cushion the blows from a mistaken accusation.

These troubles with transparency point to a pattern that should be familiar to anyone watching the range of horribles - or blessings, depending upon your perspective - that the Internet is visiting upon us. So, too, does the response. The pattern is familiar. The network disables a certain kind of control. The response of those who benefitted from that control is a frantic effort to restore it. Depending upon your perspective, restoration seems justified or not. But regardless of your perspective, restoration fails. Despite the best efforts of the most powerful, the control - so long as there is "an Internet" - is lost.

Consider, for example, the dynamic that is now killing newspapers, or more precisely, the business model for newspapers, caused either by the explosion of more efficient technologies for doing what newspapers used to profit from, or by the inevitable explosion of competition driving papers to make free what they used to charge for. Until quite recently, newspapers were among the most profitable local businesses. As one commentator calculated, average operating revenues even as late as 2000–2007 were 27.3 percent. But a raft of technologies that were seeded about a decade ago are now pushing newspapers over the brink. In 1995, a San Francisco geek named Craig opened a community website where people could list items to sell, for free. With much better coverage, space, and (obviously) price, Craigslist quickly began to dominate newsprint in markets where both went head to head. There was little that the physical paper could do to respond. A formerly lucrative cross-subsidy was gone.

A complementary story could be told without blaming Craig. People buy newspapers for the stories, not for the ink. As innovators on the Internet began offering free access to those stories, the demand for ink-staining versions declined. Why should I buy *The New York Times* when its content is available for free on its site? And if the content of The New York Times is not free on the site, no problem: I can get (essentially) the same stories elsewhere. Or worse, for local papers: if I can get access to a range of papers at a click (see Google News), why would I buy any one in particular? A business that had relatively little competition because of the costs of local markets now has almost endless competition, driving the price for this freely distributed good (as economists would predict) to zero.

Both dynamics – together they are the consequence of what we might call the "free content movement" – have had a predictable effect. First on the chopping block is investigative journalism, with its risky return, and even when successful, a return not measured in cash. Less than 10 percent of large daily newspapers in America have four investigative journalists or more. More than 40 percent have no investigative journalists at all. One need not hate the Internet to be deeply worried about the repercussions of this development for democracy.

Or think about recorded music. Until the late 1990s, the record industry had a happy fate. Every couple of years a new format would best an earlier leader – eight-track beating the LP; cassettes beating the eight-track; CDs beating cassettes. Consumers would then eagerly migrate to the new thing. With that migration, new content would have to be bought. Old content had to be replicated. Music was like old library books that you would have to check out again and again and again – except that this lending was not for free.

Along comes digital technology, and this model of profit was significantly threatened. The nature of digital is perfect copies, freely made. The nature of certain popular technologies – Napster, and then peer-to-peer (p2p) more generally – was to encourage literally millions of people to make literally billions of perfect copies and then share them for free. Such behavior could not help but dampen the demand for some recorded music (even if it spurred the demand for other recorded music – namely, music that wouldn't have been discovered if the price of admission had been a $20 CD). And it couldn't help but inspire a richly different "free culture movement". An industry that had become addicted to the blockbuster album was obviously allergic to a technology that threatened this promise of reliable profits.

Both of these developments have inspired Luddite-like responses. There is a regular call to close free access to news on the Web. There are principled objections to Craigslist, even if they are faint and confused. And there are politically well-supported objections to peer-to-peer file-sharing, seeking both laws and technology to kill the p2p "market". In all these cases, the response to the problem is to attack the source of the problem: the freedom secured by the network. In all these cases, the response presumes that we can return to a world where the network did not disable control.

But the network is not going away. We are not going to kill the "darknet" (as Microsoft called it in a fantastic paper about the inevitable survival of peer-to-peer technologies). We are not going to regulate access to news, or ads for free futons. We are not going back to the twentieth century. In a decade, a majority of Americans will not even remember what that century was like.

But then what? If we can't go back, how do we go forward? For each of these problems, there have been solutions proposed that do not depend foolishly upon breaking the network. These solutions may not produce a world as good as the world was before (at least for some). They may not benefit everyone in the same way. But they are solutions that remove an important part of the problem in each case, and restore at least part of the good that is recognized in the past.

With p2p file-sharing, scholars such as William Fisher and Neil Netanel have proposed models of compensation that would achieve the objectives of copyright without trying to control the distribution of content. Filesharing would be legal, at least in some contexts. But then artists would be compensated for the harm caused by this file-sharing through systems that track the popularity of downloads. Britney Spears would get more money than Lyle Lovett (the mysteries of taste!), with revenue coming either from a tax or from fees paid by key nodes in the network. The Electronic Frontier Foundation has a related proposal for a "voluntary collective license": pay a certain flat amount, and you secure an immunity from prosecution for non-commercial file-sharing. The Green Party in Germany has taken this idea one step further, and proposed a "cultural flat rate" that would apply to culture on the network generally, securing compensation for the artists and immunity from prosecution for the kids. All these changes would render legal the behavior your kids are engaging in right now (trust me), and assure some sort of livelihood for artists.

With journalism, the answers are less clear. There is growing legislative support for allowing newspapers to become (intentional) nonprofits, thus enabling tax-deductible donations to support their mission, and allowing the mission to be more securely set, free of the demands of stockholders or commercial return. Likewise, there has been growing support for nonprofits such as ProPublica, which fund investigative journalism that is then released freely to partner newspapers. As with music, the aim in both cases is to find a different way to fund the creation of what economists call "public goods." And as economists will tell you, no way is perfect. Each has its benefits and its flaws. But both alternatives have the singular virtue of accepting the architecture of the Internet as it is, and working out how best to provide the goods we need given this architecture.

So is there an analogous solution to the problems created by transparency? Is there an answer that accepts that transparency is here to stay – indeed, that it will become ever more lasting and ever more clear – but that avoids the harms that transparency creates?

In the context of public health, where doctors are forced to reveal any connection with industry, I cannot begin to imagine what that solution would look like. The citizenry is not remotely willing to fund publicly the research necessary to support drug development today. Close to 70 percent of the money for clinical drug trials in the United States comes from private industry. Private funding here seems inevitable – and with it, the potential for perceived conflicts. That potential will inevitably require more and more transparency about who got what from whom.

In the context of public officials, however, the solutions are obvious, and old, and eminently tractable. If the problem with transparency is what might be called its structural insinuations – its constant suggestions of a sin that is present sometimes but not always – then the obvious solution is to eliminate those insinuations and those suggestions. A system of publicly funded elections would make it impossible to suggest that the reason some member of Congress voted the way he voted was because of money. Perhaps it was because he was stupid. Perhaps it was because he was liberal, or conservative. Perhaps it was because he failed to pay attention to the issues at stake. Whatever the reason, each of these reasons is democracy-enhancing. They give the democrat a reason to get involved, if only to throw the bum out. And by removing what is understood to be an irrelevant factor – money – the desire to get involved is not stanched by the cynicism that stifles so much in the current system.

The current version of this very old idea – Theodore Roosevelt gave us its first prominent play in 1907 – is called the Fair Elections Now Act. Sponsored in the Senate by Dick Durbin and Arlen Specter, and in the House by John Larson and Walter Jones, the bill would grant to qualifying candidates a certain grubstake to fund their campaigns. In addition to that initial stake, candidates could raise as much money as they want, with contributions capped at $100 per citizen per cycle. Thus Roosevelt meets Obama, with a proposal that marries the ideal of neutralizing any appearance of improper influence with the energy that small contributions add to any campaign.

The only significant flaw in this bill, at least in my view, is its title. Waving the "fairness flag" in front of the Supreme Court is the proverbial red flag in front of the bull. What possible reason is there, the Court will ask, for allowing Congress to regulate "fairness" – at least where "fairness" seems so clearly to benefit one side in most political debates? And the concern is a good one. There is too much incumbency protection built into our politics already. It would be much worse if the state were putting a thumb on one side of a political scale.

But the objective of these proposals is not, or should not be, fairness. The objective should be trustworthiness. The problem that these bills address is that we have a Congress that nobody trusts – a Congress that, in the opinion of the vast majority of the American people, sells its results to the highest bidder. The aim of these proposals should be to change that perception by establishing a system in which no one could believe that money was buying results. In this way we can eliminate the possibility of influence that nourishes the cynicism that is anyway inevitable when technology makes it so simple to imply an endless list of influence.

As with ProPublica or nonprofit newspapers, or a "cultural flat-rate", or a compulsory license to compensate for file-sharing, proposals for public funding can thus be understood as a response to an unavoidable pathology of the technology – its pathological transparency – that increasingly rules our lives and our institutions. Without this response – with the ideal of naked transparency alone – our democracy, like the music industry and print journalism generally, is doomed. The Web will show us every possible influence. The most cynical will be the most salient. Limited attention span will assure that the most salient is the most stable. Unwarranted conclusions will be drawn, careers will be destroyed, alienation will grow. No doubt we will rally to the periodic romantic promising change (such as Barack Obama), but nothing will change. D.C. will become as D.C. is becoming: a place filled with souls animated by – as Robert Kaiser put it recently in his fine book *So Damn Much Money – a "familiar American yearning: to get rich."*

But if the transparency movement could be tied to this movement for reform – if every step for more transparency were attended by a reform that would disabuse us of the illusion that this technology is just a big simple blessing, and set out to make transparency both good and harmless – then its consequence could be salutary and constructive. When transparency and democracy are considered in this way, we may even permit ourselves to imagine a way out of this cycle of cynicism.

Reformers rarely feel responsible for the bad that their fantastic new reform effects. Their focus is always on the good. The bad is someone else's problem. It may well be asking too much to imagine more than this. But as we see the consequences of changes that many of us view as good, we might wonder whether more good might have been done had more responsibility been in the mix. The music industry was never going to like the Internet, but its war against the technology might well have been less hysterical and self-defeating if better and more balanced alternatives had been pressed from the beginning. No one can dislike Craigslist (or Craig), but we all would have benefited from a clearer recognition of what was about to be lost. Internet triumphalism is not a public good.

Likewise with transparency. There is no questioning the good that transparency creates in a wide range of contexts, government especially. But we should also recognize that the collateral consequence of that good need not itself be good. And if that collateral bad is busy certifying to the American public what it thinks it already knows, we should think carefully about how to avoid it. Sunlight may well be a great disinfectant. But as anyone who has ever waded through a swamp knows, it has other effects as well.

Lawrence Lessig (@lessig) is professor of law and director of the Edmond J. Safra Center for Ethics at Harvard Law School, and the author most recently of Remix: Making Art and Commerce Thrive in the Hybrid Economy *(Penguin). He is on the advisory board of the Sunlight Foundation and on the board of Maplight.org.*

---

[1] This article originally appeared in *The New Republic*, October 21, 2009. Used with permission.

#16

OBJECTIVITY, TRANSPARENCY, AND THE ENGAGEMENT WITH DEMOCRACY[1]

David Weinberger

Fellow, Harvard Berkman Center for Internet & Society

When you pick up a respectable newspaper, the news articles make an implicit claim: What you are reading is true, and it is untainted by the political leanings of the reporter. Indeed, that implicit claim of objectivity is a big part of what makes a newspaper respectable. But, outside of the realm of science, objectivity is discredited these days as anything but an aspiration, and even that aspiration is looking pretty sketchy. Transparency is becoming the new objectivity, and not just for journalism. The effect on government is quite direct.

The problem with objectivity is that it tries to show what the world looks like from no particular point of view. But, we are perspectival creatures. We always see from a point of view. Sometimes we recognize our biases, but some prejudices are buried too deep within language and culture. So, the notion of pure objectivity has been pretty well debunked over the past couple of generations, especially when it comes to story-telling activities such as journalism. Nevertheless, objectivity — even as an unattainable goal — has served an important role in how we come to trust ideas and information.

It was also a major component of the value newspapers offered us. You can see this in newspapers' early push-back against blogging. We were told that bloggers have agendas, whereas journalists give us objective information. Of course, if you don't think objectivity is possible, then you think that the claim of objectivity is actually hiding the biases that inevitably are there. That's why when, during a bloggers press conference at the 2004 Democratic National Convention, I asked Pulitzer-prize winning journalist Walter Mears whom he was supporting for president, he replied (paraphrasing!), "If I tell you, how can you trust what I write?" Of course, if he doesn't tell us, how can we trust what he blogs? The idea of a political blogger hiding her political standpoints is as odd as a traditional political reporter telling us his.

So, that's one sense in which transparency is the new objectivity.

What we used to believe because we thought the author was objective we now believe because we can see through the author's writings to the sources and values that brought her to that position. Transparency gives the reader information by which she can undo some of the unintended effects of the author's ever-present biases. Transparency brings us to reliability the way objectivity used to. Perhaps transparency doesn't bring us to as high a degree of certainty, but it's arguable that objectivity never really brought us all to as much reliability as we liked to believe. When it comes to understanding our world, we are likely to achieve more certainty through a transparency that acknowledges uncertainty than through an objectivity that promises certainty.

The change goes beyond how we read newspapers. That is simply where we are seeing most vividly an overall change in the role of authority in belief.

Objectivity is part of a broader system of knowledge that was aimed at solving the fundamental problem that there's too much for any one person to know. So, we developed techniques that enabled our inquiries to stop. What's the order of the planets? Ask an astronomer. And once the astronomer has told you, you can stop researching the question. It's been answered. Better, rather than annoying your local astronomer, look it up in a book. The book was written by an authorized astronomer, and it wouldn't have gotten published if the editors hadn't had good reason to believe what the book says. This system of credentials is designed to give us reasonable stopping points for inquiry so that we can get on with our studies and with our lives.

That system obviously works. We've gotten quite far as a civilization with it. But, we thought that that was how knowledge works. It turns out that it's really just how paper works. Paper is literally an opaque medium. You can't see through text printed on it to the sources of its ideas. Yes, you can look up the footnote, but that's an expensive, time-consuming activity more likely to result in failure than success. Most often we use citations in footnotes simply as reassurance that the point is supported and requires no further inquiry. So, during the Age of Paper, we got used to the idea that authority comes in the form of a stop sign: You've reached a source whose reliability requires no further inquiry.

But now we have links. In the Age of Links, we still use credentials and rely on authorities because those are indispensible ways of scaling knowledge - that is, the system of authority lets us know more than any one of us could authenticate on our own. But, increasingly, credentials and authority work best for vouchsafing commoditized knowledge, the stuff that's settled and not worth arguing about. At the edges of knowledge — in the analysis and contextualization that journalists nowadays tell us is their real value — we want, need, can have and expect transparency. Transparency puts within the report itself a way for us to see what assumptions and values may have shaped it, and lets us see the arguments that the report resolved one way and not another. Transparency — the embedded ability to see through the published draft — often gives us more reason to believe a report than the claim of objectivity did.

In fact, transparency subsumes objectivity. Anyone who claims objectivity should be willing to back that assertion up by letting us look at sources, disagreements, and the personal assumptions and values supposedly bracketed out of the report.

We are getting so used to transparency that objectivity without it increasingly will look like arrogance. Why should we trust what one person — with the best of intentions — insists is true when we instead could have a web of evidence, ideas and argument?

Objectivity is a trust mechanism you rely on when your medium can't do links. Now our medium can.

Governments are not immune to this change, for they have been authorities as well. We trust the census figures and the booklets in which we look up how much money we owe in taxes. But governments are highly charged politically, and are subject to tremendous forces of corruption. So, now that hyperlinks have made transparency so easy, a failure of the government to let us go behind its facts and figures looks like a guilty attempt to hide information. Transparency is becoming the norm, the default.

But the rise of transparency's most important effect on government is less direct. It undoes some pernicious anti-democratic assumptions that have snuck into our thinking and into our institutions.

The system of knowledge by authority is also an economy. It bestows value on those who serve as stops: The expert who answers our questions confidently and correctly makes a good living and is highly respected. Nothing wrong with that, except that it's in the interest of the experts to inflate their own value. We start to think that those people are a special caste, high priests, people who are essentially unlike us. Between us and them is (we think) an unsurpassable gap. They are the experts. We can't know what they know, and we can't retrace how they know what they know. We can only cross the chasm by believing them. That is their value: We can believe what they say and not only don't we have to look further, we lack the ability to check their work: How are you going to figure out the order of the planets independently? The opaqueness of authorities makes us passive.

A class system and citizen passivity is exactly what we don't want for our democracies. If we can trust authorities to know things - so much so that their words end our inquiry - then perhaps we can trust them to decide things as well. After all, decisions should be based on knowledge. If knowledge truly belongs to the elite, the few, the authorities, then perhaps decisions are best left in their hands as well. The system of authority tends to lead to a belief that deciding on government policies is a job for specialists.

On the other hand, a hyperlinked transparency puts before us invitations to continue. If and when we stop, it's not because we've reached the end but because our inquiry has to stop somewhere; we have other things to do - and perhaps other patches of the never-ending wilderness to explore. We are stopped not by the gap authority insists on for itself, but by the sense that now we know enough to make a decision, but always with the understanding that "knowing enough" is relative to the seriousness of the matter at hand, and that "knowing more" is always a possibility. In a hyperlinked, transparent ecology, we may choose to go no further for now, but the possibility of proceeding is always active, not passive.

Further, a hyperlinked transparency tells us that behind a claimed knowledge is not an unbridgeable gap, for the links that we see are bridges we can travel. Rather, behind a claim of knowledge are other people's ideas behind which are yet more ideas, without end. An expert knower is just another person in a web of ideas and information. Of course, an expert is in a richer web, makes more sense of that web, is intimately familiar with it, and is treated as a hub in ways that we, as non-experts, are not. But it is still one continuous fabric, now that we can see the weave and warp of it. Therefore, knowing and deciding are left up to us humans, some more expert than others, but none with an unbridgeable claim on truth and authority. Every claim of knowledge is subject to all of the errors definitive of our species. We have no one to do the knowing and deciding for us. We have to do it ourselves. That's why we have democracies.

A hyperlinked, transparent ecology thus reminds us of democracy's essential truth: We are each individuals with our own needs, perspectives and limitations. We only have ourselves. There is no hope except through engagement in our own process of governance, but with that engagement, there is every hope.

David Weinberger (@dweinberger) is a fellow at Harvard Berkman Center for Internet & Society. He is co-author of the international bestseller The Cluetrain Manifesto. *His latest book is* Everything is Miscellaneous.

---

[1] A version of this chapter appeared as a post on David Weinberger's blog on August 19, 2009. http://j.mp/MuwE3

Section III

Democratizing Government

#17

DEMOCRACY 2.0

Michael Friis
Founder, Folkets Ting

Democracy in ancient Greece was of the direct variety: Citizens of the polis would meet up every once in a while, draw lots on who should be officials and debate and vote on decrees. The modern western democracies are of the representative type: Every couple of years citizens elect representatives to a parliament where laws are debated and passed. A government is chosen, either directly by the electorate or amongst members of parliament. The government hires officials and bureaucrats to help it exercise and uphold the laws. Citizens usually have no direct say in legislation, although they can form lobbying organizations and try to indirectly influence government and parliament members. This indirect form of democracy is tolerated because political entities have grown in size from city-states to countries and even unions, and because political franchise has been expanded to include most of the population. This makes regularly gathering all citizens for debates a rather impractical proposition. Further, running modern societies apparently requires legislation of a scale and complexity that makes keeping up a full time job. The pragmatic solution is for the citizenry to elect full time representatives by some form of popular vote. The elected representatives then meet in a legislative assembly where they debate and pass legislation. The Free Press monitors representatives' actions to make sure they are aligned with the wishes of the electorate.

The premise of Democracy 2.0 is that citizens can use the Internet and Web 2.0 techniques to reenter the political fray and participate in ways reminiscent of ancient Greece. Democracy 2.0 has two overarching objectives: First, foster direct citizen oversight of politicians independently of the Press; Second, involve citizens directly in the legislative process. This chapter will outline why the author believes these to be attractive objectives and why he believes Web 2.0 technology has placed them within reach. The chapter will then describe how Democracy 2.0 websites can achieve these objectives and discuss successful real-world examples. The chapter is based on the author's experience building "Folkets Ting" (Peoples Parliament), a website[1] covering the Danish national parliament (in Danish: "Folketinget") and his analysis of other, related sites.

Do we necessarily want to drag our political processes onto the Internet and subject them to meddling from nosy citizens? This chapter argues "Yes" for the following reasons. First, traditional political journalism is in decline. Newspapers are cutting staff or closing and focus is shifting towards consumer and entertainment stories that are easy to monetize with ads. Remaining political coverage is increasingly lighthearted and focused on perceived personal conflicts between politicians. For these reasons, it is important that citizens have information and tools that let them directly monitor the legislative process and hold their elected representatives accountable for their actions. Second, democratic participation, as measured by party membership and voter turnout, is waning in many parts of the world, often most markedly amongst the young. The legitimacy of a political system rests on citizens' active sanction and support. Making democracy an accessible and online proposition will make more people participate in a greater variety of ways. Active participation by citizens itself, is likely to increase interest in politics and boost support for democratic institutions. Third, modern lawmaking involves politicians, bureaucrats and organizations with vested interests interacting in ways that are not always entirely transparent. This process should be moved onto the Internet and opened up to input from more participants such as NGOs and private citizens with specialist knowledge. Such a move would produce better laws that incorporate and address concerns from a greater part of society.

What are the innovations that make Democracy 2.0 feasible? To start with, the Internet has made publishing any amount of information a trivial task. Publishing parliamentary meeting minutes, revisions of laws, video of debates and all the other media accumulated by a parliamentary bureaucracy is entirely feasible. To make sense of the flood of information generated by cheap online publishing, several techniques have evolved. The traditional one is powerful textual search, as exemplified by Google indexing the entire Internet. In recent years, websites have employed a plethora of more user-powered "Web 2.0" techniques that are, in some ways, even better at finding information relevant to users. Examples are Amazons "Customers who bought this item also bought...," phototagging on Flickr, collaborative filtering of news-articles on Digg and Reddit, and people sharing relevant content with friends and family on social networks such as Facebook and Twitter. All these are examples of users deliberately or incidentally digging out, filtering and presenting relevant information from the vast content-sea of the Internet. If Web 2.0 can help make sense of what goes on out there on the Internet at large, surely it can profitably be applied to information generated by the political process too.

An interesting detail is what the Internet does to the so-called "Long Tail," i.e. marginal content with a very narrow audience. Since publishing costs are negligible and because the total audience is very large, it makes perfect sense to publish Long Tail content online, and the search and filtering tools mentioned above makes it possible for interested users to find it. Democracies too, have a Long Tail of legislation that is not publicly debated in any detail, typically because it affects few people. Democracy 2.0 can make these laws discoverable and open them up to debate amongst the narrow groups of citizens and organizations they affect.

Besides filtering, categorizing and finding information, Web 2.0 also lets users collaborate and interact: Amazon lets people rate and review products, news-articles on Digg and Reddit and photos on Flickr can be commented on and discussed and so can content posted to Facebook and Twitter. Whatever you may think of the intellectual prowess of the average Internet denizen, a well-curated and moderated online discussion will, more often than not, yield interesting insights and links to relevant content. Discussion amongst friends on Facebook and Twitter satisfies a basic social need to voice and share opinions and be reinforced or challenged in ones beliefs. There is no reason similar rating, reviewing and commenting cannot be applied to parliament debate minutes, laws or live video-feeds from parliament debates. Won't any online discussion of something as contentious as politics invariably drown in nonsense and invectives? Not necessarily: Amazon manages to reliably show the most relevant product reviews first by asking users to rate the reviews themselves, and Digg and Reddit does something similar for comments. Collaborative self-moderation by users can keep discussions relevant and enforce a tolerable tone of debate.

Wikipedia, the user written and edited encyclopedia, is an even more compelling example of the potential of online Web 2.0 style collaboration. Instead of just augmenting existing content with comments, reviews and tags, thousands of wikipedians have collaborated to write millions of encyclopedic articles from scratch. Many articles are about very divisive topics, yet Wikipedia is proof that – with good tools and policies – people can work together online. While it may be some years into the future, one can envision a process whereby groups of citizens draft and revise laws which are then adopted into the traditional legislative process for further refinement. In the end, political discussions are part of the DNA of any democracy and online debate of parliamentary minutes and laws will extend and inform these discussions.

Technologies and techniques like cheap publishing, powerful search, filtering, sharing, commenting and online collaboration complement each other and have the potential to revolutionize political processes and upgrade our democracies to version 2.0. The recent Obama presidential campaign heavily leveraged social networks and other Web 2.0 technology and demonstrated how this can reinvigorate politics and dramatically increase participation. The following paragraphs will take a more detailed look at features of Democracy 2.0 sites that are already up and running. Individual features will not be discussed in great technical depth, the focus will be on their potential to engage and empower citizens.

What content belongs on Democracy 2.0 websites? Basically anything that help achieve the first objective of facilitating citizen oversight of the political system. Fundamental content is stuff like texts of laws in their various revisions, parliamentary debate minutes and parliamentary voting records. Many parliamentary systems let opposition members pose questions to government ministers. These questions tend to put a finger on relevant issues, and should be included too. Sites like Folkets Ting, TheyWorkForYou.com[2] and OpenCongress[3] publish laws, debates and questions to the extent that they are available from bureaucracies. Parliaments routinely record video or audio of all meetings. TheyWorkForYou lets users match up video clips with the relevant debate minutes, so other users can watch video for speeches while reading the transcripts, another relevant feature. Political campaign donations are a canary-in-the-coalmine for citizens wary of undue influence of politicians and, if possible, should be available too. Claimed personal expenses by politicians, while tangential to actual politics, are great because they can be used to gauge the profligacy of individual parliament members. The Guardian, a newspaper, has created a superb site[4] ("Investigate your MP's expenses") where parsing and registration of receipts is crowd-sourced to the British taxpayers. Earmarks (provisions in laws mandating money be spent on particular projects, often in geographic locations where politicians are elected) are another good way of monitoring spending. "Earmark Watch,"[5] by the

Sunlight Foundation, lets Americans track US congressional earmarks.

Much of the information listed above is already published online in many countries by parliaments, election commissions and similar organizations. To access the data, most existing Democracy 2.0 organizations "screen-scrape" and "parse" the relevant government websites. Screen-scraping is a process somewhat similar to what Google does when it crawls and downloads pages on the Internet to figure out what words are used where. Parsing involves picking out relevant data from the downloaded pages, for example to figure out how particular politicians voted for a law. Screen-scrapers and parsers are typically automated robots running nightly, although they may require human help as in the case of the UK parliamentary expense claims.

An important point is that the various types of content need not be aggregated onto monolithic omnibus sites, but can be useful – and often more accessible – when presented in isolation. On the other hand, some of this information becomes a lot more interesting when aggregated. Combining campaign donations and earmarks may, for example, reveal donors buying government orders through politicians. The author can say from personal experience that one of the most memorable milestones in the development of Folkets Ting was when aggregated news-feeds for politicians were made to work. On the Danish parliament website, politicians votes, speeches and questions are shown out of context on different parts on the site. The aggregated feed on Folkets Ting presents a clear chronological overview of all the politicians' actions, dramatically increasing the utility of the information that goes into making it. OpenCongress and TheyWorkForYou similarly provide aggregated profiles for politicians.

Politicians' actions and opinions matter a lot to voters, and their profiles should have as much information as can be gathered. "Congress Speaks," another site[6] by the Sunlight Foundation, has word-clouds for each politician with commonly used words in bigger font than less frequently used ones. This is a great tool for giving users a rough idea of what topics a particular politician is most concerned with. Voters are also interested in knowing the general activity level of their elected representatives, so profiles should have graphs showing, month-for-month, the number of votes cast, words spoken, questions asked and so forth.

A particular problem is identifying, from the many votes cast by a politician, how the politician stands on a particular topic of policy (e.g. the War on Terror). Figuring this out is interesting because voters will want to make sure that politicians actual votes match up with the public stances they take on various issues. The Public Whip (another British Democracy 2.0 site[7]) has come up with an innovative solution to this problem: Users can define "policies" (e.g. "Ban fox hunting") and then assign particular parliamentary votes to that policy, designating whether a yes-vote would be "for" or "against" the policy. This makes it easy to determine where a politician stands on particular issues because the relevant votes can be aggregated into a simple score for that politician.

Another matter of great interest to voters is whether elected politicians are keeping promises made on the campaign trail. The Obameter[8], run by the St. Petersburg Times, tracks the more than 500 promises made by Barack Obama during his election campaign and rates them based on whether they have been fulfilled or broken. While not a true Democracy 2.0 site (the promises are judged by the papers reporters, not by users), it takes a good stab at an area where more oversight and account-keeping is sorely needed.

As Democracy 2.0 sites usually take their point of departure in parliament records and documents, they tend to reflect how these institutions work, even while attempting to mix and mash data in new ways. Parliamentary processes and traditions have evolved over centuries and are often highly idiosyncratic (filibusters were known to the ancient Romans and are still with us). An important mission for Democracy 2.0 is to de-contextualize politics from these strange old ways and present what is going on in parliament in easily accessible formats that are useful to citizens who are not policy wonks. Aggregating many votes into a few relevant policies or showing clouds of words commonly used by a politician are good examples of this.

To aid citizens in keeping up with parliament, Democracy 2.0 sites should offer RSS feeds and email alerts wherever possible, including for new laws, passed laws, new questions, answered questions, individual politician activity and so forth. Laws in the Danish Parliament are not categorized in any useful way, so Folkets Ting lets users tag laws (tags could be "health-care" or "transport"), making it easier for other users to navigate and follow laws by interest. As a further aid to navigation, sites can show lists of "hot" content, i.e. laws with many new comments or politician profiles with lots of recent visits.

What features should Democracy 2.0 websites have to let citizens make themselves heard? First off, users should be able to vote on laws under review. This will let politicians know how citizens feel about a particular law on its way through parliament. Second, if written questions are part of the parliamentary process, a self-respecting Democracy 2.0 site should let user pose their own questions, including provisions for opposition's politicians adopting these questions and forwarding them to government ministers. Third, users should have the opportunity to comment on all law-texts and debate minutes. OpenCongress has pioneered a technique (since copied by Folkets Ting) where comments appear under individual paragraphs in texts instead of at the end of an entire law. Comments can also be threaded so users can comment on other users' comments. This system permits very detailed discussion about particular points in laws and debates. To moderate the discussion, users are able to rate other users comments as good or bad, in the same way that reviews are rated on Amazon. Comments whose score falls under a certain threshold can be hidden by default and only shown if requested. Users also have the option of reporting offensive comments to be handled by site moderators.

Users will often be very interested to know whether politicians read and respond to their comments and questions. For this reason, politicians' profiles should include lists of most debated content, letting them quickly determine how people feel about what they are up to and optionally respond. Or, as is done by WriteToThem.com, the site can send faxes or emails with citizen messages to politicians.

How can active user participation be encouraged? Besides political discourse being an almost universal human activity in itself, there are several things a site can do to promote interaction. One way is to give users points or "karma" for comments and questions upvoted by other users. Another is to give users a page on the site where their recent comment and voting activity is displayed. These are extremely simple measures, yet they have proved massively effective on question/answer sites like Stackoverflow.com. Even though they have no bearing on real life, users consider the points a sign of prestige and use the personal activity feeds as vehicle to demonstrate their cleverness. Another way to promote participation is to integrate closely with social networking sites. Folkets Ting lets users post comments on the site directly to their Facebook feeds. Seeing friends commenting on laws and speeches is likely to draw more users into the discussion.

So far, almost all Democracy 2.0 sites have been built by citizens or NGOs (a notable exception is the New York State Senate web site[9]). It may seem logical to demand that the parliament bureaucracies gathering data should also make it available on their websites in the ways described above. There are several reasons why this is may not be a good approach however. Parliament web sites are usually run by librarian-types concerned with archiving stuff for posterity. Their goal is to create tools that make political processes function as smoothly. Having citizens clog up records with spurious comments looks more like a liability than like a benefit. Politicians, who usually closely oversee running of parliament, cannot be counted on to reliably support Democracy 2.0 efforts either. Politicians may feel intimidated by increased oversight and scrutiny of their activities (or lack thereof), or feel that Democracy 2.0 may compromise their ability to work effectively with lobbyists. Active moderation (deleting offensive comments, for example) could potentially become a very prickly subject if carried out by state-employed site moderators seen to be curbing the freedom of speech. Much better that Democracy 2.0 sites are built and run by engaged citizens who understand Web 2.0 and are concerned solely with increasing transparency and participation. Parliaments and politicians do have an important role to play however, in making sure that the necessary data is available, either through proper APIs or through web sites that are reasonably easy to scrape automatically.

This essay has outlined why we should build Democracy 2.0 websites and how we can go about building them. The core ideas of Democracy 2.0 is to grab political data, analyze it, aggregate it and mash it up so citizens can use it to monitor politicians and let them know how they feel about the way they are being represented. By empowering citizens with Web 2.0 tools, we can level the playing field and re-enter the political arena in force.

Michael Friis is a prolific hacker and writer living in Denmark. Michaels projects include LINQtoCRM, a popular LINQ query provider for Dynamics CRM and "Popcorn", a Facebook application for cinema ticket discovery and reservation. He has hijacked several million EU public procurement contracts from "Tenders Electronic Daily" and created a Google Maps mashup at tedbot.itu.dk. Michaels latest project is "Folkets Ting" (Peoples Parliament), a better website for the Danish parliament. On Folkets Ting, citizens can track politicians, ask questions and debate laws and speeches.

---

[1] http://folketsting.dk/
[2] http://www.theyworkforyou.com/
[3] http://www.opencongress.org/
[4] http://mps-expenses.guardian.co.uk/
[5] http://earmarkwatch.org/
[6] http://www.congressspeaks.com/
[7] http://www.publicwhip.org.uk/
[8] http://www.politifact.com/truth-o-meter/promises/
[9] http://www.nysenate.gov/

#18

FOCUSING ON CITIZENS[1]

Joanne Caddy
Counsellor, OECD

The current financial, economic and - increasingly - social crisis has added a new sense of urgency to the search for governance arrangements fit for the 21st century. Governments alone cannot deal with complex global and domestic challenges, such as climate change or soaring obesity levels. They face hard trade-offs, such as responding to rising demands for better quality public services despite ever-tighter budgets. They need to work with citizens and other stakeholders to find innovative solutions. The race is on and time is of essence.

The good news is that governments are not alone. They can call on a wider pool of talent, expertise and experience to develop new solutions for both intractable and emerging policy problems. To do so will require them to unlock the doors of their policy making processes and adopt new roles in facilitating autonomous action by others acting in the public interest.

The bad news is that many governments are saddled with a serious deficit in public trust. Better educated, well-informed and less deferential citizens are judging their governments on their "democratic performance", i.e., the degree to which government decision-making processes live up to democratic principles, and their "policy performance", i.e., their ability to deliver tangible positive outcomes for society.[2] On either measure, citizens in many countries have found their governments to fall short of their expectations.

Investing in more open and inclusive policy making offers part of the answer to both challenges. More often promoted as a means of improving democratic performance (which it is), open and inclusive policy making can do much more. It offers a way for governments to improve their policy performance by working with citizens, civil society organisations (CSOs), businesses and other stakeholders to deliver concrete improvements in policy outcomes and the quality of public services, e.g. through co-design and co-delivery.

Open and inclusive policy making is transparent, accessible and responsive to as wide a range of citizens as possible. Openness means providing citizens with information and making the policy process accessible and responsive. Inclusion means including as wide a variety of citizens' voices in the policy making process as possible. To be successful, these elements must be applied at all stages of the design and delivery of public policies and services.

OECD member countries' experience indicates that open and inclusive policy making can improve policy performance by helping governments to:

- Better understand people's evolving needs, respond to greater diversity in society and address inequalities of voice and access to both policy making processes and public services.
- Leverage the information, ideas and resources held by businesses, CSOs and citizens as drivers for innovation.

- Lower costs and improve policy outcomes by galvanizing people to take action in policy areas where success crucially depends upon changes in individuals' behavior (e.g. public health, climate change).
- Reduce administrative burdens, compliance costs and the risk of conflict or delays during policy implementation and service delivery.

Openness, while necessary, is not sufficient to ensure inclusive public participation. Inclusion is important for reasons of efficacy and equity. Efficacy, because the true value of opening up policy making lies in obtaining a wider range of views (beyond the "usual suspects") as input for evidence-based decision-making. Equity, because defining the "public interest" in a democracy requires governments to make extra efforts to reach out to those who are least equipped for public participation (e.g. new citizens, youth).

Granted, there are many good reasons for people not to participate in policy making and public service design and delivery. Two broad groups may be identified: People who are "willing but unable" to participate for a variety of reasons such as cultural or language barriers, geographical distance, disability or socio-economic status; and people who are "able but unwilling" to participate because they are not very interested in politics, do not have the time, or do not trust government to make good use of their input.

To engage the "willing but unable", governments must invest in lowering barriers (e.g. by providing multilingual information). For the "able but unwilling", governments must make participation more attractive (e.g. by picking relevant issues, providing multiple channels for participation, including face-to-face, online and mobile options). Above all, governments must expect to "go where people are" when seeking to engage with them, rather than expecting people to come to government.

One of the places people are is online and the emergence of the participative web has profoundly changed what people do there. No longer just passive viewers, people of all ages and walks of life are rapidly becoming active producers, rankers, raters and linkers of content.

Some governments have been swift to grasp the transformative potential offered by this enhanced interactivity. A number have begun to explore this new frontier (e.g. the UK Prime Minister's Office on Twitter @DowningStreet) and begun to develop guidance for their civil servants (e.g. New Zealand's 2007 Guide to Online Participation[3]). Governments have even gone so far as to enshrine their ambitions in joint policy declarations, such the 2008 Seoul Declaration for the Future of the Internet Economy. Issued by Ministers from both OECD and non-OECD member countries, the Seoul Declaration underlines the potential of the Internet, and related information and communication technologies (ICT), to improve citizens' quality of life by "Enabling new forms of civic engagement and participation that promote diversity of opinions and enhance transparency, accountability, privacy and trust."[4]

The tools and practices of the participative web can help make both online and face-to-face public participation more open and inclusive. The participative web is transforming three factors, which have always underpinned successful policy making and service delivery namely:

- Knowledge, which flows freely in a digital world with the move from an "economy of scarcity" to an "economy of surplus".
- Connections, which are no longer binary, private and hierarchical but multiple, public and networked.
- Actors, who are not just isolated "atoms" but are embedded in a dense network of loose links with many others.

There are at least three main benefits of participative web approaches for public policy making and service delivery:

- Efficiency: Turning the many separate strands of bilateral 'traffic' between individual citizens and government into a public information resource can help reduce administrative burdens for both the administration and the citizen (e.g. FixMyStreet.com, a UK website which allows citizens to pinpoint problems on a virtual map and then automatically sends it to local councils). For example, by publishing online the results of a specific request filed under access to information legislation, others can avoid having to file a new request and governments can avoid the burden of having to respond to identical requests in the future (e.g. ePeople.go.kr, Korea's one-stop online petition service). An approach that could offer significant benefits for all non-personal data transactions.

- Accountability: The symbolic power of government seeking to enhance transparency or develop policy on an online 'public space' is itself an important asset in establishing public trust (e.g. Recovery.gov, US Recovery Board website which tracks billions of dollars in federal government spending). So is the level of accountability exacted by online 'reputation managers' where all participants are rated on, and held accountable for, their comments and submissions (e.g. GovLoop, a US-based social network for government 2.0 issues, see Steve Ressler's chapter). Actors outside government are also beginning to develop online tools for linking publicly available information in innovative ways and with geospatial information (e.g. MapLight.org linking campaign contributions and legislators' votes in the US).

- Participation: Online collaborative tools, such as wikis and data-sharing sites, allow asynchronous collaboration with actors inside and outside government (e.g. New Zealand's ParticipatioNZ wiki[5]). They can be used to pool knowledge and ideas but can also harness the power of tagging, ranking, data visualization and state-of-the-art search engines to

> sort through information, analyze data, establish priorities and develop recommendations (e.g. the US Open Government Initiative[6]).

The participative web is now producing new tools and functionalities at a bewildering pace. Who would have thought just a year ago that there would be a need for government guidelines on the use of Twitter?[7] Navigating such rapids requires nerves of steel and a solid set of principles as a rudder.

Back in 2001, the OECD published a set of ten guiding principles for information, consultation and active participation in policy making, which have since been widely cited and used.[8] To follow up on these, we recently conducted a survey that asked government respondents how they had fared when implementing them. Based on responses from 23 countries, and feedback from civil society organisations in 14 countries, the principles have been updated and re-released (see end of this chapter).

Our survey showed that, over the past six years, for the majority (58%) the greatest progress had been made in establishing rights. Indeed, all 30 OECD countries except Luxembourg (where drafting is underway) now have legislation to ensure rights of access to information. The second most important area of progress was that of active citizenship, cited by over a third (38%) of respondents, followed by commitment, cited by a quarter (25%).

When asked which principles proved hardest to apply, almost half the respondents (45%) pointed to a lack of resources while over a third (36%) saw time factors as the most challenging. Almost a third (32%) felt that evaluation was the hardest. Overall, governments appear to be saying: "we have established rights, we have active citizens and a commitment to engage them in policy making but we face challenges of resources, time and a lack of evaluation."

The value of open and inclusive policy making is now widely accepted among OECD countries. Translating that commitment into practice remains a challenge. Governments now need to:

- Mainstream public engagement to improve policy performance. Real investments are needed to embed open and inclusive policy making as part of government's "core business", build skills among civil servants and establish a supportive political and administrative culture.
- Develop effective evaluation tools. Evaluating the quality of open and inclusive policy making processes and their impacts is a new frontier for most governments. Countries need to pool their efforts to develop appropriate evaluation frameworks, tools and training.
- Leverage technology and the participative web. Blogs, wikis and social media do not automatically deliver public engagement. The conceptual models underpinning the participative web (i.e. horizontal vs. vertical; iterative vs. sequential; open vs. proprietary; multiple vs. binary) may be more powerful, and of wider application, than the tools themselves.
- Adopt sound principles to support practice. "One size fits all" is not an option. To be effective, open and inclusive policy making must be appropriately designed and context-specific for a given country, level of government and policy field. Yet a robust set of principles can guide practitioners when designing, implementing and evaluating their initiatives.

Whatever their starting point, governments in all countries are at a crossroads. The creative collision of three broad agendas – public sector reform, technology and public engagement – is generating new ways for them to achieve tangible improvements in people's lives. Successful adoption will require a shift from "government-as-usual" to a broader governance perspective. One which builds on the twin pillars of openness and inclusion to deliver better policy outcomes and high quality public services not only for, but with, citizens.

GUIDING PRINCIPLES FOR OPEN AND INCLUSIVE POLICY MAKING[9]

These Guiding Principles are designed to help governments strengthen open and inclusive policy making as a means to improving their policy performance and service delivery.

1. Commitment: Leadership and strong commitment to open and inclusive policy making is needed at all levels – politicians, senior managers and public officials.
2. Rights: Citizens' rights to information, consultation and public participation in policy making and service delivery must be firmly grounded in law or policy. Government obligations to respond to citizens must be clearly stated. Independent oversight arrangements are essential to enforcing these rights.
3. Clarity: Objectives for, and limits to, information, consultation and public participation should be well defined from the outset. The roles and responsibilities of all parties must be clear. Government information should be complete, objective, reliable, relevant, easy to find and understand.
4. Time: Public engagement should be undertaken as early in the policy process as possible, to allow a greater range of solutions and to raise the chances of successful implementation. Adequate time must be available for consultation and participation to be effective.
5. Inclusion: All citizens should have equal opportunities and multiple channels to access information, be consulted and participate. Every reasonable effort should be made to engage with as wide a variety of people as possible.
6. Resources: Adequate financial, human and technical resources are needed for effective public information, consultation and participation. Government officials must have

access to appropriate skills, guidance and training as well as an organizational culture that supports both traditional and online tools.

7. Co-ordination: Initiatives to inform, consult and engage civil society should be coordinated within and across levels of government to ensure policy coherence, avoid duplication and reduce the risk of "consultation fatigue". Co-ordination efforts should not stifle initiative and innovation, but should leverage the power of knowledge networks and communities of practice within and beyond government.
8. Accountability: Governments have an obligation to inform participants how they use inputs received through public consultation and participation. Measures to ensure that the policy-making process is open, transparent and amenable to external scrutiny can help increase accountability of, and trust in, government.
9. Evaluation: Governments need to evaluate their own performance. To do so effectively will require efforts to build the demand, capacity, culture and tools for evaluating public participation.
10. Active citizenship: Societies benefit from dynamic civil society, and governments can facilitate access to information, encourage participation, raise awareness, strengthen citizens' civic education and skills, as well as to support capacity-building among civil society organizations. Governments need to explore new roles to effectively support autonomous problem-solving by citizens, CSOs and businesses.

Joanne Caddy (@joannecaddy) is currently Counsellor and Communications Manager at the OECD Directorate for Education. She led work on open government and public engagement at the OECD's Directorate for Public Governance and Territorial Development for close to a decade. In 2006, she was seconded to the New Zealand State Services Commission (SSC) for a year, where she served as Senior Advisor and helped draft the SSC "Guide to Online Participation" on a wiki, with inputs from a broad community of practice. Joanne is a Board member of E-Democracy.org and a member of IAP2.

She earned a BA in Natural Sciences at Cambridge University (UK), an MA in Political Science at The Johns Hopkins University and a doctorate in Political Science at the European University Institute in Italy.

---

[1] The opinions expressed in this chapter are the sole responsibility of the author and do not reflect those of the OECD or of the governments of its Member Countries. This chapter is based on *Focus on Citizens: Public Engagement for Better Policy and Services* ISBN 978-92-64-04886-7 © OECD 2009. The full report includes 14 in-depth country case studies to illustrate current practice while short opinion pieces from 18 government and civil society practitioners provide rich insights into current challenges. For more details, multilingual summaries and a video see: http://j.mp/13BNMv

[2] Klingemann D. and D. Fuchs (eds.) (1995), *Citizens and the State*, Oxford University Press.

[3] State Services Commission of New Zealand (2007), Guide to Online Participation, see http://j.mp/4nlIp

[4] For more information see: http://www.oecd.org/FutureInternet

[5] http://wiki.participation.e.govt.nz/wiki

[6] http://www.whitehouse.gov/Open/

[7] http://j.mp/3wpN14

[8] The ten guiding principles published in 2001 were: commitment, rights, clarity, time, objectivity, resources, co-ordination, accountability, evaluation and active citizenship, *Citizens As Partners: Information, Consultation And Public Participation in Policy-Making*, ISBN: 9789264195394, © OECD 2001, p. 15.

[9] The Guiding Principles were reviewed by the OECD Public Governance Committee prior to publication in the 2009 report Focus on Citizens: Public Engagement for Better Policy and Services ISBN 978-92-64-04886-7 © OECD 2009, p. 17. They have not been subject to OECD Council approval and, as such, do not constitute a legal instrument and are not binding on OECD Member countries.

#19

E-PARTICIPATORY PLANNING: NECESSITY AND ADVANTAGE

Rolf Lührs, Bengt Feil & Harald Rathmann
TuTech Innovation GmbH

The European Union is an area inhabited by approximately 500 million people, which translates as a density of 114 inhabitants per square kilometre[1], making it one of the most densely populated areas in the world. In such an environment, and especially in urban areas, the decision-making processes related to the use of land are beset with conflicts and competing interests. Spatial planning is therefore a core task of public administrations in Europe.

To address this difficult situation, the European Union and its member states have put in place highly formal procedures, which are aimed at resolving the conflicts and problems in the field of spatial planning. These procedures are codified in European, national and local law, and establish and clearly define the need for public involvement in spatial planning processes. From the 1970s on, the participatory aspects of planning "began gaining in importance as the recognition of differences in the identity and knowledge base of people became a central issue."[2] Consequently, public administrations at different organisational levels in Europe, and especially at the local level, are obliged by law to open up participatory channels in their spatial planning processes.

In this chapter we argue that electronic tools can provide many advantages over the traditional analogue way of organising formal participation in spatial planning by discussing the different expectations and needs of the stakeholders involved and describing the positive impact of electronic tools. Furthermore, the discussion will show how electronic tools in formal participation in spatial planning can bridge the gap between e-Participation and e-Government by simultaneously meeting the sometimes varying needs of all stakeholders. The different legal frameworks, which require that participation by the general public and public agencies is formally organized by law in the European Union, will be discussed.

The findings will be illustrated and validated using the trial project "Spatial Planning Online Pilot" (BOP)[3] in Hamburg/Germany as an example. This project employed an online participation platform to transfer the offline process of mandatory participation in spatial planning to the web.

The participatory elements in the spatial planning process try to fulfil a number of different aims in this conflict-laden field[4]. The three main aims are:

- Fulfilling the democratic need: Spatial planning has a direct influence on the public, businesses and the environment, for example. Since the results of planning have a direct impact on the public, there is a democratic need to open up participatory channels to prevent public planning proposals that are in conflict with the public interest.
- Producing better plans: By involving public agencies, the general public and other stakeholders, such as parts of the public administration not directly involved with spatial

planning, energy suppliers or environmental NGOs, the quality of the planning proposal is improved. For example, public agencies are able to provide additional information about the planning area or specific circumstances related to the plans under discussion.

- Improving the acceptance of planning decisions: By allowing the public to get involved early in the planning process, the level of acceptance for the final decision on how a certain area should be used is improved. Both public agencies and the public are able to feed in their comments and criticism in a formalised way.

The clear need for participation by both the general public and public agencies in spatial planning is represented in legal frameworks at the different organisational levels in *Europe*. The EC directive on the assessment of the effects of certain plans and programmes on the environment states that "it is necessary to provide that authorities with relevant environmental responsibilities and the public are to be consulted during the assessment of plans and programmes."[5] The 2003 directive for public participation in respect of the drawing up of certain plans and programmes relating to the environment supports this point[6]. Therefore public involvement is necessary in every case in which environmental impact could be possible.

The law concerning participation in spatial planning at national level has to be compliant with these EC directives and in many cases builds upon a long history of participatory elements. Germany and England will be used as examples for legal frameworks, which govern participation in spatial planning. In Sweden[7] and Denmark[8] similar procedures can be found.

In Germany, the Baugesetzbuch (Planning and Building Law) states in §3 that the public should be informed early in the planning process and should have the possibility to comment on the planning proposals[9]. In §4 the same is stated for public agencies[10]. In 2004 the above mentioned EC directives were incorporated into the German legal framework. In summary, the participatory methods instituted by German law are an effective process which has been improved by the legislator and secures a high level of participatory quality[11].

The basis for participation in spatial planning in England is the "Town and Country Planning Act 1990" (TCPA)[12]. The TCPA states that all natural persons should have the possibility of influencing the planning process at an early stage. The law orders the local planning administration to consult the "local people" and "other interested bodies" in the planning process. This situation will be further developed by the Planning Bill introduced by Secretary of State for Communities and Local Government Hazel Blears in 2007, which clearly indicates the duty to consult the local community[13].

The aforementioned legal frameworks in some cases already refer to the possibility of using electronic tools in the participatory process. The directive for public participation in respect of the drawing up of certain plans and programmes relating to the environment requires that "the public [be] informed, whether by public notices or other appropriate means such as electronic media."[14] Another example is the German Baugesetzbuch, which states that electronic information technology may be used, and that the public agencies involved and the general public may provide their feedback using electronic communication methods (§4, Abs. 4).

The discussion in the field of participation and spatial planning suggests, that "participation can be enhanced through the use of geographic information technologies (GIT)."[15] The example given later in this chapter will support the argument that geographical information systems (GIS) have a positive influence on the quality and efficiency of participation in spatial planning.

The European Union is working on harmonising the Geo Data Infrastructure (GDI) in Europe through the INSPIRE project[16]. The INSPIRE directive has to be ratified by 15 May 2009 by all member states[17]. The directive clearly defines the goal for a consolidated European GDI, including exchange standards between the different organisational levels. The ratification of the directive in all member states will therefore force local and national administrations to improve and modernise their GDIs to be INSPIRE compliant. These modernisation efforts will also have a positive influence on the development and implementation of electronic tools for participation in spatial planning.

Hybrid of e-Government and e-Participation

Three main parties are involved in official planning processes. These are the public administration responsible for managing planning, public agencies representing specific interests in the community and the members of the public affected by the planned project. These three groups have different and sometimes conflicting expectations and interests related to the spatial planning action; thus the participatory elements of this process should allow them to submit their comments and criticism. This chapter will discuss these different expectations and interests and argue that electronic tools can help all three involved parties to reach their own goals and produce a better overall result from the planning process. The information presented is mainly based on the results of the BOP project.

Public administrations organize the planning processes and the participatory elements according to laws and regulations. Besides fulfilling the legal obligation to involve the community in the planning process, the administration also gains a number of advantages through e-Participation. By consulting the public agencies, the administration collects useful information, for example about possible environmental or infrastructure issues which may have been overlooked in the planning process. Furthermore, the public administration is dependent on the acceptance of the final planning decision both by public agencies and by members of the public affected. The in-depth information and participatory channels help to secure this acceptance and identify issues of the proposed plan, which may be in conflict with the public interest[18].

The workload for the public administration is very high for every planning process. In the city of Hamburg, for example, the average length of a planning process is 2.3 years and more than 6000 sheets of paper are sent out to the involved parties if just one participatory action is required. Comments from public agencies and the public reach the administration in many different formats (letters, email, telephone calls, etc.) and the administration is forced to organise this fragmented flow of information. Electronic tools can drastically improve the efficiency of the planning process for the public administration by reducing paperwork and bringing consistency into the stream of information. The Hamburg case showed that, even though this was an early attempt and the involved parties had to get used to the system, the costs to the public administration were considerably reduced. In addition to the gains in efficiency, the quality of information provided by the participants can be higher using electronic tools. In particular, the possibility of incorporating Geo Information Technology into the tool, allowing the participants to add geographical data to their comments, is very useful in this respect.

For Public Agencies, the involvement in planning processes is important for reasons other than those applying to public administrations. As public agencies represent a specific profession or interest group, they are interested in making sure that their specific recommendations and views are taken into account by the public administration. In many cases the public agencies involved are units inside the public administration, as for example the environment agencies. However, external parties such as the local energy supplier or NGOs are also involved.

Often the involvement in planning processes is also mandatory for the public agencies, which results in a significant amount of resources having to be committed. Accordingly, it is in their interest to improve the efficiency of planning processes. By providing all necessary information on specific plans, feedback channels and information about the status of planning processes through electronic tools, the public agencies involved can improve their own workflows. A large majority of the involved parties in Hamburg agreed that the efficiency of planning processes would be greater if such tools were used. Public agencies are highly specialised organisations that in many cases make use of GIS tools themselves. For example, energy suppliers use GIS to manage their power line systems and environmental organisations to keep track of pollution. By using Geo Information Technology in the planning process, these systems can be linked directly into the process, helping to improve the quality of comments and remarks and therefore supporting the specific recommendations made by public agencies.

The third involved party is the *members of the public affected*. The input of this party is very important to ensure that planning actions do not violate the public interest and that local circumstances are taken into account. The two main advantages for the public are that they are informed in detail about the planning action and that, by participating in the planning process, they are able to intervene and influence the outcome of a plan which directly affects them in their everyday lives. They can also use the feedback system to bring their own individual interests to the public administration's attention. In addition to these advantages, the act of participating in important decisions at local level is an important element of participatory democracy[19].

The general public may be the group gaining the most improvements from the use of electronic tools to organise mandatory participation in urban planning. In many cases, as for example in Germany[20], there is no requirement for public administrations to inform the public about ongoing planning processes other than by a notice in the administrative building and an announcement in the official administration publication. The plan under discussion can then only be viewed and commented on by members of the public during office hours in the public administration's facilities. Consequently, the visibility and accessibility of the planning process and the related provisions for participation are dramatically improved by offering the information and feedback channels online. This allows members of the public to review and comment on plans on their own terms and opens up the participatory channels to those who would have not been able to use the analogue channels. The visualisation provided by GIT as part of an electronic tool can help members of the public understand the issues related to the plan better and also provide them with a more haptic way of interacting with the planning material. This assessment is strongly supported by the results of the Hamburg test.

The different expectations and needs of the involved parties range widely, from efficiency in administrative processes to better local democracy through community involvement. As electronic tools for participation in spatial planning do not seek to reform the participatory process itself, but to support it by opening up new and easy to use channels to all parties involved, they can be seen as a hybrid between e-Government and e-Participation. While electronic tools help to reduce the workload of public administrations related to mandatory participation, they also open up channels for members of the public to participate in local democracy.

Development and test in Germany

The city of Hamburg started the project "Spatial Planning Online – Pilot"[21] (BOP) in November 2007. The aim of the project was to develop an e-Participation solution for the spatial planning process in the Hamburg metropolitan area.

The city's goals were to improve the information available to members of the public and public agencies, and include them in administrative decisions. Hamburg decided that electronic tools (e.g. Internet-based ones) were the best way to achieve these goals. This strategy was in line with city policy, as including the public in the spatial planning process via e-Participation has been a part of Hamburg's e-Government strategy since 2005.

The spatial planning process in Hamburg is very complex and involves many different participants. Each planning process involves several public agencies and the members of the public affected. The city administration carried out an in-depth analysis of all conditions and processes related to spatial planning before starting to implement an electronic participation operation.

The first step of the BOP project was a business transaction analysis of the spatial planning process in the city of Hamburg[22]. The analysis showed that the planning process consists of three building blocks - information, communication and coordination - and that formal participation procedures can be responsible for up to 60% of total planning costs.

Based on these results, TuTech Innovation GmbH developed a concept for an Internet-based participation platform for the spatial planning process in the city of Hamburg. The development used the rapid prototyping approach, which meant that all stakeholders in the planning process were involved in the development of the platform from the earliest stages of the project onwards. Discussions were held with all stakeholders and the functions of the individual departments were examined. After the development phase, the platform was tested in 2008 using two genuine formal participation processes concerning spatial planning in Hamburg. The first test was aimed at involving the public agencies and the second at the general public. Both tests were highly successful.

The participation platform presents all relevant planning documents and makes them available in one place and in a selection of formats. The comments of public agencies and members of the public on the respective plans were delivered electronically and could therefore be used for further processing without any conversion. Statements could be referenced both to specific parts of the planning texts and the actual maps of the plan. The combination of digital statements and web mapping exceed the possibilities realised in other municipalities to date. The developed platform offered extensive possibilities for overlaying personal geodata with the existing plan data using international standardised interfaces (OGC conformity[23]). For the representation of the spatial plans used, the new German standard XPlanung[24,25] was used for the first time in Hamburg[26].

In Hamburg, 60-90 public agencies have to take part in each planning process. The contact data for all these agencies was managed in a central register by the planning authority and users were provided with an account to log in on the Internet platform. In most cases, the planning documents were not sent in printed form. Only if the agency explicitly asked for the material was it also provided on paper. After registration, public agencies had access to all planning documents on the platform. Furthermore, public agencies were able to involve others in the planning process. Comments were stored as drafts on the platform and could be sent to the planning authority after a final check by the agency.

In order to keep the hurdle for the participation by the general public as low as possible, users were allowed access to the platform without registration. All planning documents for the public participation were available freely. Comments could be made in relation to text documents or a point in the web mapping tool. The user was asked to give his or her name, address and valid email address when submitting a statement on the draft plans.

The planning agency must consider the submitted comments and prepare them for tabling before the decision-making bodies (town planning committee)[27]. All submissions were administered in a special area on the platform, which could only be accessed by the staff members of the administration. Various functions for administering the submissions were available to planning authority personnel. All steps taken by personnel were separately saved in a database to make sure the process was transparent. The planning authority provided its answer to the comments directly on the platform. In the final step, the list of the comments and answers to them were prepared for the decision-making bodies in printed form using the export features of the platform. This list of comments and answers could be exported into any office suite or be archived in the Hamburg document management system.

In the context of the project, many requirements of the involved parties were identified and in most cases directly incorporated into the system. An efficiency analysis confirmed that the system made good economic sense. The Hamburg pilot project will be finished by early 2009. Afterwards the participation platform is scheduled to be merged into the Hamburg IT-infrastructure and launched as part of the participation process for spatial planning affairs.

The tool developed in Hamburg has won the second price in the 8th e-Government Competition held by Cisco and Bearing Point[28] in late 2008.

The Hamburg participation platform is a fully developed e-Participation solution for spatial planning. A first independent version, called DEMOS-Plan, has already been implemented in another German region.

This chapter touches on a number of interconnected topics and seeks to provide a step-by-step argument in favour of electronic tools for participation in spatial planning and outline the advantages which all stakeholders could gain from implementing these tools. The results of this discussion, and the recommendations which can be derived from them, are laid out in this chapter.

The legal frameworks at the European level[29] clearly state that public participation in spatial planning is mandatory for every planning action in which environmental impact could be possible. As almost every planning action could have an environmental impact of some sort, this is a de facto call for public participation in all public planning. National law in the member states of the European Union in many cases already contains language which makes participation in planning mandatory, as shown by examples from Germany and England. Some legislative texts at European and national levels also explicitly mention the possibility of using electronic tools to organise the participatory elements in the planning process. These findings lead to the recommendation that planning authorities in public administrations should work on setting up or improving the participatory elements of their planning processes and try to make use of electronic tools.

Another conclusion of this article is that participation in spatial planning involves a set of different parties with strongly differing and even competing interests in participating in the planning action. These interests range from the gathering of professional information from public agencies and the need for public administrations to build acceptance for a plan among the local population, to the wish by members of the public to be involved in local democracy. These differing views translate to the varying advantages that could be gained by the different parties from using electronic tools for participation in spatial planning. The Hamburg case shows that these needs have to be taken into account and integrated when implementing an electronic tool for this purpose.

Electronic tools for participation in spatial planning must and can cover the different and competing needs and interests of the involved parties. They could be seen as a hybrid between e-Government and e-Participation tools. This ability could lead to mandatory participation through electronic tools being seen as a first step into the field of e-Participation for public administrations because it answers a specific requirement they have to fulfil, while for members of the public it opens up a participatory channel related to an issue that directly affects them. Other forms of e-Participation, such as idea generation or participation in the legislative process, could be added later to the e-Participation profile of a city or region that came to the subject via spatial planning.

Finally, mandatory participation in spatial planning is an important field both for e-Participation and e-Government related activities and opens up possibilities for public administrations, public agencies, the general public and electronic tool providers to improve the quality of planning and local democracy in a profound way.

Rolf Lührs (@somed) heads the department of Interactive Communication at TuTech Innovation GmbH, Hamburg's agency for knowledge and technology transfer. Rolf has worked for almost a decade in the fields of social science, technology assessment and online research. He holds a diploma in sociology and has been involved in many different national and European research and development projects. During 1999-2003, Rolf was the scientific and technical manager of the European eDemocracy project DEMOS (Delphi Mediation Online System). Since 2008 he is the coordinator of PEP-NET, the Pan European ePartición Network.

Bengt Feil (@bengtfeil) holds a diploma in political science and works at TuTech's department Interactive Communication since 2007, mainly in the field of E-Democracy and increased citizen participation in planning and decision-making processes. Mr. Feil has experience in the fields the social web, internet and democracy and web-technologies. His work combines social, political and technological understanding.

Harald Rathmann holds a diploma in environmental sciences and has a strong focus on the topic citizen participation on the Internet. Before he came to TuTech he worked as a specialist for internet based geographical information systems and gained intensive experience regarding the fields of regional planning and geographical informatics. At TuTech, he is involved in several e-participation and e-democracy projects and is an expert for public participation in urban land-use planning.

[1] http://j.mp/3Hb4G

[2] Lethonen, S. (2005). Public Participation in Urban Planning and Strategies – Lessons from medium sized cities in the Baltic Sea Region, online: http://j.mp/2FLAyL, p. 2.

[3] In German: Bauleitplanung Online Pilot (BOP). The German abbreviation will be used in the article.

[4] Hagenauer, M. (2006). Instrumente der Öffentlichkeitsbeteiligung im Verfahren der Bauleitplanung. Die Rechtslage in Deutschland und England, Würzburg: Hemmer/Wüst, p. 1.

[5] DIRECTIVE 2001/42/EC OF THE EUROPEAN PARLIAMENT AND OF THE COUNCIL (27 June 2001), on the assessment of the effects of certain plans and programmes on the environment, online: http://j.mp/2GLpHi

[6] DIRECTIVE 2003/35/EC OF THE EUROPEAN PARLIAMENT AND OF THE COUNCIL (26 May 2003), providing for public participation in respect of the drawing up of certain plans and programmes relating to the environment and amending with regard to public participation and access to justice Council Directives 85/337/EEC and 96/61/EC, online: http://j.mp/18m9a7

[7] Becker, R; Rebsch, S. Was geht mich das an? – Öffentlichkeitsbeteiligung bei der Umsetzung der Wasserrahmenrichtlinie. Online: http://j.mp/6Y8Y2, p.1.

[8] graenselandsportal.eu. Raumplanung in Dänemark. Online: http://j.mp/6Bpwn

[9] Baugesetzbuch §3, Abs. 1: „Die Öffentlichkeit ist möglichst frühzeitig über die allgemeinen Ziele und Zwecke der Planung, sich wesentlich unterscheidende Lösungen, die für die Neugestaltung oder Entwicklung eines Gebiets in Betracht kommen, und die voraussichtlichen Auswirkungen der Planung öffentlich zu unterrichten; ihr ist Gelegenheit zur Äußerung und Erörterung zu geben."

[10] Baugesetzbuch §4, Abs. 1: "Die Behörden und sonstigen Träger öffentlicher Belange, deren Aufgabenbereich durch die Planung berührt werden kann, sind entsprechend § 3 Abs. 1 Satz 1 Halbsatz 1 zu unterrichten und zur Äußerung auch im Hinblick auf den erforderlichen Umfang und Detaillierungsgrad der Umweltprüfung nach § 2 Abs. 4 aufzufordern."

[11] cf. Hagenauer, p. 108

[12] United Kingdom (1990), Town and Country Planning Act, online: http://j.mp/3y7vHv

[13] Planning Bill (2007). introduced by Hazel Blears, Department for Communities and Local Government and Baroness Andrews, Communities and Local Government, online: http://j.mp/oXKjl

[14] DIRECTIVE 2003/35/EC, article 2.

[15] Howard, D. (1998). Geographic Information Technologies and Community Planning: Spatial Empowerment and Public Participation, A Paper Prepared for the Project Varenius Specialist Meeting on Empowerment, Marginalization, and Public Participation GIS, p. 1.; cf. Roeder, S; Voss, A. (2002).Group Decision Support for spatial planning and e-government. In Global Spatial Data Infrastructure (GSDI), online: http://j.mp/2lwI1I, p.3.

[16] http://inspire.jrc.ec.europa.eu/

[17] DIRECTIVE 2007/2/EC OF THE EUROPEAN PARLIAMENT AND OF THE COUNCIL (14 March 2007), establishing an Infrastructure for Spatial Information in the European Community (INSPIRE), online: http://j.mp/VVFZQ

[18] cf. TuTech Innovation GmbH (2008). Bauleitplanung Online – Pilot Projektbericht – Version 1.0 (BOP Project Report), not public on December 10th 2008.

[19] Comparable to the concept of "strong democracy" by Benjamin R. Barber.

[20] Bundesrepublik Deutschland. Baugesetzbuch. Last changes: 21.12.2006 (BGBl. I S. 3316) m.W.v. 01.01.2007.

[21] A project description will be provided to ePractice.eu in early 2009.

[22] Giesenhagen, A. (2006). Geschäftsprozessanalyse und eGovernment Potenziale des Planfeststellungsverfahrens für Bebauungspläne in der Freien Hansestadt Hamburg, Management Summary, Knowlogy Solutions AG / B.I.T. Consult GmbH, Hamburg.

[23] Open Spacial Consortium (OGC). Official Website. Online: www.opengeospatial.org

[24] XPlanung E-Government Project. Official website. Online: www.xplanung.de

[25] Deutschland Online (2008). Deutschland Online Vorhaben Geodaten, Teilprojekt XPlanung – Austauschstandard in der Bauleitplanung, Berlin.

[26] Geschäfts- und Koordinierungsstelle GDI-DE (2007). Abschlussbericht zum Modellprojekt "XPlanung", Frankfurt.

[27] Freie und Hansestadt Hamburg, Behörde für Stadtentwicklung und Umwelt (2008). "Planen Sie mit", Hamburg.

[28] http://www.egovernment-wettbewerb.de/

[29] 2001/42/EC and 2003/35/EC

#20

Washington Goes to Mr. Smith: Glimpses of the Future of American Democracy?

Matt Leighninger
Executive Director, Deliberative Democracy Consortium

In the movie *Mr. Smith Goes to Washington*, our innocent leading man, played by Jimmy Stewart, becomes a senator almost by accident. He has only one legislative priority: setting up a summer camp for boys in his home state. In order to accomplish his goal, and ensure that the voices of his constituents are heard, he is forced to shout above the din of big media and corrupt politicians. During a dramatic filibuster, the strength of his conviction shines through, and he wins the day.

For a variety of reasons, a growing number of federal managers are trying to reverse the roles in Frank Capra's script. In order to keep public decisions from turning into political debacles – and in order to make their own voices heard over the din of activists and the media – they are bringing those decisions directly to citizens. They want citizens to take on an intermediary role in policy development, somewhere between utter ignorance and absolute control.

They want ordinary people to become more informed about the issues, settle some of their disagreements, and appreciate the tough choices that officials are forced to make. In agencies as diverse as the Centers for Disease Control, Environmental Protection Agency, Federal Highway Administration, and the National Nanotechnology Coordinating Office, Washington is going to Mr. Smith.

This trend has been evident for some time, but the 2008 presidential election and the advent of the Obama Administration have given it added momentum. The election showed that the new attitudes and capacities of ordinary citizens could be harnessed as part of a national electoral strategy; the challenge of the new administration is to transfer that energy into the day-to-day work of democratic governance.

When they turn toward Mr. (and Ms.) Smith, managers generally have several goals in mind:

- Gathering policy input from a broad cross-section of citizens
- Defusing tension and conflict around particular public decisions
- Rebuilding public trust and helping citizens understand how difficult the role of government can be
- Gaining a better understanding of the language and ideas they would need to use in order to reach even larger numbers of people
- Encouraging citizens (and the nonprofit organizations, advocacy groups, businesses, and faith-based groups they belong to) to take actions that support and complement public policies.

All of these goals respond to, and capitalize on, the new capacities and concerns of 21st Century citizens. The change in citizenship is most evident at the local level, where ordinary people are playing increasingly active roles – sometimes productive, sometimes disruptive – in public decision-making and problem-solving. Citizens may have less time for public life, but they bring more knowledge and skills to the table. They feel more entitled to the services and protection of government, and yet have less faith that government will be able to deliver on those promises. They are less connected to community affairs, and yet they seem better able to find the information, allies and resources they need to affect an issue or decision they care about. The bottom line is that citizens are better at governing, and worse at being governed, than ever before.

At the local level, these trends have been evident for some time. For the last fifteen years, this shift in citizen attitudes and capacities has created new tensions between residents and elected officials, produced new public actors and problem-solvers, and inspired a new generation of civic experiments. The limitations of the traditional, 'child-parent' relationship between citizens and government are becoming more obvious, and we are struggling to establish more productive 'adult-adult' forms of governance[1].

The National League of Cities, the International City/County Management Association, and Philanthropy for Active Civic Engagement have described this work in reports like *Changing the Way We Govern*[2] and *The New Laboratories of Democracy*[3].

To address these challenges and opportunities, public officials, public employees, and other kinds of leaders are trying various ways – some successful, some not – of working more productively with citizens. Several successful principles have emerged from this work:

1. Recruiting people by reaching out through the various groups and organizations to which they belong, in order to assemble a large and diverse "critical mass" of citizens. The best involvement projects map their communities, figure out what people belong to, and convince leaders within those groups and organizations to recruit people they already know.

2. Involving those citizens in a combination of small – and large-group meetings: structured, facilitated small groups

for informed, deliberative dialogue and large forums for amplifying shared conclusions and moving from talk to action. One of the worst practices in traditional citizen involvement has been to use large meetings for things (like dialogue) that can only be effective in small meetings and vice versa.

3. Giving the participants in these meetings the opportunity to compare values and experiences, and to consider a range of views and policy options. People have to be able to connect these issues to their own lives and what matters to them.

4. Encouraging and effecting change in a number of ways: by applying citizen input to policy and planning decisions; by encouraging change within organizations and institutions; by creating teams to work on particular action ideas; and/or by inspiring and connecting individual volunteers. The result of this more comprehensive approach is essentially policy with a small 'p,' meaning not just laws and ordinances, but all the things that all of us can do to solve public problems.

Resources like *Democracy, Growing Up*[4], *Where Is Democracy Headed?*[5], *Funding and Fostering Local Democracy*[6], and *Democracy as Problem Solving?*[7] describe how these shared strategies evolved, spurred by changing citizen attitudes and capacities. The core principles underpinning these projects are described by Will Friedman[8], who points out that our attempts to involve citizens in federal issues should capitalize on, and help to strengthen, these local democratic structures and opportunities.

Many of these efforts use online tools and technologies as a way to complement face-to-face meetings. Others are purely online experiments: Public Agenda's Center for Advances in Public Engagement (CAPE) [9] categorizes these different kinds of projects and offers practical suggestions for conducting them. Some of the most exciting and sustained projects are online neighborhood forums like the ones described by Steven Clift[10]. Overall, the Internet has been under-utilized in this work; online technologies offer terrific potential for tracking and measuring public engagement, providing new incentives for people to participate, helping participants find the information they need, and providing new venues for dialogue and deliberation.

Though many of these examples show how democracy can work more effectively and equitably on a temporary basis - on a single issue for a short period of time - there are fewer instances where the new strategies have been 'embedded' into the way that governments and communities function. In his *Empowered Participation*, Archon Fung[11] describes several communities where this has happened, and identifies some key ingredients for success. Understanding neighborhood governance is an essential part of this question[12].

We shouldn't neglect the democracy lessons being learned in other parts of the world, particularly in the Global South. "Reversing the Flow"[13] makes this argument eloquently, and a number of studies[14] summarize some of the work being done to revitalize governance and strengthen democratic accountability in other parts of the world. The British organization *Involve*[15] has also produced many excellent reports on the attempts to reform democracy in the U.K.

This work has introduced new twists on timeless questions about power, justice and equity. Do these forms of engagement provide powerful new opportunities for people who have traditionally been excluded and disadvantaged, or can they actually exacerbate long-standing divides and inequities? Alison Kadlec and Will Friedman recap[16] this conversation, and lays out new directions for aligning democracy, equity and justice.

Building on these principles will be critical if we want to enhance democracy at the federal level. The federal agencies with the most experience in citizen involvement tend to be the ones that make local decisions - how to manage a toxic waste cleanup, for example, or whether to protect an old-growth forest - and their interactions with citizens usually focus on those local policies rather than national ones. However, citizen participation projects dealing with state and federal policies are on the rise, partly because some officials at those levels of government are now feeling the same kinds of pressures as their local counterparts. Leading agencies like the U.S. Environmental Protection Agency and the U.S. Centers for Disease Control and Prevention (CDC) have incorporated some of these strategies into their work. In his *Investing in Democracy*, Carmen Sirianni provides a comprehensive overview and offers substantiated proposals.

Several other reports supply recommendations of, and for, pioneering federal managers. On March 30-31, 2009, at an event called "Champions of Participation," thirty-four managers from 23 different federal agencies and departments came together to develop recommendations[17] for the President's Open Government Directive. Also, on May 12, 2009, nineteen senior leaders from 13 federal agencies and departments came together at the headquarters of the Transportation Security Administration to offer ideas[18].

In August 2009, around 100 American experts and advocates of democracy reform came together to create new momentum and plans for strengthening democracy by engaging all citizens in the selection of their leaders, influencing laws and regulations, and taking public action. At the *Strengthening our Nation's Democracy* conference, key leaders from the Obama Administration shared their plans and accomplishments in the area of democratic participation and reform. The participants, in turn, created a set of priorities for advancing democracy reform and open government, which they presented to Administration leaders. The conference resulted in a practical agenda for addressing the increasing loss of peoples' trust in – and sense of connection to – our systems of politics and governance. Participants developed 10 detailed recommendations and action steps for both the Administration and the democracy reform movement itself[19]:

1. Involve the American public in meaningful deliberations about important policy questions
2. Support and promote an electoral reform agenda
3. Improve federal public participation and collaboration
4. Explore lessons from the Open Government Dialogue
5. Recognize and support engagement carried out by traditionally disenfranchised communities
6. Create a report on the health of our democracy
7. Build skills and capacity for public engagement
8. Increase the availability of federal funding for democratic participation
9. Convene an international democracy conference
10. Create an ongoing mechanism for sustaining leadership

These attempts to reach out to citizens are, on one level, a reversal of *Mr. Smith Goes To Washington*. But they are motivated by many of the same impulses apparent in Jimmy Stewart's character: the need to understand and explain citizen values in Washington, and the desire to rebuild trust and communication back home. The new dynamic in 21st Century politics has given us a new urgency, and new opportunities, to recast the relationship between citizens and government.

Matt Leighninger is the executive director of the Deliberative Democracy Consortium. Portions of this essay were adapted from his book, The Next Form of Democracy *(Vanderbilt University Press).*

---

[1] For a brief, humorous video describing this transition, see http://j.mp/AIqgH
[2] http://j.mp/2QZVXa
[3] http://www.pacefunders.org/publications/NewLaboratoriesofDemocracy.pdf
[4] http://j.mp/1Mpqj
[5] http://j.mp/vy9GA
[6] http://j.mp/vxc09
[7] http://mitpress.mit.edu/catalog/item/default.asp?ttype=2&tid=11627
[8] Will Friedman (2006) "Deliberative Democracy and the Problem of Scope," Journal of Public Deliberation: Vol. 2: No. 1, Article 1.
[9] http://j.mp/20p5u
[10] http://stevenclift.com/?p=152
[11] http://press.princeton.edu/titles/7762.html
[12] The Promise and Challenge of Neighborhood Democracy. http://j.mp/d806d
[13] http://www.alliancemagazine.org/node/2259
[14] See for example, http://j.mp/1SncBt and http://j.mp/1f3khr
[15] http://www.involve.org.uk/
[16] Alison Kadlec and Will Friedman (2007) "Deliberative Democracy and the Problem of Power", Journal of Public Deliberation: Vol. 3: No. 1, Article 8.
[17] http://j.mp/7IMHM
[18] http://j.mp/KL286
[19] Archon Fung et al (2009) Working Together to Build a Stronger Democracy: A Preliminary Report on Ten Proposals for Strengthening our Nation's Democracy. August 14, 2009. http://j.mp/booDZ

#21

PEOPLE POWER CAN REBOOT A NATION

Lee Bryant
CEO, HeadShift

We are lucky to have a stable and relatively functional political system in the UK, for all the recent drama, and we should avoid throwing away that heritage in pursuit of change for its own sake.

But in addition to the obvious short-term challenge of rebuilding faith in our political and economic system, we face some difficult long-term issues that require 21st century solutions.

Faced with the plunder of the banks, the government's answer has been to bail out the bankers and hope (again) for trickle down effects, rather than invest in people and services to create value and wealth. They have spectacularly failed to deal with both boom and bust, and they continue pulling their big 20th century levers despite the fact these are no longer working. Although the government realizes the internet has a key role to play, the recent Digital Britain report[1] shows just how little they understand the online world. Aside from the obvious conclusion that universal broadband (which should be 8Mb as a minimum) is a necessary enabler to an inclusive digital economy, the report seems firmly located in the 1990s world of 'content providers', copyright restrictions and network operators. We need to show the political elite what to do, and get on with fixing things before they get much worse.

Over the past decade, we have learned a lot about how network thinking and specifically the social web can dramatically reduce the costs of co-ordination and collective action, allowing new ways of involving people in organizational, democratic or social processes. Many people have argued that government and industry should take advantage of these innovations to create more people-powered organizations. Now, in the face of serious crises in both the economy and the political system, and faced with a recession that calls into question whether we can even afford 'business as usual', it is time to take a serious look at how we can leverage human talent, energy and creativity to begin rebooting the system to create sustainable, affordable, long-term mechanisms for public engagement.

We have been talking about e-government for years, and have made steady progress with some of the enablers, such as online service provision, the Government Gateway[2] and a growing awareness among civil servants about online public engagement. But so far, this work has remained very much within existing organizational boundaries. It has focused on how to enable communication and limited interaction between government and citizens, but has not yet changed either the workings of government or the role of citizens in that process.

The next stage must be to look at how we leverage the vast human resources that exist both within government and among citizens to accelerate progress and help develop modern, affordable services.

Debates about the role of government have traditionally focused on the rather fatuous issue of 'big government' versus 'small government', more investment in public services or cuts. Yet, there is plenty of scope for government that is 'big' in terms of whom it includes, but 'small' in its approach to investment and bureaucracy.

Smarter, simpler social technology has a key role to play here. In the 1980s and early 1990s, we saw ideologically motivated cuts in key public services, and the effects of these are with us today in the form of social problems and a growing gap between rich and poor. From 1997 onwards, we have seen that it is possible to spend a great deal of money on the supply side of public services with diminishing returns at the point of delivery, as the managerial class soaks up a large proportion of this spend. Perhaps more worrying, we have also seen a gradual disempowerment of front-line staff in favor of targets, 'best practice' and centralized, process-based thinking.

We can have both bigger and smaller government at the same time. Our society is capable of running itself better, and cheaper, if we trust people to be part of the solution, rather than passive 'consumers' of services who just get to swap their representatives every four years or so. We need to see government as an enabler or a force multiplier that can combine with the energy and resources of ordinary people to improve governance and public service delivery. There are many examples of how we waste energy and resources by treating citizens as passive recipients of services. Call centre-style communication is one example that has been badly copied from the private sector, where government spends a great deal of money centralizing a communication function that prevents interaction and treats people like children. At the other end of the line, citizens are forced to waste minutes (often hours) of their time for little benefit. Similarly, in healthcare, 'customers' are often highly motivated and want to take an active role in their diagnosis and treatment, but they are not always allowed to do so. This area alone is one in which the potential for participative approaches to service design and delivery could save many millions of pounds, whilst producing better clinical outcomes, since feeling empowered and involved tends to make people feel less ill.

But this also means re-balancing our expectations of government and encouraging (and possibly educating) us to take more individual and collective responsibility for our society.

Social tools supporting real conversation between government and citizens can help this process and help people develop realistic expectations, rather than unlimited demands (e.g. Scandinavian services with American taxes). We have already been educated as passive consumers, rather than equal participants in the process of identifying and solving problems. Taking more responsibility for our own lives is not always easy, but it is better than simply throwing demands at government and then being surprised when they cannot meet them all.

The first and most important thing we can do is to make better use of government spending to make it go further. Government procurement should be treated as a stimulus fund, and used to deliver social and economic benefits as well as products and services. Big ticket projects in areas such as IT, Health and Defense have a high failure rate, which is made worse by the tendency to select a large supplier and require them to spend all the money up front in one big hit. Instead, it makes more sense to adopt an investment mindset and provide seed funding to various potential suppliers (ideally community groups and small companies as well as generic corporations that specialize in outsourcing contracts), and then provide more substantial first and second round funding to those projects that show potential, until a clear winner emerges. This way, funding can be leveraged to stimulate innovation as well as deliver a service, and an iterative multi-round approach is more likely to pick winners than just handing over the whole thing in one go. Perhaps, drawing on the lesson of Social Innovation Camp[3] and 4iP[4], a proportion of all departmental budgets should be earmarked for open innovation funds in the hope that we might discover the next SureStart[5] or similar idea.

If we are to target spending on public services better, then we also need better ways of surfacing and identifying need. Too many public sector bodies are created as part of a shiny political initiative and then waste huge sums of money consolidating their own position, rather than helping people, before finally being wound down after a few years. The logic of the Vendor Relationship Management movement[6] – that people express their needs and intent and then invite service providers to fulfill them – has potential to create more efficient public service delivery mechanisms. If government wants to use social media, then a good starting point is to listen and learn. Beyond that, there should be more thinking about how to sample needs and demand in general, rather than the purely supply-side focus that governments are used to.

The second thing we can do is harness people power to improve existing democratic and public services. One of the best lessons of the social web is the idea of rapid feedback-driven iteration as an evolutionary model. The launch of a service is just the beginning of a process whereby user involvement and feedback is used to make improvements and refinements. Giving feedback need not be onerous. There is a wealth of (often ignored) behavioral and usage data that can provide useful feedback to developers and designers, even where it needs to be anonymized. Instead of 'experts' gathering requirements, obtaining a huge budget and then spending it all in one go, this evolutionary model seeks to co-create services with users. There is a lot of good thinking emerging around concepts of service (co-)design in the public sector, and perhaps it is time to apply this on a bigger stage. There is both a cost and a quality rationale for citizens to be participants in the process of service delivery, which implies going way beyond the current practice of occasional consultation.

But creating user-driven organizations is not just about rapid feedback from external users; it must also apply internally as well.

In government, as in business, we suffer from organizational models that are too expensive and inefficient to succeed in the current climate. We need to place people above process and – assuming we have hired the right individuals and trained them well – let them get on with their job. Key to this is the introduction of simple, social tools that let people develop their own networks within organizations and use these to get things done. Corporate IT has become a blocker, not an enabler, and we urgently need a new, more human-scale approach to internal communications and knowledge sharing within organizations in both the private and public sector. The boom times of recent years have hidden a great deal of inefficiency, and as revenues recede, we need flatter, more agile organizational structures instead of the stultifying middle management bureaucratic machines that exist because organizations fundamentally don't trust their own people, let alone their customers and users.

The third priority for action has been well documented and argued in the Power of Information Taskforce Report[7] (see Richard Allan's chapter), which is the need to open up data of various kinds that government collects and holds. It should be a requirement of all government-funded projects that they share their data openly, even if it needs to be anonymized. Projects such as Gapminder.org show how hidden statistical data can be opened up to create new insights, and the Show us a Better Way[8] proof of concept project shows just how much value could be unlocked by encouraging new and innovative uses of existing data sets.

The big question, though, is how to achieve any of this. In the United States, federal CIO Vivek Kundra has outlined plans for pursuing these ideas, which is unsurprising since the internet was crucial to Obama's spectacular refactoring of the US body politic. The US data.gov initiative has set the bar high in terms of access to data, and it is reasonable to expect that this translates into better government and public services over the medium term. In the UK, the recent Cabinet Office initiative, prompted by Tim Berners Lee's advocacy of open data to Prime Minister Gordon Brown over the summer, is also a good start. Their new data site[9] makes over a thousand data sets available for developers to build on, many of which have been converted from older, less accessible formats. This is a good start, if small compared to the traditional IT spending that continues day in and day out elsewhere in government.

In the UK, we are still laboring under a late 20th century government in its final phase, so we should not expect too much. Perhaps it is better for all of us to simply get on with it and create our own structures and services, as mySociety.org and others have pioneered, until we have a government that understands the internet.

Lee Bryant (@leebryant) is co-founder and director of Headshift, now part of the Dachis Group, and is aiming to focus on the emerging area of social software and social networking. He has been playing with words and computers since the age of 10, and has a strong belief in the empowering potential of the internet. He is also a board member of a social enterprise, Involve, and a trustee of the Foundation for Science Technology and Culture.

---

[1] http://j.mp/xaQUv
[2] http://www.gateway.gov.uk/
[3] http://www.sicamp.org/
[4] http://www.4ip.org.uk/
[5] http://www.surestart.gov.uk/
[6] http://j.mp/BGKsM
[7] http://j.mp/1rTEPi
[8] http://showusabetterway.com/
[9] http://hmg.gov.uk/data

Section IV

CO-CREATION, INNOVATION & VALUES

#22

PUBLIC ADMINISTRATION: LET THERE BE E-UNIFICATION, AGAIN AND AGAIN

Olov Östberg
Professor Emeritus, Mid Sweden University

The Government of Sweden in 2008 decided[1] to reclaim world leadership in the e-Gov ranking circus by 2010. Easier said than done; policy documents alone will not overcome the age-old gaps between the three layers of public administration containing some six hundred independently managed agencies.

At best, the agencies in the state sector capability cloud may be managed to march to the whole-of-government tune. Among the problems faced in the attempted paradigm shift are nevertheless (i) unrealistic time scale, (ii) governance not possible without enterprise architecture, (iii) modeling end user needs cannot be left solely to individual agencies, (iv) clusters and federations must be defined by means of federation level agreements as well as service level agreements, (v) low adherence level to EU's directives on Services and Public information re-usage will be rewarded with low e-Gov EU ranking, and (vi) there are very few mandatory standards and profiles for Swedish agencies and no Swedish National Interoperability Framework at the horizon. Among the positive signs are that very ambitious work is taking place in the defense and e-health sectors. To compensate for the unrealistic time scale, and to secure public value, it's an absolute must that forums for e-Gov discussions, architecting work and information exchange get established as soon as possible.

The term e-Gov(ernment) has been around long enough to have earned the epithet 'traditional'. In the case of Sweden, there have been four action programs tailored to ever more sophisticated use of computing machines in the public administration. Action program #1 came about when a social democrat government in the 50ies embarked on a massive welfare program, and starting in 2009, a centre-right government is implementing program #4 so as to firmly position Sweden as an international e-Gov leader. On the other hand, since almost all of our everyday tasks involve the use of information and communication technology, it has been argued that it is meaningless to use the prefix 'e' as a descriptor. Yes, it is possible to discuss public administration modernization and paradigm shifts without ever using that 'e', but then it merely becomes an exercise, just as when the French author Georges Perec in 1969 managed to write a long novel without ever using the vowel 'e'.

Coming of age. As indicated by the series of action programs in Sweden, today's e-Gov thrust has a sixty year's history, and that's not just in Sweden. The International Council for Information Technology in Government Administration (ICA[2]), a non-profit organization established to promote the information exchange of knowledge, ideas and experiences between Central Government IT Authorities, in October 2009 held its 43rd (!) annual conference in Brussels. Internet in terms of the TCP/IP protocol has been around for forty years, and the World Wide Web protocol HTTP for twenty years.

One for All, All for One. This slogan has ever has since 1902 been considered the motto of the Federal State of Switzerland. The motto has been used to evoke a sense of duty and solidarity and national unity in the population of the young nation. It can also be used as a catchword for a federation in general — and for what seems to be happening in today's networkization.

A motto may be seen as a 'tool' to create an aura. In the senses of the perceivers, all material or immaterial objects and concepts have auras. In his seminal 1935-essay *Work of Art*, German culture critic Walter Benjamin (1892-1940) noted[3] that:

> *"Just as the entire mode of existence of human collectives changes over long historical periods, so too does their mode of perception. The way in which human perception is organized the medium in which it occurs is conditioned not only by nature but by history. The era of the migration of peoples, an era which saw the rise of the late-Roman art industry and the Vienna Genesis, developed not only an art different from that of antiquity but also a different perception. [...] The stripping of the veil from the object, the destruction of the aura, is the signature of a perception whose sense for all that is the same in the world so increased that, by means of reproduction, it extracts sameness even from what is unique."*

In the writings of Marshall McLuhan (1911-1980), and in particular through "the media is the message" message, the aura deformation traits of technology were extended and popularized.

Today's digital gadgets and social software are doing just that; spreading of tools and artifacts, tagging for sameness, instant sharing, etc. In 2009, Sweden actually saw the formation of an *e-Community of Interest* political party — the Pirate Party[4], winning one seat in the EU parliament – sharply focused on the view (i) that *One for All, All for One* overrides intellectual property laws, (ii) that citizens' rights to privacy shall be respected, and (iii) that the patent system needs an overhaul. As of October 1, 2009, Pirate Parties have been established in 35 countries[5].

The overarching 2010 objective for the Swedish e-Government Action Plan [2008] is "*As simple as possible for As many as possible.*" Not too different from that of the Pirate Party. Perhaps this is the first sign of a worldwide *Reclaim the Government* concept in the making — p-Gov?

Not just the e-Gov aura is reshaping itself, the very time scale also seems to be changing. The equivalent to the development that took place in the past thousand years will probably be completed within the coming hundred years. Developments are simultaneously and interactively taking place in disciplines at an accelerating pace, making it futile to make predictions, even about the near future.

Ray Kurzweil[6] talks about "a future period during which the pace of technological change will be so rapid, its impact so deep, that human life will be irreversibly transformed." Neither utopian nor dystopian, he describes how this epoch will transform "the concepts that we rely on to give meaning to our lives, from our business models to the cycle of human life, including death itself."

To quote the Singularity Institute[7]:

> *"The Singularity represents an 'event horizon' in the predictability of human technological development past which present models of the future may cease to give reliable answers, following the creation of strong AI or the enhancement of human intelligence."*

As noted in the introduction, the Government of Sweden in 2008 decided to reclaim world leadership in the e-Gov ranking circus by 2010. Strangely enough, the Government of Sweden already in 1994 set the same goal for the very same 2010. Well, perhaps not so strange in the light of *Alice's Adventures in Wonderland* (Lewis Caroll, 1865):

> *"Well, in our country," said Alice, still panting a little, "you'd generally get to somewhere else — if you run very fast for a long time, as we've been doing."*
>
> *"A slow sort of country!" said the Queen. "Now, here, you see, it takes all the running you can do, to keep in the same place. If you want to get somewhere else, you must run at least twice as fast as that!"*

The e-Gov challenge is to become better at becoming better. Together.

Olov Östberg (@OlovOst) serves as international liaison to the program on Public Information Systems at Mid Sweden University. Prior this position as Prof. Emer., Olov for twenty years held positions as e-Gov adviser to the Swedish Central Government Offices, notably on e-Democracy and the 24/7 e-Gov agenda. Before that he had a prolific academic track — including a CV listing 236 publications and professor positions in Sweden, UK, USA, and Japan — in areas related to Human Factors.

---

[1] In January 2008, the Minister for Local Government and Financial Markets, Mats Odell, announced the Swedish Government's "Action plan for eGovernment – New grounds for IT-based business development in Public Administration" (Handlingsplan för eFörvaltning – Nya grunder för IT-baserad verksamhetsutveckling i offentlig förvaltning). English description, see http://j.mp/njwjA.

[2] http://ica-it.org/

[3] Walter Benjamin (2008) Work of Art in the Age of Its Technological Reproducibility, and Other Writings on Media. Harvard University Press. Originally published as *Das Kunstwerk im Zeitalter seiner technischen Reproduzierbarkeit* in *Zeitschrift für Sozialforschung* in 1935.

[4] http://j.mp/jA3d9

[5] http://j.mp/1PXLaC

[6] Ray Kurzweil (2005) *The Singularity is Near.* Viking Penguin

[7] "In the coming decades, humanity will likely create a powerful artificial intelligence. The Singularity Institute for Artificial Intelligence (SIAI) exists to confront this urgent challenge, both the opportunity and the risk." http://www.singinst.org/

#23

Co-Production of Public Services and Policies: The Role of Emerging Technologies

Tony Bovaird

INLOGOV, University of Birmingham, UK

Elke Löffler

Governance International, UK

James Downe

Cardiff Business School, Cardiff University, UK

Co-production is rapidly becoming one of the most talked-about themes when working in public services and public policy in Europe, North America and Australia, as our recent Policy Paper for UK government demonstrated[1]. However, as yet there has been no coherent approach at government level or in the academic community to bring together the evidence on the potential – and the limitations – of user and community coproduction of public services and public policies.

This chapter[2] explores two very different theoretical strands in current thinking on co-production, which can deliver very different roles and outcomes. The first approach - user co-production - focuses on how co-production can deliver individualized benefits from the design and operation of public services, while the second approach - community co-production - concentrates on more collective benefits which co-production can bring. We show that this second approach is currently under-developed and then go on to explore how the potential benefits of 'collectivized' co-production might be more effectively captured by public service organizations. We suggest that the technological solutions required for 'collective co-production' are distinctly different from those involved in 'individualized co-production' and that collective co-production based on Web 2.0 applications may in the future offer major improvements to public service outcomes.

The academic literature has viewed co-production through the perspectives of economics - looking at jointness in production; service management - where Richard Normann has argued[3] that service effectiveness depends critically on mobilizing the contributions which users are uniquely able to provide; and consumer psychology - which suggests that giving users a major role in service design and/or operation brings more user satisfaction and commitment to the service. But these approaches have severe limitations - they share the assumption that co-production depends on individuals interacting with service professionals, either as users or as volunteers in the community. This means that the outcomes of user and community co-producers can be calculated as the sum of users' outcomes.

However, this radically oversimplifies public service co-production. First, the user is often not the only person to benefit from the way the service is co-produced - many others in the community may also benefit. Secondly, much co-production is engaged in because of desire to help others, rather than simply to produce benefits for oneself.

In practice, improved user's outcomes produce a series of different types of benefits for others. These external benefits include:

- Those close to the user (carers, friends, volunteers, etc.), who experience two kinds of benefit when the user's outcomes improve:
    - A reduction in the level of effort they need to make to maintain the service user's quality of life
    - Pleasure in the user's improved quality of life
- Other users who can learn how to make better use of the service by the example set by the service co-producer (e.g. the 'expert patient' who has learnt to cope with chronic diabetes or self-administered dialysis)
- Other citizens who anticipate that they may need to use the service at some time in the future and receive benefits from seeing that the service can be more cost-effective than they had previously suspected.

These benefits to society are real and they are important. But how are they to be produced? They are reaped by others than the person whose behavior produces them. Co-production which is engaged in as a philanthropic, rather than selfish, act, is not easy to rationalize under the normal analysis of welfare economics or public choice (unless one hypothesizes the existence of some direct return to the active giver by way of 'feelgood factor', which unfortunately is not measurable and is almost tautological – we only suspect it is there because the giver's behavior suggests it is there). However, much 'collective co-production' behavior, such as volunteering, is of this type and produces collective benefits which can be of major significance.

Some light is thrown on the level of co-production in practice by a recent research project[4] undertaken for the European Presidency, comparing the current state of user and community co-production in the Czech Republic, Denmark, France, Germany and the UK, based on a survey of about 1,000 citizens in each of the five countries, focus groups with service professionals and managers in each country, and some in-depth interviews with a range of officers of public service organizations (in public, private and third sector organizations) and with representatives of users and community groups.

The study focused on three different sectors which reflect distinctly different types of government functions:

- *Community safety*, as an example of coercive action on the part of the state
- *Local environment*, as an example of the regulatory function of the state
- *Public health*, as an example of the welfare improvement function of the state.

Co-production by citizens in community safety, local environment and public health may involve a whole range of activities, from helping to identify the problems, helping to prevent the problems, right through to solving the problems and dealing with the damage done by the problems. In the survey, given the limited resources available and the short time afforded by telephone interviews, we decided to survey all citizens, rather than survey service users only (since it is much harder to achieve representative samples of the latter). The survey focused particularly on preventative activities of citizens, asking them what they currently do – and what they would be prepared to do in the future – to help public agencies to *prevent problems* from arising. However, in the community safety questions, citizens were also asked about how they personally dealt with some problems, specifically how they react when they come across crime and anti-social behavior – do they try to help the police to deal with the problem (or even take some form of direct action themselves)?

How important is the role of citizens in public service delivery?

When we asked this question of the focus groups in the five countries, the overall reaction of professional service providers was "we don't know ... but probably rather limited." A few participants even complained about the relevance of this question. In particular, in the three Danish focus groups sessions, representatives of public agencies initially had great difficulty in understanding the topic to be discussed. The same applied to the focus groups focusing on health issues in most countries, where participants had to be challenged again and again by the facilitators to come up with examples of citizen involvement in service delivery. Only the German and UK focus groups on health issues shared the view that prevention has become a more important area in health care and that citizen involvement plays an important role in this area.

However, in dramatic contrast, when we asked citizens about their level of involvement in prevention activities related to community safety, local environment and health, and when we asked them how they co-operate with the police when being confronted with crime or anti-social behavior, the results showed a significant level of co-production by citizens in the five countries studied, in all three sectors.

Looking at what kind of contributions citizens make on a regular basis in each of these sectors, an interesting pattern emerges. In general, European citizens in the five countries show particularly high levels of engagement when they can undertake activities which do not need much effort by themselves and do not require getting in touch with third parties. This applies, for example, to locking doors and windows in their home before going out, recycling household rubbish and saving water and electricity, which about 80 percent of citizens indicate as doing often. All these activities do not require interactions with other citizens or public sector organizations.

When it comes to making changes to the personal lifestyle, there is a sharp drop – e.g. in the number of citizens who walk, cycle or use public transport, change to a more healthy diet or try to exercise. Just about 50% of citizens reported undertaking these often.

Clearly, there are also activities that citizens are less inclined to undertake, at least on a regular basis. Interestingly, all the activities at the bottom of the ranking list imply getting involved with others – be it a neighbor, a doctor, the police or strangers.

At the very bottom of the responses on prevention activities is 'seeking advice from the police on safety issues.' Only 5% of European citizens often ask the police for advice on how to best protect their property, while 14 percent sometimes do so. UK citizens are most inclined to make use of this free service provided by the police, whereas Danish and Czech citizens are the most reluctant. In particular, the Czech case is interesting. As the citizen survey shows, Czech citizens feel relatively unsafe in their neighborhood and we know from national crime statistics that property-related crimes made up 70 percent of all crimes in 2004. Even though the number of police staff dealing with crime prevention has increased in recent years, crime levels have stayed persistently high. In this difficult situation, the Czech Ministry of Interior launched the 'Safe Locality' Program in 2007, which encourages citizens to take action to protect their property. According to a Czech survey on safety perceptions of the population, 40 percent of citizens know about this program (see the interview with the Czech Ministry of Interior at www.govint.org). However, as representatives of the local and national police and other participants suggested in Prague during a discussion on the role of citizens in public safety issues, levels of trust in the police are still low, which may be why only 1.3% of Czech citizens in the survey often contact the police for crime prevention advice.

There are quite a few other activities with rates of response similarly low to those in citizens seeking advice from the police. In particular, there were very low numbers of respondents who participate regularly in groups, whether the topic is community safety, local environment or health. This clearly demonstrates that seeking to tackle these issues simply through organized associations has major limitations – and these limitations are likely to persist. This indicates the importance, to which we will return later, of getting people involved on an individual basis, and not simply through third sector organizations.

It is interesting to see how many people are prepared often to take steps to encourage others to behave more appropriately, e.g. telling them not to drop rubbish (26%) and intervening to stop anti-social behavior (17%). Given that these are high effort actions, and not to be undertaken lightly, this indicates that there is a significant group of the population who see themselves as real 'activists', at least in those areas about which they genuinely care. It also suggests that the deterrent to involvement in group activities is not inherently the effort involved.

In many cases, these 'activists' might be identical to the so-called 'usual suspects', a group found in all European countries. However, some countries seem to have more than others. We can see that the level of regular participation of European citizens in groups and organizations is highest in health (9.7%), followed by environment (7.9%) and then safety (5.9%). This is an interesting finding since the index of overall co-production activities of European citizens is highest in local environment and not in health. The fact that more citizens 'co-produce' in health by getting organized may indicate a lack of availability of individual forms of co-production, which may partly be due to the attitudes of professionals working in health care as participants in several focus groups on health issues suggested.

The number of 'organized activists' in community safety and environmental issues is lowest in Denmark (2.4% in safety-related organizations and 3.5% in environmental organizations), whereas the UK has the highest proportion of citizens who often take part in organizations to improve safety in their neighborhood (12.2%). This finding is not surprising, given that there are more than 10 million members in UK neighborhood watch groups. The UK also has the highest number of citizens who often get involved in environmental groups and organizations (9%), but also a high proportion of Czech citizens often participate in groups or organizations to improve the local environment (8.4%).

As far as the participation of citizens in groups and organizations dealing with health issues is concerned, 13.5% of Czech citizens indicate that they participate often in such groups whereas in France only 6.5% of citizens do so, with citizens in other countries falling between these figures.

In summary, the survey has shown that:

- There is already a lot more citizen involvement in public service delivery than the professionals taking part in our focus groups wanted to acknowledge. This is particularly evident in local environmental and health issues but also, though to a lesser degree, in community safety issues.

- There is likely to be more citizen involvement in service delivery in the future due to the demographic changes taking place in most European countries. The involvement of citizens in delivering public services clearly increases with age, so that the 'ageing society' is good news in terms of increasing levels of 'co-production'.

- Citizens are most willing to make a contribution towards improving public services when it involves them in relatively little effort and when they do not have to work closely with other citizens or staff, or professionals in the government.

What does this imply for public service delivery and the attempts which have been made to improve service quality? So far, the quality improvement approaches in most public services have tended to focus on how *professionals* can improve service quality and outcomes. Indeed, the most commonly used quality assurance systems tend to view service users and society from the perspective of what results are achieved *for them*, rather than viewing them as a resource. Once they are seen as a resource, working with them has a very different set of implications for the management and governance of public services. However, this perspective is still far from universal – as our focus group participants suggested, not all professionals working in public services are prepared yet to give service users a more active role.

Relative public value of 'individual' and 'collective' co-production

While the results above indicate that citizens are less inclined to spend their co-production efforts in group activities, this does not mean that such collectivized co-production is unimportant. As examples of how important it is to the creation of public value, in the UK there are about 350,000 school governors, who not only serve on committees to help run schools, but also have a legal liability for the affairs of the school; about 5.6m people help to run sports clubs; 750,000 people volunteer to assist teachers in schools; 170,000 volunteer in the NHS, befriending and counseling patients, driving people to hospital, fund raising, running shops and cafes, etc. Of course, these activities often bring individual benefits, too – for example, school governors often have children in the school and parents often help run sports clubs in which their children are active – but the point remains that they undertake activities which have potentially important collective benefits.

Admittedly, these numbers are small (with the exception of the sports club volunteers), compared to the 1.8m regular blood donors, the 8m people signed up as potential organ donors, and the 10m people within Neighborhood Watch schemes, all of which are more 'lonely' activities, which do not need to be programmed to the same extent within a person's daily timetable.

Nevertheless, the value of the contribution made by co-producers cannot be estimated simply by a head count. The potential 'external' benefits listed in an earlier section suggest that collective co-production may be sufficiently attractive to make its increase an appropriate target for public intervention, if the costs were kept commensurate. In the next sections, we consider how this might be achieved.

There are a number of different theoretical approaches, which can help us to explain what lies behind the marked differences in citizen responses in respect of individual and collective co-production:

Social network theory: interactions between network agents lead to system behavior that is non-predictable from individual expectations because of the character of the links between actors in the network.

Social movement theory: mobilization of mass action is achieved through individual word of mouth and commitments to small-scale joint action, in connected chains of actors, leading to major collective actions, which reinforce the commitment of the actors to their localized choices.

Complexity theory: small changes in initial conditions can lead to very different system behaviors where actors are connected as complex adaptive systems, e.g. where confidence in medical advice is undermined in relation to one immunization (like MMR), which is therefore shunned by some citizens, although other vaccinations continue to be popular and unproblematic.

What each of these theoretical approaches has in common is that it is based on a non-linearity between the initial inputs to the system and the eventual outcomes. While the mechanisms by means of which this non-linearity takes effect differ between the theories and the models derived from them, they each result in the characteristics of collective behavior being very different from those of the individual behaviors, which triggered it.

The implications are important for public service organizations – for maximum returns from the potential of co-production, these collective behaviors may need to be activated, through some form of system meta-interventions[5].

Of course, there are not only positive synergies – where negative synergies occur, which threaten to drive systems towards stasis or even destruction, by the same logic there is a need for system meta-interventions which make these effects less likely or less powerful.

Possible strategies for activating the positive synergies, which could make user and community co-production more cost-effective, would include:

- Increasing the incentives for collective behavior
- Decreasing the disincentives for collective behavior
- Increasing the connectivity of those giving rise to positive synergies in collective behavior
- Decreasing the connectivity of those giving rise to negative synergies in collective behavior.

We here focus on the latter two strategies around connectivity. Its importance derives from the fact that connectivity determines the level (and direction) of nonlinearities in the system through three different characteristics:

- strength of the connectivity
- degree of non-linearity ('curvature') in the connectivity relationship
- likelihood of changes of direction in system behavior over time (determined by the 'recursiveness' of the system, broadly the number of 'turning points' in the underlying relationship, or 'equation', describing system behavior).

In ordinary personal relationships, these characteristics can be seen respectively in terms of how the relationship is viewed by an individual:

- a strong relationship will lead more often to positive reciprocal behaviors (such as the giving of meaningful presents) than a weak relationship, while a weak relationship will lead more often to negative reciprocal behaviors (such as trading insults in public)

- a highly non-linear relationship will mean that quite small changes in behaviors by one or other person will produce marked responses from the other person (e.g. a hint of overworking by one person will lead to an offer of sharing of some tasks from several colleagues)
- a highly recursive relationship will mean that a stimulus by one person will, over time, result in unexpected switches in behavior by the other person (e.g. allowing a colleague to miss a deadline at work because of family circumstances means that a similar excuse is often wheeled out in the future, without any forewarning being given).

These characteristics can be embedded in the relationship in one of two ways – they can either be a result of the 'personalities' of the two actors in the relationship (i.e. their predisposition to act in particular ways), or they can be a result of the mechanisms through which they interact (i.e. the 'technology' of the relationship).

In this chapter, our interest is in how the latter of these two mechanisms, the technology of the relationship between actors, might influence the balance of 'individual' versus 'collective' co-production.

In a personal relationship, the key way in which the strength of the relationship is reinforced is through mutual contact. From its advent, even a simple one-to-one communications technology like the telephone greatly increased the possibility of frequent contact between people in any kind of relationship (at least, for those who had the means to use it). However, increased frequency is not enough to help a relationship to flourish – the content of the interaction is also important. We can hypothesize, then, that the telephone may have polarized relationships – where the content of calls was regarded as positive, the increased frequency was likely to produce stronger bonds, while weaker bonds (and even outright antipathy) may have been produced in those cases of increased contact where the content was regarded as unattractive.

As regards the effect of the telephone on the 'curvature' of relationships, we need to ask if the intensity of relationships was in any way enhanced by the advent of the telephone.

The evidence base is not detailed or scientific, but nevertheless very compelling – people found that it was very much more personal and intimate to talk to each other on the telephone than to write. It seems likely that this new form of connectivity had a more than proportionate effect on the ability of people to sustain their relationships while apart.

Finally, the effect on a relationship of using the telephone to keep in constant contact is not necessarily monotonic – satiation can mean that a turning point occurs, beyond which diseconomies are experienced. For example, someone who rings too often can become perceived as a nuisance, rather than a close friend, or can evince a reaction which is either one of delight or irritation, depending on the circumstances (and irrespective of the content of the call).

It seems likely that the replacement of landlines by mobile phones has not fundamentally altered the effect of the telephone on connectivity within relationships, although it has strengthened each of the three elements of connectivity. However, the internet, and especially Web 2.0 platforms, now offer rather different potential for the three dimensions of connectivity.

First, they are likely to lead to substantially stronger connectivity because of the ease and low cost of use (at least for those people who are 'wired').

Secondly, there is likely to be very strong 'curvature' in relationships which are web-enabled, partly because of the multiple formats of web-enabled communication – email, webcam, Skype, Twitter,

Facebook, YouTube, Flickr, etc. Moreover, the potential for each partner to introduce other actors into any given conversation is greatly expanded – the power of the 'Reply to all' button in email, something which is still very restricted on the telephone, where conference calls are possible but not easy (and not cheap). Twitter actually broadcasts all tweets automatically to everyone who wants to access them.

Finally, the recursiveness of web-enabled relationships is more difficult to estimate a priori. On the one hand, it is just as possible to get too many emails (or tweets or Facebook messages) from some contacts as it is on the telephone. However, emails have the useful characteristic that there is no expectation that the person to whom one writes will be online and able to reply immediately. Therefore, emails retain a 'batch processing' expectation, which means that they can be dealt with when one wishes to, without necessarily hurting the feelings of the person who is waiting. (Of course, not replying to reminder emails has more or the less the same effect on a relationship as not replying to a reminder telephone call). It may be that this latter phenomenon reduces the recursiveness of internet-enabled connectivity.

Taking these characteristics of internet-enabled connectivity into account, we might expect that not only would the internet increase the potential for collective co-production, it might also broaden its reach to a wider range of potential co-producers. This argument suggests that collective co-production is likely now to be more practical to mobilize than in previous periods. It remains to be seen whether these improvements in connectivity will be enough to overcome the individualist preference-based obstacles to collective-based co-production, which we outlined from the European survey.

Public interventions to promote internet-enabled collective co-production

Our European study revealed that policy makers and practitioners are still very ambivalent about the contribution which co-production makes and could make to public service improvement. While they recognize that co-production exists, and can both ensure that services are more in line with user needs and are more fully resourced than they otherwise would be, they are also reluctant to admit to the volume of co-production activity and the contribution which it makes to public value.

However, a series of internet-enabled interventions are emerging which have the effect of enhancing collective co-production. We list here some examples mainly from the UK, but similar developments can be found in the other countries in our European study, using a framework for different types of co-production[6].

Co-planning: South Bristol Digital Neighbourhoods has been working with Bristol City Council to help local residents to use the council's consultation site AskBristol.com, which is part of the EU e-participation project Citizenscape, and allows residents' comments to influence council decisions. The current consultation project focuses on traffic noise pollution, and the website uses video, sound bites, images and discussion forums to encourage debate. Residents can nominate their favorite quiet areas of the city and plot them on a map - and this map is hosted on the interactive information touch screen at local shopping centers for those who don't have Internet access at home. The information gathered feeds in to how Bristol implements the city's noise action plan.

Co-design: The Birmingham's 'Open City' project was developed by Digital Birmingham to create new digital resources, going beyond forums and blogs, which will enable citizens better to contribute to local decision-making. It develops an online community that allows people to influence the planning and delivery of services, through an interactive approach which generates discussion and debate between web users.

Co-commissioning: experiments in internet-based participatory budgeting (PB) are becoming more common, especially in Germany, where Berlin-Lichtenberg has run its PB process through the internet, by post and through local meetings and, more recently, Köln has run a purely internet-based PB exercise, which is currently being evaluated.

Co-managing: a 'Smart Community' is a neighborhood where the residents are better connected to each other and to the businesses and agencies that serve them, including local TV channels and local information and online services, with specialist provision for those who need it. It is intended to make residents feel more a part of their local neighborhood and to make the area as a whole more desirable as a place to live. It is achieved through a local high bandwidth network connecting all homes, businesses and other service providers, which also enables cost-effective management of the digital services delivered to individual homes. Originating in San Diego in the US, this approach has now been developed and piloted in Scotland[7].

Co-delivering: Cheltenham Borough Council initially discovered the power of Web 2.0 in July 2007, as a result of massive local flooding, when its old web site could not respond to the flow of news and information, so it set up a 'flood blog' to provide a responsive and fast service to residents. Subsequently, this has triggered widespread adoption of Web 2.0 by Council staff and the public. Residents can publish images to the Cheltenham Flickr feed and movies through the Cheltenham YouTube channel – directly to the Council's site, all controlled via its content management system.

Co-monitoring: websites such as FixMyStreet.com allow residents to report problems in the street scene, e.g. tipped rubbish bins, potholes in the road, incorrect street signs, etc., including posting photos of the problem on the website, so that fast action can be taken.

Co-evaluating: websites such as patientopinion.com allow NHS patients to post their experiences of healthcare on the internet for other users to read and benefit from, and they can rate NHS services on criteria such as standard of medical care.

In each of these cases, while individuals have been helped by the internet to co-produce public services with professionals from public agencies, the co-production process has had a collective character and had outcomes for more people than those who directly took part in the co-production process.

This chapter highlights the limitations of 'self-interested' co-production and suggests that a more systematic and coordinated approach to collective co-production is needed if it is to rise above the levels which will result from purely 'self-organizing' activities. It suggests that collective co-production is likely to have particular significance for the public sector, where it can be encouraged, but the behavior of citizens is more likely to give rise to individual co-production, unless encouragement is given to mechanisms which lead to more collective co-production. Internet-enabled technologies fulfill the requirements that make collective co-production easier and more likely.

Tony Bovaird (@tonybovaird) is Professor of Public Management and Policy, INLOGOV and Centre for Public Service Partnerships, Birmingham University. He has advised OECD and UK government on assessing the performance of e-government and directed the UK component of the recent EU Presidency project on user and community co-production of public services.

Elke Loeffler is Chief Executive of Governance International, a non-profit organization based in the UK, which promotes good governance, participatory budgeting and citizen co-production of public services. She has advised the UK Cabinet Office and many European governments on citizen participation and directed the recent EU Presidency project on user and community co-production of public services.

James Downe is a Senior Research Fellow at the Centre for Local & Regional Government Research, Cardiff University. He is an expert in local government policy and managed the recent meta-evaluation of Local Government Modernization Reforms in England, on behalf of the Office of the Deputy Prime Minister and the Department for Communities and Local Government.

---

[1] Tony Bovaird and James Downe (2008), Innovation In Public Engagement And Co-Production Of Services. Policy Paper to Department of Communities and Local Government. London: CLG.

[2] Our thanks go to the Department of Communities and Local Government and the French Presidency of the EU, both of which sponsored some of the research on which this chapter is based.

[3] Richard Normann (1984), Service Management: Strategy and Leadership in the Service Business, John Wiley and Sons.

[4] Elke Löffler, Tony Bovaird, Salvador Parrado and Greg van Ryzin (2008), "If you want to go fast, walk alone. If you want to go far, walk together": Citizens and the co-production of public services. Report to the EU Presidency. Paris: Ministry of Finance, Budget and Public Services.

[5] Tony Bovaird (2005), "E-government and e-governance: organisational implications, options and dilemmas" in Mehdi Khosrow-Pour (ed), Practicing E-Government: A Global Perspective, New York: Idea-Group Inc for OECD.

[6] Tony Bovaird (2007), "Beyond engagement and participation – user and community co-production of public services", Public Administration Review, 67 (5): 846-860 (2007).

[7] http://www.smartcommunityfife.org.uk

#24

OPEN VALUE CREATION AS A STRATEGIC MANAGEMENT APPROACH

Philipp S. Müller
Center for Public Management and Governance

In 2008, I was working for Terri Takai, California's CIO, on the question of how we can implement social media and massive collaboration as a tool to improve interaction between Mexican and US border states. At the time, debating open value creation in government seemed slightly foreign. In 2009 we are confronted with new management approaches in mediated policy initiation and formulation (Obama's Open Government Initiative[1]), distributed intelligence gathering (the US intelligence communities Intellipedia[2]), crowdsourcing of accountability (The Guardian's British Parliament invoice scandal platform[3]), citizen involvement (participatory budgeting in 160 cities in Germany) or peer produced political campaigning (the Obama Campaign), and even social media enhanced revolutions (Iran). Not everything that business or government does can be addressed by these new mechanisms, but with technologically mediated open value creation we have been handed a powerful tool to make the world a better place[4]. Tim O'Reilly asks the pertinent questions in Forbes (and in his chapter in this book):

> *How does government itself become an open platform that allows people inside and outside government to innovate? How do you design a system in which all of the outcomes aren't specified beforehand, but instead evolve through interactions between the technology provider and its user community?*

The idea of government (or business) as a platform necessitates an open value creation process. Open Value Creation consists of Open Policy Making (participation) and an Open Value Chain (collaboration). The distinction is slightly arbitrary but useful. It allows us to differentiate between coming up with a value generating process (policy) and repeatedly creating the value (value chain).

- Open policy making aims to open all aspects of the policy process (initiation, formulation, implementation, evaluation) to outside inputs and scrutiny. It assumes that this allows better informed policy making that is more legitimate and less costly.
- The open value chain opens the implementation process (inputs, process, outputs, impact, outcome) to outside contributions under the assumption that a co-produced public value is less costly and more effective.

Open value creation can be achieved if it is applied in all phases of the policy cycle and the value chain. At the Erfurt School of Public Policy[5] we refer to the IDCA framework (ideation, deliberation // collaboration, accountability) for this purpose:

1. Ideation (policy)
Ideation is the process of collectively coming up with ideas and developing them. What is need is a platform that allows participants to post ideas, to comment and to weed out the bad apples.

2. Deliberation (policy)

We understand deliberation best, because it has its analog in the offline world and there is sufficient text about it. The idea is to create a space in which the better argument and not the structurally advantaged position wins. What is needed is a platform to present ideas, discuss them both syn- and diachronically, and to weigh them in concordance with the underlying governance principle (think Digg-style, Reddit-style, or IMDB-style).

3. Collaboration (value chain)

We have most difficulties with collaboration, because it is new. Collaboration allows access to the work-flow by self-selected outsiders. The idea is to make the work flow modular, granular and redundant, so that very different contributions can be integrated without endangering the quality of the output. A collaboration platform must be governed by a combination of self-enforcing code, simple but strong core principles, and an inclusive culture (think Canonical's Launchpad or Wikipedia).

4. Accountability (value chain)

Accountability is often not well understood. We see it as a danger and not a strategic asset. By accounting to our stakeholders, we decrease our error rates by adding free expertise and increase legitimacy, and public pride and ownership.

Core Technologies of Open Value Creation

Open value creation is possible because of new technologies that allow us to structure idea generation and information aggregation in digital form. The core technologies of open value creation are the wiki (principle-based, user-generated platforms, with flexible moderation capacity), the forum (question driven user-generated knowledge platform), blogging (core message with feedback/discourse loop), and work flow management and visualization tools (Government resource planning, government process mapping tools, think SAP, Oracle, SugarCRM, etc.). Together they allow us to structure policy and administrative public value creation processes, by enhancing ideation (idea-generation), deliberation (commenting and discussion), collaboration (generating public values), and accountability (parsing data to hold government accountable).

In order to fully utilize open value creation radical transparency is necessary. Radical transparency is a management approach in which all decision making is carried out publicly and the work flow has open application interfaces. It is a radical departure from existing processes, where (a) decision making was never fully open, to ensure security and the discretion of the decision makers and (b) the work flow was a black box, where outside intervention would be looked upon as outside meddling.

Decision Making (policy cycle)	Ensure access to draft documents, allow commenting and include the public in final decisions.
Work Flow (value chain)	Design application interfaces that allow the public to access the work flow in real time and participate in a granular and modular fashion.

What is the value added of the approach?

It is important to realize that radical transparency is not a requirement put upon a process from outside stakeholders, but an actively chosen strategy. So why go transparent? Radical transparency impacts value identification, capacity and legitimacy of any project.

Value definition	Value definition profits from the wider discussion. Group thinking is potentially avoided.
Legitimacy	It increases legitimacy, because stakeholders are involved in the decision making process and trust is increased.
Capacity	Capacity is increased if radical transparency allows you to integrate "self-selected experts" into your decision cycle and resulting work flow. It saves costs!

When to apply it?

As with any management strategy, radical transparency is not a panacea. So the question is what types of problems are amenable to the approach and what types of problems are better left in the dark.

Coordination Issues	In today's world, many issues are coordination issues. The legitimacy and quality of standard-setting will approve dramatically.
Consensus Building	Many issues today have become trans-national and cross-sectoral. This means that there are no established and institutionalized decision making procedures. In such situations, radical transparency can dramatically increase the legitimacy (and effectiveness) of the procedures.
Uncovering distributed expertise	In today's world expertise is not anymore monopolized by professionals. However, finding this distributed expertise is expensive. By utilizing radical transparency (in combination with functioning quality control), one allows for self-selection of expertise.
Utilizing the love of the amateurs	There are topics where we know that amateurs will be very willing to cooperate. Think of the inclusion of amateur astronomers in the identification of new meteors.

When not to apply it?

There are other issues, where it is best not to pursue a radical transparent approach:

Security	If radical transparency endangers (national) security, the topic should be off-topic. However, it makes sense to clearly and openly delineate the boundaries of such limitations.
Privacy	If there is no way of ensuring the anonymity of data and if the issue would impact the privacy of individuals, the approach should not be used.
Secrecy	If the competitiveness of an enterprise depends on the secrecy of the process (think the Coca Cola formula), radical transparency shall not be used.
Design	If the design of the output should follow a specific (totalitarian) idea, it is not sensible to open up the process. Apple Computers uses this approach.
Capture	If the platform is relevant enough that it can be captured by off-topic participants, management of the process becomes tedious. This has happened with the UFO believers and the Obama birth certificate debaters on the Open Government Initiative.

How to design radically transparent procedures? (A rough guide to implementation)

At this point in time, we are not yet very good at designing open value creation policy cycles and value chains. For every successful example, there are many failures. Therefore, a very careful implementation strategy is necessary. I have developed the following framework from the more than 10 projects we have been working on in the last year.

Scope	Define what data you will free.
Trajectory	Explain the limitations explicitly, outline the next steps to full transparency.
Open Access	Make sure you make all data available in machine-readable format, ideally in real-time. Do not massage or edit it!
Engagement Principles	Do not define who will be able to access your data, let your collaborators self-select. But, define standards for participation, do this in code and convention.
Moderation	Structure the conversation, define expectations, but allow for flexibility and participation in the debate about the core principles of the collaboration. Do not ask open questions like "what do you think of Europe? How do we integrate minorities?"[6]
Reflexivity	Design reflexivity into the process. Use work flow mapping and meta-data on the deliberation processes to mirror the community back at its members. Sophistication will increase.

Using these frameworks we are working on many such projects with municipal (participatory budgeting, crowdsourcing security), state level (knowledge management, cross-border collaboration), and federal level stakeholders (legal ramifications of new forms of collaboration, strategy development) worldwide. Open value creation has become a mainstream strategic management approach.

Philipp S. Müller (@philippmueller) is visiting professor for public policy at Erfurt University, tenured associate professor at the Graduate School for Public Administration and Public Policy of Tecnológico de Monterrey, Mexico (EGAP – Tec de Monterrey) and adjunct professor at the Salzburg School of Management, where he runs the Center for Public Management and Governance. In his research, he focuses on policy making in network society. He has published Unearthing the Politics of Globalization *(LIT 2004) and* Criticizing Global Governance *(Palgrave MacMillan 2005).*

---

[1] http://j.mp/3mkJnQ
[2] http://j.mp/3ckFU
[3] http://mps-expenses.guardian.co.uk/
[4] http://j.mp/12c2UT
[5] http://www.espp.de/
[6] http://j.mp/Lngvh

#25

REAPING THE BENEFITS OF GOVERNMENT-LED CHANGE: ENGAGING THE PUBLIC IN CREATING VALUE FROM INVESTMENTS

Chris Potts

Corporate Strategist, Dominic Barrow

Governments invest public money in changing some things for the better while keeping others the same. Their publics - including taxpayers and voters - are becoming used to having information in the palms of their hands, and with it the power to make new or different choices. How should governments best provide their "2.0" publics with evidence that the changes they are investing in are the most efficient way of delivering the value they promised? And how can they harness everyone's increasing power as consumers, to maximize that value?

Governments preside over a balance of change and stability. But they understandably assume that we vote for them, and judge them, based more on what they promise to do differently than what they will keep the same. For example, Barack Obama's 2009 US presidency campaign rallying call, "Yes We Can," was talking primarily about change, not the challenge of keeping things as they were under George W. Bush.

Change is an easy thing for newly-elected governments to promise with credibility. Conversely, one of the big challenges facing any long-term government, such as the British government under Gordon Brown, and similarly its Conservative predecessors, is how to credibly promise, execute and deliver the benefits of changes to the status quo, when this was themselves. Their main rationale for change must be founded on factors in the wider environment – for example, economic, cultural, technological – to which the government must respond differently than before.

"Government 2.0" is all of these things. In reverse order, the technological innovations that initiated "2.0" very rapidly translated into cultural changes that are starting to deeply affect the economic systems over which governments have primary stewardship. Consumers, with new forms of information in their hands and (often free) tools with which to wield it, are taking both individual and collective control of processes and choices that were until recently assumed to be in the hands of governments and of commercial organizations. Some of those organizations, and the markets they are in, are reacting better to this shift in power than others.

Consider the US market for telephony. Consumers, armed with information about the relative benefits and costs of mobile telephones and landlines, are increasingly giving up their fixed-line phones. As The Economist observed[1], this technology decision is also a socioeconomic one. The more that Americans abandon the fixed-line phone network, the more fragile it becomes as its fixed costs have to be met by fewer and fewer subscribers. The consequences are the subject of governmental and societal, as well as commercial, interests: landlines are the platform for many public services, such as emergency response; taxes on landlines provide subsidies that ensure a "universal service", meaning an affordable phone line for all.

Government 2.0 (like Enterprise 2.0 for commercial organizations) means a new settlement between institutions and the public. While governments are investing in changes on behalf of the public, the public is empowered to make more choices that significantly impact government. How can governments make sure that everyone benefits?

For a start, by recognizing that the genie is out of the bottle. In time, the balance of power between government and public will settle at a new and different equilibrium than before. Governments who seek to convince their publics that they are 'granting' them more choice will be increasingly off the pace. We, the investors in, and consumers of, government services are already taking those choices on ourselves. Better to inform and channel the energy of our choices, than assume that it is still within your gift to give them to us. Government strategies for investing in change must shift more towards harnessing the emergent choices of the public.

In making choices and investing in changes, there are many valuable ways in which governments differ from commercial enterprises, but in this respect they are very similar: they divide their resources into servicing today's operational needs, and making changes for the future. The difference with governments is that they are investing public resources, not their own. Make these investments transparent to the public, and they are more likely to understand how their own choices affect government decisions (for example, the longer-term consequences of giving up fixed-line telephones), also to take a more active role in contributing to those decisions and the changes that come from them, and in maximizing the value of government-led investments in change.

So, with Government 2.0 comes a need to be much more transparent about investments in government-led change: the resources that are being invested, the efficiency with which the value of changes is being delivered, and what choices we, the public, can make that maximize the benefits of those changes both to ourselves and to society as a whole.

For this, we need a reasonably straightforward summary: why our government is investing in changes on our behalf; the anticipated value of those changes to us; how much is being invested; what benefits are actually being achieved; and how can we further contribute to maximizing those benefits? By taking stock of this 'portfolio' of investments we can assess whether our government is doing the best job it can and – if we are so motivated – more actively influence the future value of investments in change under both current and future governments.

In the US an approach that newly-elected President Obama took to this opportunity was to rapidly appoint a Federal Chief Information Officer (CIO), Vivek Kundra, who had a track record of treating government-led changes – more specifically those in Information Technology (IT) – as if they were stock-market investments. In this approach, projects are subject to ongoing, robust investment management: those that will still deliver their expected value are nurtured, while those that won't are cancelled and the investment moved elsewhere.

A key strength of a 'projects are like stocks' approach is that it brings – with vital adjustments – some long-established principles of portfolio investment into the realm of government investments in change. The fundamental purpose of the portfolio is to deliver its promised value as efficiently as possible. Investments are evaluated on their value contribution, and risk, to the portfolio (not simply on their standalone merits). Only efficient changes get backed, and projects that fall below their 'stop loss' threshold are quickly stopped. Finally, inheriting and adapting a key principle of investment theory – diversification to ensure efficiency – the portfolio is balanced across a range of value types, mitigating the risk that change projects may collectively deliver not enough of one kind of value, and too much of another.

US Government responsibilities for using IT "to improve the productivity, efficiency, and effectiveness of Federal programs, including through dissemination of public information"[2] are enshrined in US law, in the 1996 'Clinger-Cohen' Act. In June 2009, within a few months of his appointment, Kundra published on the internet a Federal IT Dashboard of how well the government was performing in the delivery of "IT investments". Initially, 20% of investments were included. By early August 2009, that had risen to 100%.

The Federal IT Dashboard provides a new - but incomplete - example of how governments can use IT to disseminate public information about the changes they are investing in. With it, the US government has established a "2.0" model of transparency and accountability about investments in change that other governments might follow.

However, the specific focus on investments in IT can only be a temporary one if the Dashboard is to be of true value to the public. Organizations that have mastered investments in change by starting with 'IT investments' know that it can be a valid initial tactic, as long as that is not where the process ends. As Kundra himself has hinted, the IT dashboard should act as a model for a much wider and more valuable approach: "... we need to adopt an evidence based approach to governance by employing platforms like the IT dashboard so we can report, analyze, monitor, and predict performance."[3]

How much a government invests in the IT elements of change is of little practical value to the public - or indeed the government itself. While IT offers people the opportunities to deliver more value, on its own it delivers none. Delivering the benefits of change demands more investment than just in IT. Also, in IT-specific dashboards, changes are naturally expressed more in technological terms making their meaning opaque to the public. An 'IT Investments Dashboard' can be a good place to start, and may be quicker and easier to compile and publish than an 'Investments in Change Dashboard' but will be of little value to Government 2.0 if the focus remains on IT alone.

As rapidly as possible, before it becomes the de facto standard, an 'IT investments' dashboard needs to be upgraded to one that accounts for total investments in change, of which IT is just one element.

So, as governments and their CIOs look to harness the energy and choices of a "2.0" public, by disseminating information about government-led investments in change, here are three things in particular worth bearing in mind:

- The "projects are like stocks" approach is only truly valuable and effective when applied to all investments in change, not just those involving IT, and certainly not when it is only accounting for the IT elements of change.

- Treating projects like stocks needs robust competencies in investment portfolio management. Like Kundra, many CIOs in both government agencies and commercial organizations have been developing these competencies, but often only for IT. If so, it's time to upgrade their focus, to the total investments in change and not just IT.

- Measures designed for choosing, targeting and measuring the value of stock market investments are not appropriate for investing in government-led change. In particular, using a single measure of 'value', such as Net Present Value, is unrepresentative of the diverse reasons that governments invest in change, and therefore of the value of those investments.

  Instead, government CIOs need to use a portfolio of different value types (typically around ten), ones that make sense to the public, as the foundation of their dashboards and their 'projects as stocks' portfolio management.

Transparency with the public about government-led investments in change is a vital element of Government 2.0. It reflects, and informs, the shift in the balance of power between governments and their publics, in parallel with a similar shift in power between consumer and companies that characterizes Enterprise 2.0.

As well as making sure our governments are transparently accounting for the investments they make in change on our behalf, and the benefits that come from them, it can help us all see what we can do to fully exploit those changes once made. However, governments need to be wary of the irony that, while IT is a major tool for achieving transparency about our government's investments in IT – and a relatively quick and easy place to start – would be of little help if that were all the information given to us with which to maximize the benefit of government-led change.

Chris Potts (@chrisdpotts) is a Corporate Strategist, who specializes in investments in change and exploiting IT. He is the author of "fruITion: Creating the Ultimate Corporate Strategy for Information Technology."

---

[1] The Economist, August 13th 2009
[2] Clinger-Cohen Act 1996
[3] Vivek Kundra blog, http://it.usaspending.gov, August 5th 2009

#26

E-GOVERNMENT AWARDS: FIVE PROPOSITIONS ON ADVANCING THEIR VALUE

Kim Normann Andersen
Professor, Copenhagen Business School (CBS)

Hanne Sørum
PhD student, Norwegian School of Information Technology

Rony Medaglia
Assistant Professor, Copenhagen Business School (CBS)

E-government rankings and awards are more popular than ever, as exemplified by the UN eReadiness rankings, the statistical indicators on the European i2010 information society, and the newly established Asia annual Government Technology Awards. Fifteen years of online services have not reduced the need to focus attention on the ongoing improvement of public sector websites. Having a high quality website is probably more important now than ever before, and governments today need to present websites that emphasize clear missions if they are to satisfy the user's needs and business goals. Evaluating public websites is also profitable work for consultants and practitioners.

With yet more web layers, rich media, and web 2.0 tools being integrated in websites, web awards are facing not only the challenge of more websites to evaluate, but also more challenging tasks, since the use of websites in government is no longer exclusively about broadcasting information to citizens, but it is also increasingly about narrowcasting and co-creating content together with citizens.

In this chapter we will put forward five propositions on the state of art of e-government web awards:

1. The value of e-government awards is linked to the technical assessment, the interaction that takes place during the award ceremony, and the ex post exposure of the award winners;
2. There is a need to respond to the fact that web awards to a large extent ignore the actual use of the websites, and therefore rarely lead to business benefits or public value;
3. The current web awards are widening the gap between the strategy and the usefulness of e-government websites by using traditional methods for website quality measurements – such as crawlers, expert opinions, pop-up user surveys, etc. – and thus ignoring the use of public websites in real settings;
4. More refined indicators of success of websites need to be developed in order to reduce an implicit positive bias favoring websites with high frequency of use, and thereby to value also web avoidance services;
5. The understanding of the dynamics of e-government needs to be extended in order for practitioners and researchers to progress from knowing who has the best website to also understanding how they manage to progress and be successful.

In the following, we will substantiate the propositions by drawing on ongoing discussions within the EGovMoNet project[1], on an ongoing study of web awards in Scandinavia[2], and on preliminary indicators from a review of the European e-Government Awards. We do not claim any external validity in the propositions; we merely see them as an input to the progression of the research body that addresses e-government maturity models and how to approach the evaluation of website quality[3]. Also, we aim at giving an input to the thinking and fine-tuning of the awards.

The European e-Government Awards

At the EU level, the European e-Government Award is handed out every second year. As shown in Table 1, about 300 e-Government cases are part of the European e-Government award process that has taken place for now six years.

	Number of submissions	Number of finalists	Number of countries represented
2003	357	66	29 of 32 eligible
2005	234	52	28 of 33 eligible
2007	310	52	31 of 34 eligible
2009	259	52	n.a.

Table 1. European e-Government Awards 2003-2009: Number of submissions, number of finalists and number of countries represented. Source: Data compiled from the ePractice portal, September 2009.

The eleven winners during the past three award ceremonies have excelled in categories such as participation and transparency, and effective and efficient administration. In Table 2 we have provided an overview of each of the award categories. At this stage in our research we have not made any explicit impact analysis of the European E-government Awards, but it can be clearly observed that the awarded cases are highlighted on the EU Commission's website as good practices, and are intended to serve as an inspiration. The winners in 2007 were divided in four categories: better public services for growth and jobs, participation and transparency, social impact and cohesion public services, and effective and efficient administration. A closer look at the individual cases of winning website provides interesting insights. The City of Amsterdam, which won the award for "better public services for growth and jobs," launched a website targeting those opening a bar, hotel or restaurant:

> *"To open a bar, hotel or a restaurant in Amsterdam, an entrepreneur needs to obtain licenses and dispensations from more than 18 different authorities, creating a difficult obstacle for those trying to set up a business. Through the HoReCa1 one-stop shop, an entrepreneur can easily find out which selection of 40 governmental documents has to be obtained through answering 20 questions and filling out one single form for seven local licenses of the City of Amsterdam. At the national level, the reduction possibilities are up to €30.2 million a year for both the administrative costs and burdens." (Source: http://www.epractice.eu/awards)*

Among the Scandinavian countries, *Mypage* from Norway and *Electronic Invoicing* from Denmark have been the winners of awards in 2007 and 2005, respectively. For the Norwegian *Mypage*, the following motivation was listed:

> *"Mypage is a user-defined and secured citizen's portal on which users can carry out personalized public eServices in one place. Norwegian citizens can also control information about them held by various public administrations. From May 2007, some 200 services from more than 40 public administrations have been provided, serving more than 200,000 registered citizens. Through citizen participation and increasing demands, services already in place and competition between the administrations, the administrations will open registers and create new services. The goal is that all relevant services from all levels of administration will be available through Mypage by the end of 2009." (Source: http://www.epractice.eu/awards)*

In the submitted documentation from the Danish *Electronic Invoicing* award winner in 2005, it was stated that:

"Electronic invoicing became mandatory in Denmark on 1 February, 2005. 15 million transactions that were previously handled in paper are now managed electronically. The new system has resulted in savings of an estimated € 120-150 million per year. Electronic Invoicing is now compulsory in Denmark, and is supported by a recent law which gave the Minister of Finance the authority to establish a legislative framework for electronic invoicing. EID was the result of a public/ private partnership that made use of successful and established technology. The central infrastructure uses dedicated networks (VANS) and offices called Read-In Bureaus. Documents sent across this network are based on a standard variant of XML, OIO-XML. By providing security and convenience for the supplier, this system enables all public sector partners to computerize all internal work processes and systems. This example of a national government showing readiness for eGovernment also demonstrates how organizational transformation and back office innovation takes place across the public sector."
(Source: http://www.epractice.eu/awards)

The three award winners from Netherlands, Norway and Denmark well exemplify the variety of websites submitted and bring attention to the variance in readiness from different parts of government. What at first hand could be interpreted as a very advanced solution from Denmark, the electronic invoice case, is probably most of all interesting and could serve as inspiration due to the use of political and normative instruments in getting e-government processes digitalized by asking private sector to submit electronic invoices and, through this external shock, pushing back-office innovation in the public sector.

Year and place of EU ministerial conference	Overall theme	Categories of winners	Winner
2007 (19-21 September 2007 in Lisbon)	Reaping the Benefits of e-Government	Better public services for growth and jobs	"HoReCa1," One-stop-shop for Hotel Restaurant Café licenses, submitted by the Economic Development Department, City of Amsterdam, The Netherlands[4].
		Participation and transparency	"Mypage: Self-service Citizen Portal," submitted by Norge.no, portal of the Ministry of Government Administration and Reform of Norway[5].
		Social impact and cohesion public services	"Besancon.clic," submitted by the City of Besançon, France[6].
		Effective and efficient administration:	"DVDV - German Administration Services Directory," submitted by BIT the Portal of the Federal Government of Germany[7].
2005 (Manchester, UK November 23-24)	Transforming Public Services	The right environment	KSI ZUS - Complex Computer System (KSI) for the Social Insurance Institution (ZUS) in Poland, Social Insurance Institution (PL)[8].
		Government readiness	EID - Electronic Invoicing in Denmark, Agency of Governmental Management (DK)[9].
		Service use	Kadaster-on-line, Kadaster (NL)[10].
		Impact	ROS - Revenue Online Service, ROS, Revenue Commissioners (IE)[11].
2003 (Como, Italy July 3-4)	Good Practices for Improving Public eServices and Transforming Government	The role of e-Government in European Competitiveness	Bremen On-line Services, Senator for Finances - Department for New Media and e-Government (DE)[12].
		A Better life for European Citizens	HELP - Virtual Guide to Austrian Authorities and Institutions, Federal Chancellery (AT)[13].
		European, Central and Local e-Government e-Cooperation	Tax Information between Public Administrations, Agencia Tributaria, Departamento de Informática Tributaria (ES)[14].

Table 2. European e-Government Awards 2003-2007: Place of Award Ceremony, Overall Theme, Categories of Winners and Winners. Source: Data retrieved from http://www.epractice.eu/awards

Scandinavian Web Awards

Focusing on the national web awards in Scandinavia, it is striking to notice how many of these web awards are complementary in how they measure website quality and have overlapping target groups. Although each of the awards aims at adding a sense of objectivity in the award assessment, the transparency and feedback from the assessment varies from extensive documentation of methods and results, to more informal feedback. In general, the public awards (organized by governments) are well documented in the way that the results from the evaluation process are detailed and publicly available on the Internet, in comparison with most of the private ones. On the web one can also find previous results from the awards organized by the government, so that they can be compared with prior results for each of each of the websites participating in the competition. The public awards are also generally more extensive with respect to the number of websites covered and the means to get websites involved.

Regarding accessibility and the use of WAI (Web Accessibility Initiative) principles, which is a central evaluation criterion, so far this has been primarily related to the evaluation of public websites organized by the government itself. One example of this is that the Norwegian government stated that, by the end of 2007, 80 % of all official websites should meet *Norge.no*'s quality criteria regarding accessibility. Accessibility has been one of the three main quality criteria in the yearly evaluation and ranking of about 700 public websites, organized by the government in Norway (The Agency for Public Management and e-Government). Using this as an evaluation criterion for public websites is one way of focusing on website quality aspects that the government finds important in order to satisfy citizens with various needs. In the Norwegian case, there is a large use of very technical evaluation criteria (e.g. downloading time, number of clicks, etc.), at the expense of the assessment of website contents.

Denmark features a very similar type of quality assessment of public websites on a yearly basis, with the web award "Best on the Net"

(*Bedst på Nettet*). In Denmark the results from the evaluation process are made publicly available. The prizes for best website are handed out at a one-day conference, which is also an important occasion for the participants for networking and social interaction.

Table 3, although it does not cover all the awards in the three Scandinavian countries Norway, Sweden and Denmark, provides an example of the types of websites assessed in each of the ten awards listed. In the awards covering both public and private websites, the number of public ones seems to be in minority.

Country	Web Award	Organizer of the Award	Assessing public websites	Assessing private websites
Norway	Norge.no	The Agency for Public Management and e-Government	X	
	Farmandprisen Beste Nettsted	Farmand Activum	X	X
	Årets nettsted	The Norwegian Communication Association	X	X
	Rosingprisen	The Norwegian Computer Society	X	X
	Gulltaggen	The organization for interactive marketing	X	X
Sweden	Guldlänken	Vinnova and the Swedish Association of Local Authorities and Regions	X	
	Topp 100	IDG Internetworld	X	X
Denmark	Bedst på Nettet	The National Danish IT and Telecom Agency	X	
	E-handelsprisen	The Danish Distance Selling and E-business	X	X
	Digitaliserings-prisen	Rambøll Management Consulting	X	

Table 3. Scandinavian web awards in 2008: Organizers and Private/ Public Sector Scope

A great number of websites is assessed every year in the three Scandinavian countries analyzed, Denmark, Norway and Sweden, greater than the number assessed within the framework of the

European e-Government Awards. Around 600 websites are assessed in the Danish web awards yearly, while around 300 are assessed for the European e-Government Awards (see table 1).

The use of evaluation criteria to measure the quality of a website presentation is mostly carried out through objective measures, that is, measures that allow the assessments to be replicated with almost identical results, regardless of who are the evaluators. The actual user's voice (subjective opinion) seems to be ignored in the evaluation process in these awards. The methods used and evaluation criteria are therefore based on objective, rather than subjective measures. After an initial screening process, all the participants are ranked by quality and then, eventually, an expert jury selects the winner(s) of the award. In most of the awards there are a number of evaluation categories, e.g. best public website, most innovative website and best e-business provider.

Five propositions on how to extend the value of e-government awards

Web awards are an increasingly popular phenomenon that public and private institutions across Europe gather around, receiving widespread attention from the media, the participating agencies and practitioners involved in the e-government policy area. Despite this, little research has focused on studying web awards, even though such phenomenon can be deemed to provide very important insights into a variety of aspects of e-government policy development. These aspects include, but are not limited to, the implicit criteria underlying e-government policies in different national contexts, the adequacy of existing assessing methods, the impact of Web 2.0 and citizen involvement on e-government evaluation, and also the role of social networks in creating shared definition of "e-government excellence." The overview of well-established web award contests at European level and at national level in Scandinavian countries included in this paper has provided a first body of evidence to substantiate some insights on crucial issues related to the future of e-government design and evaluation. Drawing on this evidence, we can substantiate the five propositions on the state of the art of e-government web awards presented in the introduction.

Regarding proposition (1), the motives for participating are not necessarily unevenly distributed among the private and public awards. In public web awards the websites do not have to sign up for participation, which is something they have to do in the private awards. In the Danish public sector award it is mandatory for public sector websites to participate, whereas in the Danish e-business award the participating companies pay a fee for their voluntary assessment. In Norway, the rating by Norge.no is not voluntary, but it is a high-publicity event in which the results are made public. Therefore, the quality of public websites can be compared back in time to when the initiative first took place.

With respect to the second proposition (2), it is surprising that what are considered to be traditional Scandinavian methods (living labs, situated practice, user involvement, etc.) are not addressed. This calls for additional research on whether the way website quality is measured lacks credibility within the information systems development circles or whether it would lead to any benefits for the business. The winners of national web awards are highlighted as best practice examples and serve as inspiration for many practitioners. Detailed results from the awards (evaluation process) organized by the Norwegian and Danish government are made publicly available, and therefore public website providers have an opportunity to learn from each other, in order to develop a high quality public website, seen from a government point of view. A discussion that naturally could be raised is the one about to what extent the use of evaluation criteria in these awards actually improve quality, and how and to what extent the participants can use the feedback for quality or business improvements.

Regarding the third proposition (3), we propose that the traditional and conservative choice of variables and methods can lower the website quality and endanger the future for institutionalized web awards. Web 2.0 technologies allow users (and others) to form ad hoc communities to give their feedback, even blunt, on the websites. Factoring in this feedback (by using blog crawlers, etc.), and using this as part of the awards has been ignored so far, but appears to be a road to explore in future research and practice. Consequently, there is a need to extend our knowledge of practice by studying e-government services in use, and our proposition is that we should supplement the pop-up surveys and phone-based surveys with engaged studies of the often low-key technological solutions, such as SMS services and/ or public school extranet services that attract a high and returning number of users.

Regarding the fourth proposition (4), the awards share an implicit bias, according to which the more use and the more users a website has, the better. While in some cases this can contradict the overall rationale for government, it is also conflicting, for instance, with the web strategy for the Danish Ministry of Taxation, which aims at having as few users online as possible. On the contrary, their strategy is to do as much information collection and back office computing as possible, and to ask citizens to do as few interactions with the Ministry of Taxation website as possible. Thus, there is a need to develop methodologies on how to measure and award web avoidance, that is when governmental units use back office operations to reduce or eliminate the need for citizens to be online, and governmental units that use Web 2.0 proactively to increase citizen self-governance. The necessity of focusing on this proposition could also help addressing the worrying figures from the i2010 information society indicators on declining number of citizens using public e-services in 2008.

Regarding the fifth proposition (5), the understanding of the dynamics of e-government needs to be extended in order for practitioners and researchers to progress from knowing who has best website, to also understanding how they managed to progress and be successful. Web awards and catalogues of the websites participating (and ranked) in the national and EU awards can form a solid basis for studies on who, why, and how some manage to stay at the top every year and get awarded in one or more of the national awards for two/ three years. Is it because they manage to attract additional funding/ staff due to the fact that they won the previous year? Or it is because the units developing, implementing and updating the websites get a closer and more constructive collaboration after winning an award?

Dr Kim Normann Andersen (@andersenCBS) is Professor at the Center for Applied ICT (CAICT) at Copenhagen Business School (CBS), and study manager for the e-business program at the IT University of Copenhagen. He has done extensive research on drivers and barriers on uptake of IT in the public sector, engaged in various research projects and networks using normative models and evaluation to give constructive input to how government move forward in the adoption of IT.

Hanne Sørum (@hannesorum) is a PhD student at The Norwegian School of Information Technology in Oslo, where she also works as a lecturer. She will receive her PhD degree from Copenhagen Business School. Her research and publications focus on topics such as eGovernment, website evaluation and the business value of human-computer interaction (HCI).

Rony Medaglia (@Ronyyy) is Assistant Professor at Center for Applied Information and Communication Technology (CAICT) at Copenhagen Business School. His research focus is on IT in the public sector, and he has authored publications in international journals and conferences on e-Government, e-Participation and the use of Web 2.0 applications. He has been part of DEMO_net, a Network of Excellence funded under the European Commission's sixth framework program.

[1] eGovMoNet is a Thematic Network co-funded by the European Commission (CIP project number 224998, Project period: 01-05-2008 – 01-05-2010) to establish a community to review national e-Government measurement frameworks.

[2] Sørum, H., Medaglia, R., & Andersen, K. (2009). Assessment of Website Quality: Scandinavian Web Awards Right on Track? In Electronic Government (pp. 198-209).

[3] See Elling, S., Lentz, L., & de Jong, M. (2007). Website Evaluation Questionnaire: Development of a Research-Based Tool for Evaluating Informational Websites. In *Electronic Government* (pp. 293-304), and van Velsen, L., van der Geest, T., ter Hedde, M., & Derks, W. (2008). Engineering User Requirements for e-Government Services: A Dutch Case Study. In *Electronic Government* (pp. 243-254).

[4] http://www.amsterdam.nl/ondernemen/horeca

[5] http://www.norge.no/minside/

[6] http://www.besancon.fr/index.php?p=510

[7] http://www.dvdv.de

[8] http://www.zus.pl/english.pdf

[9] http://www.oes.dk/

[10] http://www.kadaster.nl/

[11] http://www.revenue.ie/

[12] http://www.bremen.de/

[13] http://www.help.gv.at/

[14] http://www.agenciatributaria.es/

#27

GOVERNMENT 2.0 AND ONWARDS

John Gøtze
Lecturer, Copenhagen Business School

Christian Bering Pedersen
Consultant, Devoteam Consulting

There is much hype, and many ideas, in the Government 2.0 area. Blog entries, books and conferences are everywhere, and new services, web pages and data sets are being launched on a regular basis. And now also this book.

"Government 2.0" has been climbing the steep incline of the hype cycle very fast. But as mentioned in the introduction to this book, a Gartner analyst has already 'seen' the peak. So what happens when we reach the top, and start to look down at the other side? When we all agree, that "Government 2.0" will not save the world, with its open data websites, its transparent government memoranda and manifestos, and its citizen consultations and focus groups. What happens, when we realize that government is just as difficult to change, if not more so, as the private organizations currently working with adopting the tools of web 2.0 as enterprise 2.0 takes hold?

It would be terrible for all this good energy to fizz out and for disillusion to set in.

What if we try to learn from the past cycles of hype and disillusion, and agree that the revolution will not be twittered, written in a wiki or released in XML-format under a Creative Commons license? What if we are realistic, and agree that even though new ways of working and new digital tools have tremendous potential to bring about change, it will still be hard work, it will take a lot of time and many people will resist the change it brings.

The 'hype experts' from Gartner say[1] that the hype cycle is inevitable and that its phases cannot be avoided, but we can at least try to dampen the effect. So how do we do this? In our view, the key is in adopting a pragmatic perspective, where the way to "Government 2.0" bliss is paved with small, incremental victories and continuous improvement. It will be an evolutionary process that will take a lot of cultural and organizational change to produce real and lasting results.

The concrete consequence of a pragmatic approach is a different strategy. It starts with the realization that no person, institution or region can force through significant change on their own, but also in realizing that until more experience is gained with the new tools and in working with Government 2.0, a lot of organizations and entrepreneurs will be exploring new territory on their own. Because of this, projects will be started that will turn out to be unrealistic; some will blow the budget, others will be mired by mistakes and controversy. This is an evolutionary process and these mistakes are unavoidable, so there will be plenty of opportunities to gain experience with what works and what does not work.

These days, we see many new services being built and released, particularly with regards to opening up the data silos of government. Making data readily available is largely a technical challenge in the beginning. Not a trivial challenge, but nevertheless mainly technical. Likewise, a number of similar initiatives about launching collaborative portals with citizens, crowdsourcing ideas and reaching out through new communication channels like YouTube or Twitter have initially focused on the technical side. This is natural, as the technical side is easy to work with and takes less political maneuvering and agreement between different parties.

Although there have been setbacks and problems, the overall experience with these tools has been good, as it is documented by many of the contributors to this book. Parts of the public is interested in interacting, the employees of the public sector are interested in using new and better tools, and it is generally easy for the people to see the point of using new tools that are more social, open and flexible. It is a very interesting time to work in and with government, and the progress that has been made recently is very encouraging.

A successful initiative on opening up government data or processes can lead to bigger things. The relative success of some projects has paved the way for the next phase, and among the early adopters of Government 2.0 some are ready to move to the next level. After the initial period of picking the low-hanging fruit is over, the work of changing how government works starts to get more challenging. Demands, both from inside and outside government, are becoming more sophisticated. When developers start using government data, there are going to be demands for the actuality and availability of this data. When citizens get used to interacting with the government on some projects, they naturally expect this interaction from all parts of the government.

So with time comes the need for serious organizational change in order to further open up government and work more closely with citizens. The organizational change is not going to happen by itself, and it is not going to be a revolution, where the millenials, Generation Y, or another particularly identifiable group, take control. It is much more likely that change will happen if the new kids on the block learn to speak the language of the old guard, and put the benefits of the new model in words that they can understand. One of the words that the people in charge understand is "return-on-investment", ROI. It is a simple question: "what is in it for me?" and it has to be answered to move forward. This should be an important priority for the early adopters who are now ready to move to the next phase of development: prove the ROI of the early projects to get funding for the next big thing.

The math may be fuzzy on how to quantify the 'value contribution' and 'business case' of a boost in citizen interaction or private entrepreneurs using government data, but value comes in many different forms, and in many cases, the value contributions will be so obvious that it does not matter if it is unquantifiable.

Both of the authors have a background in enterprise architecture, and as an enterprise architect it is intriguing, but sometimes also painful, to watch the current initiatives unfold.

Government 2.0 projects often lack time and resources to think about standards, compliance, governance, procurement, service-level agreements, scalability, security and all the more formal things that come with enterprise-level initiatives. Many projects are run by enthusiasts who already have a day job, and who are already taking on much more than what their job description says.

This means that there is a risk of constructing new silos of data, information and expertise, when there is no coordination. But there is no sense in trying to control the development of these projects or even worse stop them from happening. The energy of the entrepreneurs cannot and should not be impeded. So how can we start to apply some of the same architectural coordination to the new government 2.0 solutions that already is in place with a lot of other systems, without ruining the energy of the entrepreneurs?

This book can be seen as an attempt to aid with one important aspect: **communication**. By providing examples of what is taking place in different places around the world, we are adding to a growing body of knowledge in the area. Hopefully the communities that already exist, like GovLoop (as described by Steve Ressler in chapter 4), will help facilitate the communication. There is a big span in maturity among the different organizations working with government 2.0, and it should be possible for the more conservative to learn from the experience of the early adopters.

Another important aspect is **coordination**. Although it is impossible to establish common standards in the beginning, with some practical guidelines in place at an early stage, it may be possible to avoid the more simple mistakes. Agree on provisional standards for data formats, choose vendors that let you keep control of your data and call out the ones that use lock-in to gain a competitive advantage. Compare solutions with others and prepare to negotiate in different areas and accept solutions that are "good-enough" in the beginning, to get systems and people talking to each other.

Proving the ROI of a new initiative and identifying the future architectural challenges can make government 2.0 advance much smoother. But it is important to remember that part of the new way of doing things is adapting an iterative process. So development does not stop when a system is launched, and interaction with citizens does not stop just because the project is over. Using the constant flow of feedback that comes from opening up is key to continuous improvement. The public sector will have to change in a lot of ways to learn to use the feedback from the public, but there are a lot of positive signs that things are moving in the right direction.

Often, major innovations will be accompanied with a tag line such as "this will change everything". The advances discussed in this book certainly fall into this category. Of course, there is the question of preparedness, but generally, there is an acceptance that this will change everything.

Perhaps then, it is best to end on a note of self-control in this time of exuberance. Let us remember that there are many, many things that will not change in the Government 2.0 world. People, the electors, will still rely on the politicians, the elected, to represent them and manage the affairs of their jurisdiction. The fundamental idea of democracy doesn't change. The American government will still be a "government of the people, by the people, for the people", with a bit more "with the people". Taxes will still exist, and many times you will have many people disagreeing with the government direction.

Things, however, are really changing. We now have millions of people that rally on the internet, protest and even become a mob of sorts. However, even if millions protest against something, governments cannot interpret that as a mandate. Sure, there may be people raising their voice, like they do in the street, but there is still the rule of democracy where one person gets one vote. Millions may never join in the e-fray, but they have the right not to do so. So we must move forward remembering some of these basic democratic tenants.

Government is not a puppet to the vocal minority, the powerful few nor the e-involved. One person, one vote still works. However, politicians are faced with the risk of the bureaucracy getting closer to the citizens than they can. Government functions on the basic premise that:

A) People tell politicians what they want by electing those that promise the right things, and then

B) The elected politicians direct the bureaucrats.

Politicians, after all, have crisscrossed the land, held countless meetings, kissed babies, shook hands and made promises. They have been elected based on their ability to understand the needs of people, and convinced people that they can make it happen. In the old days (1990 and before), that worked, but now we have an accelerated democracy.

Unfortunately, in some cases, the bureaucracy is doing the talking, conducting the opinions, sharing and talking. Even if all of this is done with the permission of the politicians, we have changed the democratic model to look something like:

A) People talk to bureaucrats (via new media) and tell them what they want, then

B) Bureaucrats tell politicians what the people said, then

C) Politicians agree (after some degree of value added modifications in line with general party platforms), then

D) Politicians crisscross the land for the next election. But what should they promise? Should they say "I won't promise to do anything other than be a good listener when the time comes"?

It is called "disintermediation", and it will be an interesting challenge in the Government 2.0 world. Although, it should be said that politicians are certainly getting into the act, so maybe it is just a matter of limiting the range of (bureaucrat-citizen) dialogue that is acceptable, so as not to cause a problem.

Whatever the answer might be, we do have, however, a startling reality upon us now. We designed our democratic operational model long ago. The principles and goals are still valid, but perhaps it is time to change some of the ways we do things. We really can allow greater visibility, dialogue and participation into government, and so we should. After all, it really should be "by the people".

---

[1] http://j.mp/16qYoR

INDEX

C

D

E

F

G

H

I

J

K

L

M

N

O

P

R

S

T

U

V

W

X

Y

Visit 21gov.net

www.ingramcontent.com/pod-product-compliance
Lightning Source LLC
Chambersburg PA
CBHW051223050326
40689CB00007B/781

* 9 7 8 1 4 4 9 0 4 7 2 9 0 *